SUMMER

SUMMER

EDITED BY
ALICE GORDON AND VINCENT VIRGA

ADDISON-WESLEY PUBLISHING COMPANY, INC.

READING, MASSACHUSETTS   MENLO PARK, CALIFORNIA   NEW YORK
DON MILLS, ONTARIO   WOKINGHAM, ENGLAND   AMSTERDAM   BONN   SYDNEY
SINGAPORE   TOKYO   MADRID   SAN JUAN

All acknowledgments for permission to reprint previously published material can be found on page 251.

Suns appear courtesy of The Bettmann Archive.

Many of the designations used by manufacturers and sellers to distinguish their products are claimed as trademarks. Where those designations appear in this book and Addison-Wesley was aware of a trademark claim, the designations have been printed in initial capital letters (e.g., Perrier).

Library of Congress Cataloging-in-Publication Data

Summer / edited by Alice Gordon and Vincent Virga.
    p. cm.
  ISBN 0-201-19460-0
  1. American literature—20th century. 2. Summer—
Literary collections. I. Gordon, Alice.
II. Virga, Vincent.
PS509.S87S8 1990
814'.508033—dc20   89-27359
                           CIP

ABCDEFGHIJ-HK-9543210
First printing, January 1990

ACKNOWLEDGMENTS

MARTHA MOUTRAY, OUR EDITOR AT ADDISON-Wesley, had the idea to put summer in a book, and we feel fortunate that she asked us to assemble such a pleasurable project. Fran Kiernan worked on a preliminary shape for *Summer,* and her enthusiasm for the book informed it all along the way. Vicki Karp suggested several of the poems included here (Ray Bradbury's is the only poem written expressly for the book, his response to an invitation to write an essay). Lori Foley, senior production supervisor at Addison-Wesley and a superb professional, was a genuine collaborator in the making of this book. Editorial assistant Johanna Van Hise was invaluable for her good cheer and powers of organization. We thank all of them, and above all, we thank each writer, poet, photographer, and painter whose distillations of a season combine to make what we hope will be a *Summer* well spent at any time of year.

Alice Gordon
Vincent Virga

CONTENTS

PREFACE

IF I EVER EXCHANGE MY NEW YORK CITY address for a mailbox on a country road, it will be because I have succumbed, finally, to a river I first saw in summer. The Guadalupe is clear and green in the environs of the town of Hunt, Texas, which is really only a post office and store in the Hill Country. Much of the river is narrow and shallow, a limestone bed bubbling with artesian springs; elsewhere it is as deep as eight feet and fifty yards wide—making jade-colored swimming holes, half a mile long. Old cypress trees droop over stretches of the river; other parts of it are bounded by limestone cliffs, and as you swim beneath them you can hear canyon wrens singing from the ledges. Except during storms the water is slow-moving because it has been picturesquely dammed at irregular intervals by girls' camps and the owners of big river-rock houses built many years ago. There are also smaller houses on the river road, wooden cottages like the one I visited with my best friend and her parents the year I was twelve. That was the year this river became my future South of France, my Lake Tahoe, the place I want to be when summer comes.

I guess I had better things to do than go to Hunt in the summers between twelve and twenty-five; but since twenty-five I have tried to return every year. Very little has changed. While I am there my time is spent more or less as it was when I was twelve: I'm in the water for hours, swimming, floating, exploring, doing nothing. I've found a particularly beautiful spot on the river where no one else ever seems to go, a big flat rock jutting out under a cliff. I have swum to it again and again with various friends, and sometimes their dogs, pushing

ALICE GORDON

innertubes holding coolers full of lunch or notebooks full of work destined not to get done. Amazingly, after all this time, the Crider family's old arena, cafe, and dance floor are still down the road, and there's still a rodeo followed by a dance under the stars every Saturday night. One of the cooks in the cafe is a man I had a crush on back when he was a sixteen-year-old from Houston, where I lived then too. With a few other odd jobs he manages to make a living in Hunt during the rest of the year. I haven't asked him how it feels to live there when the summer is over or not yet begun.

Houston lost its favor after I discovered the Texas Hill Country, and yet I loved the summers I spent there as a child for being filled with peculiarly suburban pleasures: waking up to the buzz of the lawnmower and the fragrance of San Augustine grass filtering into the house through the air-conditioning; pointing the hose on our neighbor's smooth cement driveway and sliding on our backs in the water that pooled under the porte cochere; playing block-long hide and seek at dusk, or darting in and out of the fog made by the tank-like DDT machine as it lumbered through the neighborhood spraying for mosquitoes—little did we know then about fractured chromosomes. The great thing about summer is that it seems to bless you wherever you are.

Being at home and just around the neighborhood in summer meant having nothing special to do. I still have the feeling on summer mornings that I can jump out of bed and spend the whole day fooling around and seeing what's up, even—or perhaps especially—when my life must follow an orderly agenda. In spite of my adult responsibilities, editing this book was more like seeing what was up than following an agenda, for I had the privilege, as you will now, to see summer topics transformed into tales of wonderful or not so wonderful but always rich and complicated summers, summers I would love to have been a part of and now am, in a way, for having read about them. All together these writerly increments of a season made me think of something obvious, something I have been known to forget in the heat of a concrete-city noon: in summer, everything in nature is designed to grow and thrive. Everything includes us.

I HAVE FRAMED A BLACK AND WHITE SNAPSHOT of me aged ten months, sitting tilted on grass in front of my proud young parents. We're in a park beneath New York City's Queensboro Bridge—opposite the future site of the U.N.—on a hot summer's day. I know it's summer because I'm barefoot, my mother is wearing a short-sleeved, brightly patterned dress, and my dad has on a white tee shirt. I know it's hot because I'm looking down, dazed, out of the blinding glare that has the adults squinting, and I'm obviously preparing to topple into a crawl toward the nearest puddle of shade. The picture confirms for me (were confirmation called for) that my discomfort in the heat began when it and I were first introduced. Like any treasured image, it never fails to draw varied emotional responses from me. One relates to summer as a state of being, welcome or otherwise.

Summer's heat was the most frustrating thing throughout my childhood: Just when I was released from confining school schedules and had joyously become my own responsibility, it turned too damn hot to do anything but sit spellbound in darkness at the movies or hide out in a back room with a book. Since these were undeniably my two favorite occupations, a deep ambivalence prevailed for the rest of the year as I longed for summer— paradoxically my least favorite season.

When we moved to suburbia, not far from the Atlantic, I got sun poisoning on the beach, heat stroke in the playgrounds, and violent seasickness on boats. I became the best-read, movie-mad kid in my school until one day I discovered a new pastime. Suddenly, in breeze-

VINCENT VIRGA

ways or under awnings and at night, with the sun tucked away, I was dancing at parties with the graceful abandon of a tumbling wave. I quickly shucked the ambivalence routine and learned to cherish the opportunities of summer. In short, thanks to the lindy and the cha-cha, I underwent a sea change, developing an early-morning symbiosis with the ocean and its environs. Properly utilized, the flowering earth was an Eden.

My best memories of summer are bright and clear, color-fast, color-drenched, moist-lit, and heavily chiaroscuro, very like the images I sought for this book. I wanted each one to be a discrete entity—an emblem of summertime—yet to work mnemonically when combined with others, evoking both a distinct sense of place—summer as a nearby, unspoiled, friendly planet—

and a distinct mood—summer as an emotional condition, at best crisp and refreshing as a pair of new white ducks.

My antipathy to summer heat has shaped my life. It led directly to a self-employed existence that allows me to vacate the city for the entire season. I have learned to love summer unconditionally now. There are no parental figures sitting behind to restrain me from the shady pool or a temperate northern European climate. Every summer I am most aware—more than at any other time of year—that I am indeed my own responsibility and can do as I like wherever I like. I have also learned that there are many people, places, and things grander than movies or books. These days, I am often as dazed with gratitude as the infant in that old snapshot is bedazzled by the burning star overhead—for summer is a wonder.

12

13

14

1 · The Door to Summer

16

I N SAN FRANCISCO, SINCE SO OFTEN THE SUM-
mers are fiercely cold, fog-darkened, wind-whipped,
you do not really need summer clothes; heavy sweat-
ers are more in order than sheer cotton or flimsy
silk. And very likely for that reason, the fact that I
had not bought anything summery for quite a few
years, the summer that I now think of as "that summer" seems, in my mind, to have begun in a fitting
room at Magnin's. I tried on and then bought a
romantic dress, a purely summer party dress: white,
splashed with large pink dots, a floppy full skirt and
bared shoulders. A dress for a summer tan, a summer
dance. I bought that dress and some very short white
shorts, and I thought, I'm really going back there,
I'm going back to Chapel Hill for the summer. Back
to where it's warm.

On the face of it, a party dress was the last
thing I might have expected to have use for then.
My family situations were all problematic: I wanted
to leave my husband, but worried about supporting
myself and my son, then seven. Also, although for

ALICE ADAMS

every reason I wanted to go back home for the summer—it would be good for Peter, my son, we both needed a change of scene, and my stronger, more secret plan was to start a novel there—I was not at all sure of being welcomed at my father's house in Chapel Hill, where he then lived fairly happily, often drunkenly, with my stepmother.

But the trip had been set in motion some weeks before, with a visit from a woman whom I will call Marie, a German-born psychoanalyst who had rented the house across the road from my father and his wife. Marie was a woman of enormous charm—a dangerous word, I know, but no other will quite describe her very European grace of manner, her beautiful low voice, and her odd small laugh, her intense way of listening. All that was combined with an extreme intelligence and an extraordinary education, doctorates in art and literature as well as her medical training.

And so when Marie came to see me in San Francisco, without going into all my plans and fears, I simply said that I wondered if I should in fact come to Chapel Hill.

And she looked at me, in her way, and she smiled and said simply, "Come!" And so I did.

Remarkably, I think (and more remarkable that I have never noticed this before) as I now write, on my desk is a large framed photograph of Marie, taken shortly before she died. And in the picture she is wearing a white blouse with large pink polka dots splashed across it. A pure and trivial coincidence, perhaps, but I would prefer to think that it is not.

The summer deal with my father, that summer, arrived at through many complicated and confused late-night calls, was that Peter and I could have the apartment that took up one wing of my parents' house. My father

and stepmother were going to Maine. There would be only a few days when my father and his wife (let us call her Dipsy) and Peter and I would all be there together. For those few days we would be their guests, and in August Peter and I would drive to Maine to be their guests again.

Had I thought in a clear way about this project I would have seen trouble ahead, been wary of my very ambivalent father's (and Dipsy's) concept of guest. I would have known that whatever I (we) did would be wrong. But at the time I was not thinking clearly at all, I was only dreaming of sunshine and warmth. Of not being with my husband. Of, maybe, going to some southern beach.

Of possibly meeting someone. Falling in love.

And so we set off, Peter and I, with high hopes and new clothes. Books for him and my typewriter for me. Conscious and unconscious expectations.

My father met us at the Raleigh-Durham airport. Smelling strongly of pipe tobacco and of bourbon too, he could not stop talking. And even for me he was hard to understand, with his pipe in his mouth, constantly, and his extreme southern accent, spoken with great rapidity. As soon as we got into the car he offered me a slug of bourbon from his clearly new silver flask (a recent gift from Dipsy), which I turned down. The flask was then offered to Peter, a joke that did not quite come off.

I was back into family problems, then. However, even as I braced myself tensely against all that, I was far more aware of the countryside that now rushed past the car as we drove the infinitely familiar twelve miles from Durham to Chapel Hill. Southern fields, crumbling dirt through which peered tiny white or blue wildflowers; swollen, rushing brown creeks, high water swirling with a rich trash of sticks and dead winter leaves; banks heavy-laden with honeysuckle vines, sweet-smelling, thickly green; and, back beyond the fields, back from the creek, were the dark green pinewoods, now lightly swaying in the pure blue sky of early June, the gentle breeze of summer.

The apartment, actually the wing of my parents' house in which I grew up, was something of a shock: not only was it an incredible mess (interesting in itself, since Dipsy always billed herself as super-neat, as opposed to untidy me), but it was literally falling apart, holes torn in walls, pieces of floorboard missing (by the following winter, all this disarray was said to have been caused by Peter, and by me). In every room, however, stood bowls of the most beautiful, fragrant roses, a gift from Marie, we were told, who had made a rose garden in her yard across the road.

And, as the roses to a great extent made up for the general depressingness of our quarters, so the bad hours with Dipsy and my father were balanced by the long walks that Peter and I took all around town. After those walks we would come home and swim, and it did not seem to matter much that those few evenings were alcoholic, boring, quarrelsome (for me, at least; Peter was of course in bed).

And then my father and Dipsy left for Maine, and Peter and I were more or less on our own, in the odd ramshackle apartment, with my father's very old but functioning car. And our enchanting neighbor and new friend, Marie.

This was in fact the first summer that I had ever spent in Chapel Hill; when I was a child we always went to Maine for the three months of academic vacations. And while I loved Maine, the lake and mountains, birch trees and canoes, I was also curious about the southern places, especially the beaches, where most of my friends spent their summers. And an idea began to gain mo-

mentum in my head: why not drive down to Myrtle Beach, say, or Wrightsville (those were the names I most often heard) and stay for a couple of days?

Marie often came over to swim with us in the late afternoons, I suppose just after her last patient. I can see her so clearly, still: a small, rather bent-over woman (she had scholarly bad posture) shyly arriving in her white terry robe, dark wool bathing suit, slipping into the pool.

We talked rather little. What was most on my mind, how to leave my husband, was or seemed to me then unmentionable. And Marie was undoubtedly tired, and relieved not to have to respond to conversation. Yet some very strong sympathetic liking was quite clearly established between us, and I thought, more than once that summer, Oh, if only my crazy father had married you!

And one afternoon, when actually I had been thinking all day about the possible beach trip, Marie said, "Ah, Alice—" (she prefaced many crucial sentences with that small "ah!") "my friend Henry—" (naming a local writer whom I had heard of but not met) "Henry writes to me that he has a house in Windy Hill, near to Myrtle Beach. And I wondered, could not you and I and Peter drive to see him there? I think that you would like Henry."

Amazing: this seemed the gift of a fairy god-mother, which was more or less what Marie was to me, that summer.

At the time, among other things I thought, Oh good, I'll fall in love with Henry; he'll be my summer romance.

I actually began to fall in love with Henry on that drive to the coast. Almost all of that scenery was new to me, exotic: the gradually flattening landscape of bare yards and chinaberry trees, the swamps overcome with kudzu vines, the water oaks festooned with Spanish moss, its drippings mysterious gray. I took it all in with an intense excitement, a sense that anything whatsoever could happen now: summer, and I was home, and free.

What happened was that just after parking the car I got out and looked up at Henry, a tall man with a sad witty kind face; we shook hands and fell in love. (I wish I could remember what I was wearing then; it could have been the short white shorts, for that long hot trip). Since there were a lot of people around—including, even, a temporary girlfriend of Henry's, who conveniently vanished soon after that trip—all that attraction was manifest only in a great deal of talk, much laughing at nothing. It even turned out that we knew quite a lot of people in common, from a wide range of places, and we made a great deal of that.

At Windy Hill (a flat and windless place, I have no notion of the origin of that name) it was always hot, and a wide and perfectly smooth beach of the finest sand, pure white, seemed to stretch forever, an endless summer coast, beside the gently rolling, azure Atlantic.

Peter dug holes and built sand castles, the way children are supposed to do, in the summer, at a beach. He also found and collected some especially beautiful small shells, gold and white, shaped like butterflies, small golden butterflies. We all took long beach walks and swam and played about in the easy surf. And we talked a lot and laughed. We were all in love.

And then Peter and Marie and I drove back to Chapel Hill, and a few days after that Henry, who was also back in town, called and invited me to a party. I wore my new pink polka-dotted dress, and we danced a lot in a mildly outrageous way, very sexy and close but at the same time laughing at ourselves. In fact, everything about that evening seemed extremely funny to us both.

We laughed all the way home, barely able to stop and kiss goodnight, but to kiss very seriously, both almost knowing what we had begun.

The next morning Henry came over to see me—or rather, us: from the start he and Peter took strongly to each other. Henry stayed only a short time on that visit, and then he left, and then he came back again. I think he came to call, as it were, five or six times that day. "I can't believe this is happening to me," is what he said. "I have to keep checking."

Thus, so far, everything that I had wanted had come to pass, a hot southern summer and time at a southern beach, and a summer love. Everything I had wished for and considerably more, as things turned out. Even the weather was hotter than anyone there could remember. There was something called a Bermuda blanket, enclosing heat, and the Bermuda blanket became one of the things that Henry and I laughed about; I can no longer recall why it seemed quite so funny. Later Henry wrote a short story about us, and that summer, in which he said that he could remember all our jokes, and maybe he can. I would rather not ask.

As some love affairs do, mine with Henry seemed to shape itself into triangles—the other people for us being Peter and Marie. With Peter, Henry and I took long country walks together, usually after supper; we listened to the country sounds of distant hounds, and nearer to hand the crickets and tree frogs, as we breathed in the evening smells of flowers, and sun-baked dirt. Peter learned to chase and capture fireflies, to keep in a bottle in his room, and he and Henry told each other silly jokes and riddles: Would you rather be run over by an old Greyhound bus or a new one? Once I wrote a story about such a walk, and I am now unsure whether I am remembering the story or an actual walk, with Peter and Henry; the story was about why Henry and I never married, a

topic we surely never discussed on a walk with Peter, or for that matter at any other time.

And then there were other walks that Henry and I took by ourselves, in the afternoons, around the town. Peter was now enrolled in a day camp at the local Y; after dropping him off I would go to meet Henry, and happily, aimlessly, we would walk about. For privacy we especially liked the cemetery, we spent a lot of time there, gossiping about our mutual acquaintances among the dead. And sometimes we just strolled along Franklin Street, I in my short white shorts and Henry in faded khakis—both of us much too hot, and always longing for more time: specifically we needed more time to go down to the Tonga Room, a chilly local bar, for beer. Or time to drive out to his garage apartment, for love. Or both, which somehow sometimes we managed.

With Marie, our connection, mine and Henry's, was somewhat social; we went across the street to parties at her house, at which we always had a good time— although the best part was coming home to laugh (we agreed that too many formal Europeans can wreck a party, and those were the people that Marie mostly knew, and entertained).

Or, sometimes Marie would come up to my house and I would make supper for the four of us.

I had a sense that Marie was also in love with Henry, in the shy way that an older woman can love a young man from whom she does not expect love in return. (I wrote a story about this too.) Although Henry in his way did love Marie, admired and valued her enormously, as I did. Their behavior with each other was extremely formal, however, deep-southern Henry and Viennese Marie. She had a particular way of saying his name that bespoke deep affection.

But soon after I had put Peter to bed, in his room upstairs, Marie would plead fatigue, and soon after

that, Henry and I would walk her home, just down across the road, in the early firefly summer night.

The heat went on and on, and I clearly needed at least another cotton dress. And so one afternoon I went off by myself to a store called the Little Shop, where I had often shopped as a girl growing up in that town— and where I now saw a "Summer Sale" sign. I went in, and was greeted by a woman who had worked there for many years. She knew me right away, and we greeted each other very affectionately, very southern-ly, and I had a pleased sense of being, now, in my own small home town, a grown-up at last, a woman among women.

I found a beautiful cotton dress, marked down to $15 (is that possible? I think it is). Softly gathered, off-white with a pale pattern of yellow leaves. A dress that Henry loved on sight, when I wore it that night.

And then it was time for me to leave, to drive up north to Maine, with Peter.

As I should perhaps have said earlier, the extreme verbal reticence with which our love affair was conducted held great charm for both me and Henry. The precariousness and uncertainty of our situations must surely have withheld us from specific plans; Henry had at that moment neither any money nor a job, and I too lacked both those essentials, nor was I even nearly divorced. Also, two writers, we were both aware (I think) of the tendencies in our kind to wordy overkill, the perverse need to drown even true love in declarations, analyses, descriptions.

In any case, on the night before my departure for Maine I blew all that, I broke all our unspoken rules. In passion, I declared that I would always love Henry (this has turned out to be true, though not in the sense I meant it at the time), along with other statements in that vein. And Henry, while not exactly responding in kind, received what I said with love and great gentleness, thus delicately sparing me possible later shame.

Thus we parted quite without specific plans. We would see what happened, is how we both mostly felt, and what we did.

That time of happy summer love with Henry actually lasted a scant four weeks, before Peter and I drove up to Maine, and into more family trouble. But those four weeks have for me still, in retrospect, the character of an endless summer, like the summers of childhood that one remembers as having lasted forever.

In August, in Maine, I found out that my first short story had been sold, for $350, to a now defunct magazine called *Charm*. A major event for me, from which among other things I derived the courage to divorce my husband.

San Francisco's summer often takes place in the fall, and so I began my life as a separate woman in my Chapel Hill summer clothes. (I was photographed for *Charm* in the dress from the Little Shop.) And Henry and I began to write letters, as we do still. We began then to make the intricate, sometimes impossible transition from lovers to friends. Or, perhaps that is what we were really doing that summer, making friends.

Sometime later Henry had a long and in many ways difficult marriage, and I had a very difficult love affair of about the same duration. And once on the phone we were discussing our shared slowness to catch on, in matters of the heart. One of us said, I honestly do not remember which of us, "It's good we never got married; we still would be."

But on first getting the news about my story, in Maine, just a few days after leaving Chapel Hill, and leaving Henry, most of all I wanted to let him know. Selling the story seemed an important omen. My father's house had no telephone at that time, and so Peter and I hiked into Richville, the nearest town, to send a telegram. (I knew that Henry was visiting his mother, and the idea of calling him there made me very shy.)

I worked hard over the wording of the wire, I remember, but was only able to come up with a rather stilted message, despite my intentions. Something about celebrating the summer, I think—which was, after all, quite close to what I meant to say.

23

L ET'S DEAL RIGHT AWAY WITH THE OBSESSION issue. I would maintain that I am not properly described as being obsessed with chiggers. Interested in a rather intense way, yes—but not obsessed. It's true that I've never been able to think of summertime without thinking of chiggers. It's true that I talk about chiggers constantly, even in midwinter. It's true that I once responded to hearing about some refusenik being sent to Siberia by saying, "Well, at least it's too cold there for chiggers." So what?

While we're at it, we might as well deal with the morbid fear issue. I would maintain that it's not really accurate to say that I have a morbid fear of chiggers. In my opinion, an unwillingness to approach high grass in the summertime—even in Nova Scotia, where we spend our summers in a place that is, not by accident, a full fifteen hundred miles from the nearest chigger—does not reflect morbid fear but simple prudence. Of course, "morbid fear" is a fuzzy phrase anyway. A fear that is fully justified,

25

CALVIN TRILLIN

for instance, is obviously not a morbid fear—unless, of course, what is feared involves morbidity. Now that I think of it, maybe we should deal with the morbid fear issue a little later.

My wife is the one who's responsible for the impression that there's something unnatural about my interest in chiggers. She grew up in the East, which is a chigger-free zone, and she doesn't understand why I'm afraid of chiggers. This is more or less the equivalent of someone from North Dakota wondering why someone who grew up in the swamps is afraid of alligators: the simple fact is that we've seen the damage these beasts can do. My wife has a clear position on my interest in chiggers. She says that I might well have been bitten a lot by chiggers when I was a boy in Kansas City but that I am no longer a boy nor in Kansas City and that my constant mention of chiggers therefore amounts to an obsession, or maybe even a morbid fear.

That's what my wife says now. There was a time when she did not believe in the existence of such a thing as a chigger. There's a lot about Kansas City my wife doesn't believe. On visits to Kansas City, for instance, she has seen the cow on top of the American Hereford Association building with her own eyes, but she still does not believe that its heart and liver light up at night. She has never believed that the largest body of water near Kansas City, Lake Lotawana, goes up a foot and a half on the Fourth of July, when everyone gets in at once. She was particularly skeptical about chiggers, I think, because I told her that they were too small to be seen by the human eye—even a human eye wide with fear.

The fact that a chigger can't be seen may have something to do with why it's not better known to the general public—although every time I read about the concentration of the national media in the East, I toy with a conspiracy theory or two. Chiggers have missed out on the folklore that keeps mosquitoes in the public mind—folklore that is not based on itch-power but on pure size. Storytellers are always talking about mosquitoes large enough to carry off a full-grown man; what they don't tell you is that if the man was bitten during his kidnapping, the bite will only itch for an hour or two. The duration of chigger bite itch is, as I have pointed out in a scientific treatise on this subject, "just short of eternity."

The only folklore I've ever heard about chiggers is a poem that was recited to us once by my friend Tom Chaney—who grew up in Horse Cave, Kentucky, which is chigger country. It's based on the disparity between a chigger's size and its impact:

> There was a little chigger,
> And he wasn't any bigger
> Than a point on a very small pin.
> But the bump that he raises
> Just itches like the blazes,
> And that's where the rub comes in.

I thought it was a pretty good poem, even though it seriously understates how much a chigger bite itches. (According to my research, carried out with my usual scientific controls, the average chigger bite has an itch of six to eight milamoses—a milamos being the itch power of one thousand mosquito bites.)

But my wife reminded me that poems are written about a lot of subjects that are, strictly speaking, imaginary. To prove to her that chiggers exist, I had to show her the definition of chigger in the dictionary: "a 6-legged mite larva (family Trombiculidae) that sucks the blood of vertebrates and causes intense irritation." The person who wrote that definition, by the way, has obviously never been the vertebrate whose blood was sucked or he wouldn't describe the result as "intense irritation." It's the equivalent of saying that being hanged and quartered is the sort of thing that can smart. I suspect most dictionary writers are from the East.

I live in the East now, and I can't tell you what a relief it is for me to live in a chigger-free zone. In fact, it has occurred to me that the absence of chiggers in the East may have something to do with why easterners are always saying how refreshingly unneurotic midwesterners are: most of the midwesterners easterners meet are those who have moved to the East from the Midwest and who are therefore so relieved to be in a place where they can walk in high grass in August that they sail blissfully past the ordinary trials of life.

My wife wondered why she had never heard of chiggers before. That's easy: a lot of people who spent childhood summers in the Midwest have blocked chiggers out of their memories. They'd simply rather forget. I often come across passages in books by midwesterners describing those hot, lazy August evenings spent in a Midwest backyard, sipping lemonade and chasing lightning bugs. Lightning bugs! Nobody cares about lightning bugs. All of that lightning bug talk is just a way of avoiding the subject of chiggers. People who write lyrical descriptions of summer evenings can't bear to write about what's lurking in the grass, no bigger than the point of a very small pin. They can't stand to think about the tension of facing an enemy that cannot be seen and may not even be out there.

I don't blame the writers of those passages. There have been times when I've tried to blot out memories of the vacant lot next to my Cousin Kenny's house. What the Serengeti is to lions and the Atchafalaya Basin spillway is to crawfish the vacant lot next to my Cousin Kenny's house was to chiggers. I know what you're thinking: why didn't he simply stay away from the vacant lot next door to his Cousin Kenny's house?

Fine. You're right, of course. I should have simply stayed away. I knew perfectly well that there was no way to protect yourself from chiggers. Protective clothing? Chiggers scoffed at protective clothing. (A chigger scoff cannot be heard by the human ear.) Chiggers, in fact, like the most protective parts of protective clothing. They often bite along elastic. They burrow inside. They like soft spots. They love warm spots. They crave creases.

But I knew all of that then. I knew that scratching could mean infection and infection could mean spending hot summer days lying in bed, waiting for the swelling to go down. Why did I go into the vacant lot? Well, there was a lot of good stuff there. At this point, I can't remember just what, but I do remember there was a lot of good stuff. And there were no chiggers in sight. Why not risk it? There we went—my cousin Kenny and I—walking into the vacant lot on a steamy July afternoon. There we went—two vertebrates—about to have our blood sucked by 6-legged mite larvae. Dummies!

You're thinking that even if we got a lot of chigger bites we could simply put something on them to make them stop itching. Wrong! I've said again and again what would stop the itch of a chigger bite: amputation, sometimes. Not that we didn't try all sorts of remedies. During my childhood, summertime in Kansas City was a frenzied, doomed search for chigger nostrums. The one I remember best was something that came in a tiny square bottle and had a name like ChiggeRRid. It had a lot in common with clear fingernail polish. For all I know, it *was* clear fingernail polish. When you applied it, a sort of crust was formed on top of the chigger bite.

I remember when it first came out. A miracle cure! I was at Boy Scout camp at the time—Camp Osceola, B.S.A. Somehow, we got the word about ChiggeRRid. My mother assured me that she would bring me a supply when she came to Osceola for visiting day, and when my comrades heard that, they all put in an order. There was my mother, like someone with a fistful of Portuguese visas as the Nazi armies neared Paris.

She was surrounded by desperate Boy Scouts who were clamoring for their tiny square bottles.

ChiggeRRid didn't work, of course, at least not in my case. I painted it on dutifully. I spent a lot of time sharing scientific theories about how it would stop the itching by shutting off the oxygen. (We knew that a lack of oxygen could stop burning. Why not itching?) But it didn't work. I was still up all night with chigger bites—the only difference being that the crusts on my skin made a slight crackling sound as I tossed and turned in my bunk. The bites continued to itch. And itch. The itch was horrible, made more agonizing by the knowledge that it was just short of eternal. I just realized that I'm not quite ready to deal with the morbid fear issue. Maybe later.

29

SUMMER—A HIGH, CANDID, DEFINITE TIME. IT may slither out of the ambiguity, hesitance, or too early ripeness of spring and edge toward the soothing peculiarities of autumn, but summer is downright, a true companion of winter. It is an extreme, a returning, a vivid comparative. It does not signify that some are cool and some are dry and sweltering; summer is a kind of entity, poetic, but not a poetic mystery. The sun is at its zenith in the tropic of Cancer, a culmination.

I like to remember the summer season coming to those who just stay at home the year round, that is, most of the world. The plain patterns of simple domestic life meet each year with a routine. Nothing is unexpected. An almanac of memories disputes claims of the hottest day in decades or the level of the rainfall.

The furnace is shut down and the fireplace, if there should be one, is emptied and the tiles relieved of grit and polished to an oily sienna sheen.

ELIZABETH HARDWICK

Windows washed, everything aired; moths seeking the bedroom light bulb; grass and weeds pushing up out of the hard winter soil; leaves on the maples and elms—nothing special; doors latched back and covered by a flapping screen—with a hole in it and rusty hinges; voices calling out of the windows; perennials determined to exhibit their workhorse nature, if most a little disgruntled and with more stem than flower; insects strong as poison; the smell of chlorine in a child's hair—from the community pool across town.

The congratulation of summer is that it can make the homely and the humble if not exactly beautiful, beautifully acceptable. Such brightness at midday and then the benign pastels, blues and pinks and lavenders of the summer sky. Much may wither and exhaust, but so great is the glow and greater the freedom of the season that every extreme will be accommodated. There are great gardens filled with jewels as precious as those dug out of the earth and then the hand that planted the sparse petunias and impatiens in the window box—there's that, too.

I remember days from the summers in the upper South and sights from certain towns in the Middle West, in Ohio and Indiana, places just passed through long ago. There's something touching about the summer streets of middle-size towns: everything a bit worn down in July, all slow and somnolent except for the supersonic hummingbird in the browning hydrangea bush at the edge of the porch. The disaster of the repetitive but solid architecture of the 1920s—once perceived as quite an accomplishment of ownership, and suitable—comfortable according to what was possible.

The front porches. That unalterable, dominating, front-face mistake left over from the time before the absolute, unconditional surrender to the automobile and to traffic. There was a time when not everyone had a car, and to children then the traffic was interesting. The brand names, the out-of-state license plates—a primitive pleasure to take note of them, like stamping your palm at the sight of a white horse. And the family on the front porch, watching the life of the street.

This porch in front and so unsightly and useless and awful in the winter with the gray of the splintered planks and the soggy sag of the furniture often left out to hibernate in public view. The old eyesores, defining the houses, many of them spacious, with gables, and bits of colored glass from a catalogue over the door, in a fan shape. If nothing else, summer redeems the dismal overhang of the porch, for a few months, and even the darkened halls and parlors within might be glad of an escape from the heat.

Somewhere there is water. Not too far away there will be an abandoned quarry, difficult to climb into and cold as a lake in Nova Scotia. There will be a stream or a river, not very deep and muddy at the banks—middle western water.

If there are no neighbors to be seen on the streets, they can be seen and heard at the back, there on the patio where tubs standing on tripods and filled with charcoal lumps are ready to receive marinated bits of flesh. There is pleasure in all this, in the smoke, in the luscious brown of the chicken leg—on your own little plot where you fed the chickadee last winter.

These scenes, local as the unearned wildflower, the goldenrod with its harsh cinnamon scent, are not splendid. Little of the charm of the ocean view and the table set with blue linen, and the delectable salmon, so well designed for painterly display, laid out on a platter among scattered stems of watercress. Still the American town streets—those angling off the main drag seen on the way to the airport—are a landscape of the American summer. And why should we groan with pain at the sight of the plastic flamingo on the lawn or the dead whiteness of the large inflated duck coming into its decorative own nowadays? There's not much else to buy downtown, for one thing.

These things remind me of those elders who used to go abroad every summer to the same pension, to dusty interiors and dining rooms where the wine bottle with your name on it returned every night to the table until it was empty. Perhaps in Florence or outside Siena or in the north, to the band concert in the park by a German lake.

In Russian fiction people go off to the Crimea and sigh, how dull it is here. But since there is to be a plot, the scene is not to be so dull after all. In the salon, with the violin whining and the fish overcooked, the same faces take up their posts for the same complaints and posturings. Then someone new appears to the defensive snubs of the old-timers or to the guarded curiosity of the bored. It might be a sulky young girl with a chaperone or her mother; or a woman, not a girl, to be seated on the same side of the room as the tall man from Moscow, away from his family for two weeks and subject to dreaming. And it begins to begin. . . .

Summer romance—when the two words are brought together, each takes on a swift linguistic undercurrent. As a phrase, it is something akin to "summer soldier"—the romance carries away and the summer soldier runs away from duty or from the reality of things. Heaven is something with a girl in summer: a line of Robert Lowell's. The summer romance will have the sharpness and sweetness and the indescribable wonder of the native strawberry, raspberry, blueberry, and toward the end the somewhat gritty cling of the late blackberry.

The sun-filled romance is the dramatic background of much fiction. There is the accident of the meeting and the unreasonable heightening of the season. And classically there is often an imbalance of class or situation, hard, chilly truths swept away by the soft clouds, the fields, and the urgency of the burst-open water lilies.

Edith Wharton wrote a short novel called *Summer*. In it you will find a love affair between a pretty and poor young girl from the New England hills and a clever young man from the city who likes to study the old houses of the region. As always, he is alone, happily solitary, idling about in the sunshine, and she is there, as she has always been. In the way of these sudden romances everything before and ahead seems to fade. Of course, it is not to last, at least not to last for the young man, who, as it turns out, is engaged to someone of his own sort . . . and so on.

Tess of the D'Urbervilles: "Rays from the sunrise drew forth the buds and stretched them in long stalks, lifted up sap in noiseless streams, opened petals, and sucked out scents in invisible jets and breathings." This is the summer landscape that engulfs Tess and Angel Clare and finally leads to a despair of such magnitude only the genius of Thomas Hardy could imagine it and embody it in the changing seasons and the changing structure of the English countryside.

In Chekhov's story "The Lady with the Dog," the lady and the man are both married. They meet in Yalta in the summer and the romance flows along on a pitiless tide, without any possible ending except misery. When they believe the love will at last end or the devastation will have a solution, the final line says no, "it was only just beginning."

So in spite of the meadows and the picnic under the shade of the copper beech tree, the days will grow longer and there will again be buying and selling and coming and going elsewhere. The romantic ritual of the season fades, even if it will be staged again next summer with other lovers in other places. The freedom of the summer remains in the memory.

In the mountains, there you feel free. . . . Yes. Under Mount Monadnock in New Hampshire—a storm of stars in the heavens, a pattern of gorgeous gleaming

dots on the dark blue silk of the sky, all spreading down like a huge soft cloak to the edge of the field.

The mountains are perhaps not quite in such demand as they once were in summer. Too lonely and overwhelming, the pleasures offered no longer quite suitable to the extraordinary energies of those who rush to the long, long expressways on a Friday afternoon—flat roads ahead, and yet they mean getting there. The weekend, commuting distance, breads and cheeses and bottles of wine, Vivaldi on the cassette, and a lot of work to be done and gladly.

Impatience with the division of city and country, or what is more or less "country," has changed the heart of the seasons. Many face a February weekend as if it were July. There is a need for an eternal summer, some mutant need created by the demand for nature, for weekend nature, even as nature disappears along the route.

Eternal summer, kind only as a metaphor. Night is the winter of the tropics, as the saying has it. On the equator the days are twelve hours long. Withering rivers and unrelenting lassitude in the never-ending summer-time. In Bombay in January, blissful for the citizens, but to those accustomed to the temperate sections of the United States, the heat of January in India spreads around like an infamous August swelter.

The gardens, the terraces, the flowers in vases. The first peas, the lettuce out of the ground, the always too greatly abundant zucchini—and at last a genuine tomato. No doubt the taste for these has grown sharper from the fact that we have them all year round in an inauthentic condition of preservation. When the memory is never allowed to subside, according to each thing in its time, the true summer taste of vegetable and fruit is more astonishing. One of summer's intensifications. Very much like actually swimming or sailing after the presence of the sea or lake known only as a view.

Summer, the season of crops. The concreteness of it. Not as perfumed and delicate and sudden as spring and not as *triste* as autumn. Yet for the enjoyment of summer's pleasures, for the beach, the crowded airplane to Venice, most of us consent to work all year long.

35

SUMMER MORNING

I love to stretch
Like this, naked
On my bed in the morning;
Quiet, listening:

Outside they are opening
Their primers
In the little school
Of the cornfield.

There is a smell of damp hay,
Of horses, of summer sky,
Of laziness, of eternal life.

I know all the dark places
Where the sun hasn't reached yet,
Where the singing has just ceased
In the hidden aviaries of the crickets—
Anthills where it goes on raining—
Slumbering spiders dreaming of wedding dresses.

I pass over the farmhouses
Where the little mouths open to suck,
Barnyards where a man, naked to the waist,
Washes his face with a hose,
Where the dishes begin to rattle in the kitchen.

The good tree with its voice
Of a mountain brook
Knows my steps
It hushes.

CHARLES SIMIC

I stop and listen:
Somewhere close by
A stone cracks a knuckle,
Another turns over in its sleep.

I hear a butterfly stirring
In the tiny soul of the caterpillar.
I hear the dust dreaming
Of eyes and great winds.

Further ahead, someone
Even more silent
Passes over the grass
Without bending it.

—And all of a sudden
In the midst of that silence

It seems possible
To live simply
On the earth.

Every day was the same day. We were American boys in the 1950s, and we played baseball. In springtime we played it in city streets as soon as the soot-gray hardpack of snow melted away. In fall, when darkness fell early, we played it against front stoops, the light from the porch illuminating the ball as it zipped off the steps. In the winter we played it with dice and playing cards and dime-store games that came with a spinner and little markers and a cardboard replica of a diamond. But in summer, when each day rolled smoothly into the next and the sun accommodated game upon game upon game—in summer we played baseball, and we did nothing else.

The door to summer: On the last day of classes, my parents' car, a two-tone green '53 Chevy, would be parked outside my Detroit grade school with the engine running, ready to take us to our small, unheated cottage on a lake twenty-five miles from the city. Even in the mid-fifties, Detroit was hardly the place where one wanted to spend the

DANIEL OKRENT

summer. Everything we needed for three months was stuffed into the Chevy's trunk or jammed onto the shelf by the rear window. My older brother and sister, already collected from their junior high school, were in the back seat, and as I came running at top speed across the school lawn, my mother opened the door for me, issuing an invitation to Arcadia.

The drive to Cooley Lake took less than an hour, but once we arrived we were lost to civilization. Each day, my father commuted to his office in the city, while the four of us who didn't have to earn a living remained on the overbuilt shores of the mile-long lake. As summer people we were in the minority at Cooley Lake because the city was palpably close at hand, even if metaphorically distant, and the General Motors plant in Pontiac was even nearer; many of its employees tended their tiny yards dividing a row of small houses in close rank on our side of the lake, each facing south toward the water. My sister, an exceptional swimmer, lived in that water, while my brother lived on its surface, skimming across its rippling wavelets in the little speedboat he painstakingly sanded and painted each winter. But my summer life turned west, the direction I traveled each morning past two small houses and a slightly larger one with the heads of three lake-record pike nailed above the door, then some buildings I only vaguely remember from my hell-bent dash down the oiled ribbon of dirt and gravel that was our road. The houses were mostly on my left; to the right, untended fields stretched into the distance. I do remember the white house with the red trim, a house I was told to avoid. It belonged to a man who had tried to chase away the young lawyer, his immigrant wife, and their three young children when they became the first Jews to buy on this side of the lake. But it was a minefield I was willing to brave, for barely twenty yards beyond the house of the awful anti-Semite, back on the undeveloped side of the road, lay our ball field.

The field was privately owned, but local custom and quotidian practice had made it de facto community property. A wood-and-wire backstop stood near the road, and just up the third-base line reposed the faintest facsimile of a dugout, its splintered, unpainted boards giving it the look of an abandoned chicken coop with one wall missing. The grass was cut regularly by groups of kids pushing hand mowers, and where the mowing stopped in the outfield, a wavy wall of uncut hay rose to eye level. Any ball that reached the long grass in the air—an impossibility for most of us—was a home run; one that rolled or bounced in untouched was a double. If you chased after a ball into the long grass you'd likely find a group of older kids sneaking smokes in the hay. It was tempting, but only slightly. The attractions of the ball field were far more powerful.

We'd play from nine until noon, when the high sun and beckoning mothers drew us home for lunch. Barely digesting our food, we'd be back again until dinnertime; if dinner waited for my father to return from the city, I'd play until dusk made a hit baseball as small and threatening as a bullet. We had no Little League, which meant in turn we had no parents in the way. They were all out on the lake on their boats, or gathered around their patio grills, or idle in their lawn chairs with drinks in hand. We didn't have girls, either; the few tomboys—so antique a term!—on our road were off climbing trees somewhere.

The group that gathered each morning at the field varied in size from day to day, but not in any other essential way. We were all a few years either side of ten or eleven, we all oiled our gloves with the same reverence our grandmothers brought to polishing the family silver, and none of us could imagine another activity more engaging than baseball. It's strange, but I remember specific ballmates only vaguely. I suspect this is because what compelled me—maybe all of us—was less companionship

40

than activity, less the bonds of friendship than the nascent hormonal buzz of ceaseless competition.

I may not have been the worst ballplayer on our side of the lake (I could always throw pretty well), but the dozen or so kids who had more trouble with a twisting liner than I did would show up for one game at the beginning of the season, confront their ineptitude, and disappear into other activities for the rest of the summer. What we were left with, then, were some very good players, some decent ones, and me. I was small, slow, and unmuscled. Line drives hit right at me caused me to flinch in self-protection. Inside pitches backed me from the plate. But I was a glutton. I was seduced by desire, but hamstrung by it, too. Aching to conquer what was beyond me, I was crippled all the more by my desperate wanting. My brother, four-and-a-half years older than I, was as strong as I was not, a confident athlete. I was grateful that he rarely came to the field; his every success only underscored my own incompetence.

On winter weekends, I was a late sleeper. Freedom from school meant freedom from my mother's gentle nudge in the morning, or from my brother's rougher greeting, a diabolical flourish of disappearing bedclothes. In summer I was up early every day, by necessity. If I reached the field any later than nine I wouldn't get to be a captain and pick teammates, the prerogative of the first two arrivals. If I wasn't a captain, and there was an uneven number of players, I was inevitably the "official pitcher," never privileged by a time at bat unless teams were evened up with the appearance of another player. And sometimes, even then, I wouldn't bat; if the new kid was equally inept, one of us would be official pitcher, the other official catcher.

When I did get to bat, I tried, I tried, but fear dominated—fear of the ball, fear of flinching from fear of the ball, fear of the humiliation of flinching from fear of the ball. Intrepid, I persuaded myself that my mortification was really a stratagem. By the time I was eight, I knew that the worst fielders were arrayed on the right side of the diamond, and as I bailed out from pitches directly over the plate I could tell myself—and, I hoped, make clear to everyone else—that I was simply trying to hit the ball toward those who might have more trouble handling it than would the skillful shortstop or the speedy left-fielder. I thought of myself as a clever singles hitter, like Harvey Kuenn of my beloved Detroit Tigers, seeking holes in the defense the way he did. In truth, I was a singles hitter only in the sense that I couldn't hit anything more than a single.

Still, I was so smitten I found perverse joy in my lack of skill—even as official pitcher, doomed eternally to the outer orbit of any kids' baseball game, where batting is everything. On those endless August days when I pitched and pitched and pitched without relief (and without complaint), every batter had a dozen faces. The first time up he was my neighbor Mickey Howell, a big kid a year older than I, who could hit the ball into the tall grass. But as morning and afternoon wore on, I'd give him new identities. "Coming up to the plate, Willie Mays!" I'd shout, and the blond, pink-faced, perpetually overweight Mickey would (at least in my mind) don the identity of the dazzling Mays as naturally as a new cap. The next time he was Williams, and then he was Kluszewski, and then he was Stan the Man, improbably screwing himself into Musial's impossible batting stance. My own mimicry of big-league pitchers was as exaggerated as my talents were slight, my running commentary a hyperbolic (and accidental) parody of an overheated radio announcer. But my chatter and my poses and all the other elements of the daily fantasy turned every hour on the Cooley Lake field into the Tigers against the Yankees, or the All-Star Game, or the seventh game of the World Series.

It was more than that, actually; for all the single-mindedness I brought to the exercise, it could have been MacArthur returning to Bataan. Those weren't games that I played out there—they were stories, novels, millennial epics.

To my parents, at least to my mother, my endless days of baseball must have been a puzzle; she, who had emigrated from eastern Europe at eighteen, considered baseball an unfathomable mystery, one of those impossible peculiarities of American life. Thirty years later, when I wrote a book about the sport, my mother dutifully read it and then said, "Of course, I loved it because you wrote it, but I didn't understand a single word."

My father understood it perfectly well, if anything too well. He was a fairly knowledgeable fan, and after dinner he brought to my own ball-field efforts the matter-of-fact, unsentimental appraisal he brought to nearly everything. A small-beer lawyer whose grander dreams for himself had deflated by the time he reached his forties, he seemed to find comfort in living without illusions, for himself or for anyone else. It didn't take much observation for him to know that I was a rotten athlete, and his appalling honesty (not to mention a wish to interest me in academic matters, where my grasp was steadier) compelled him to let me know that he knew. There was no real disapproval in his cool evaluation of my athletic skills—teller of truth, he was merely dismissive, and consequently all the more hurtful. Seeing how I'd flinch at his appraisals, he'd try to make me feel better by explaining that athletic ability—baseball ability—wasn't important, managing both to bruise my ego and diminish that wondrous thing that I so loved.

But I didn't deter easily. I'd play through the rain and under the hottest sun, and I'd play until my mother would send one of my siblings down the road to fetch me for dinner. On those occasional days when my brother and his friends commandeered the field, bored by the wonders of the lake and the charms of the Luckies they liked to smoke in the tall grass, I'd chase foul balls for them, and on those days when the rain was so heavy you couldn't see the backstop from the leaky dugout, I'd work on the pocket of my glove, kneading and pounding and shaping it with the intensity a sculptor brings to clay. The hand-hewn Cooley Lake ball field was all the world I wanted.

Was it Oedipus that made me persist? That's possible, I suppose; there were times in my childhood when, had my father taught me to fly, I would have intentionally learned how to crash. But I would like to think there was a conscious, uncorrupted choice involved as well. I liked to swim well enough, but swimming couldn't be measured; one jump off the dock was like any other, the splash and whirl of the water anonymous responses to my exertions. On the ball field, though, each game had content and meaning, each inning a textual richness no dive from a dock could ever contain.

When there were enough of us, we played full-field games, or nearly so—with as few as fourteen players, you could manage three outfielders and four infielders, pitcher and catcher provided by the team at bat; with twelve, you'd do without first basemen, and pitcher's mound was out. With ten players, we'd give up on right field, any ball hit there in the air an automatic strike, any grounder an automatic single if it got past the second baseman. At eight, the configuration was short-third-left-center; at six, it got tough.

But that never stopped us. The next best thing to a game was the facsimile of the game. There was one-on-five, where each player was his own team, hitting into a five-man defense. You didn't run bases in one-on-five. A cleanly fielded ground ball, pop-up, liner, or fly was an out; a grounder that made it past the infielders a single;

42

a grounder past the outfielders, a double. Every eventuality was covered by a code as finely constructed as Talmudic law.

When one-on-five became one-on-four, scores tended to get ridiculous. With four players, we'd play roll-up: the player at bat stayed at the plate until someone could catch a fly, throw the ball all the way in from the spot where it was caught, and hit the bat, laid carefully on the ground at the hitter's feet.

With three, we'd turn to pickle, essentially a base-running exercise; with two, it was home-run derby, which may have entailed far too much ball-chasing but nonetheless allowed us the chance to throw (and hit) a tennis ball at speeds we'd never attain with a real baseball, and when I was alone I'd move the game from the field to my head. I'd sit in the dugout, or on the baseline, and imagine in my fantasies what I couldn't accomplish in reality. At these times I'd stand alone in the outfield, throw the ball up in the air behind me, and race back a half-dozen steps to catch it.

At the best of these last moments, I'd willfully toss the ball just a little too far, or connive to start running a bit too late. And if everything was perfect, if summer was delivering what it had promised, if school was approaching and my idyll was coming to its hurrying end—at such moments I'd lunge to make the catch, falling into a dive just like Al Kaline, my glove intersecting the path of the ball an instant before it would hit the ground, the luscious whiteness just visible in my webbing. I'd imagine the oohs and wows of my friends; I'd see my father drop his newspaper, rise to his feet, and applaud; I'd hear my mother telling her friend about it on the telephone, wrapping her Hungarian accent around the unfamiliar words as if she were singing some new national anthem; I'd hear the roar of the Briggs Stadium crowd, the "He's got it! What a catch! What a catch!" of the radio announcers, and finally the rumble of the printing presses as they

reported my Series-saving grab to an awestruck world.

Then I'd get up, make certain there was absolutely no one around, make certain that the enveloping twilight obscured me even from the view of Mrs. Peters across the road—and then, alone in my private stadium, I would do it once again.

Soon the green-on-green Chevy would be ready to be packed with the sandy bathing suits and the boxes of jigsaw puzzles and the lemonade coolers with their push-button spigots and all the other spent and tattered goods that surrounded a hopelessly middle-class American family in the summer of 1956. But along with everything else that returned to the city in the back of the Chevy, I'd take along my lonely, exquisite triumph on the ballfield at Cooley Lake.

In time, of course, I reached my teens, and inevitably baseball began to recede from my life. I was old enough to drive my brother's boat now, and I responded to the sensation of speed as any fourteen-year-old would. Then came girls, and soon cars, and by the year I turned sixteen I was spending the summer in Detroit, selling hotdogs and soda at the refreshment stand in a city park. When I reached college, my interest in baseball—as both fan and as participant—had subsided entirely, supplanted by the more compelling images of a war in Asia, inequity in the ghettos, the horrible boor in the White House, and all the other enticing targets of the age.

It was several years later, when I had begun to play softball for the company I worked for in New York, that I returned to the game. Remarkably, I turned out to be a fairly decent player; the intimidating shadow of my brother's superior skills was now as distant as my mother's indifference and my father's disdain. More, though, expecting little, I had learned not to take any of it too seriously; relaxed, I could now accomplish what the delicious and terrible agony of desire had made impossible years earlier. I began to play more and more,

44

and in time found myself on summer Sunday mornings riding the subway from my apartment in Brooklyn to Central Park.

Soon enough I found a regular game, informally organized but seriously competitive, at a diamond on the park's west side, near Sixty-fifth Street. Every weekend, the same shifting group of twenty or thirty men, linked only by their wish to play, would show up. Around us the city did what cities do, but our field in the park was an island. Again I learned to rise early, but now out of eagerness rather than desperation: the first nine players to arrive were the home team, the next nine the visitors, and the winners held the field. Latecomers, idling in the bleachers with the Sunday crossword puzzle, would make up a third team for our round-robin. No one knew each other's name, save for the nicknames that accrued as the Sundays piled up.

I was called "Jake," for reasons dim to me even then and utterly lost today. But I do remember one blistering August afternoon on a Sunday that had begun with my group of nine taking the field for the very first game, at nine-thirty in the morning. By some miraculous alignment of the planets, we played as if blessed and didn't relinquish the diamond the entire day. We bought hotdogs from a nearby vendor, gobbled them during our at bats, then took the field again, never pausing and never losing, destroying the opposition in seven-inning increments. Our dominance lasted for a full seven games, and I played all 52 innings, pitching or playing center. I clearly remember that it was 52 innings because the last game went three extra, until just past five in the afternoon, before we won it, 8–7, on a one-out, bases-loaded double over the left-fielder's head—hit by me.

Another player—he hadn't been on my side this Sunday, but we'd been teammates many times before—came up to me several minutes later as I sat exhausted and deliriously happy in the bleachers, too thrilled to go home. His *nom de champs* was Smitty, and he was a well-muscled, thin-waisted black man about thirty-five, with the narrow, pigeon-toed gait of a born athlete. Consistently the best player in our weekly game, he had nonetheless played on the losing team four times today. "Say, Jake," he asked me in apparent earnestness, "you play college ball?"

Even in my post-victory joy, the question surprised me, and then it lifted me from euphoria to sheer giddiness. No, I told him, laughing at the improbability of the question, I never played college ball.

"Then where'd you play, man?"

I could think of only one answer. "At Cooley Lake," I said.

45

MY FAMILY HAS ALWAYS PLANTED IN THE WRONG season, starting with my Chippewa grandfather, who provided for a dozen children during the Depression from his lush Turtle Mountain truck farm. Every January he decided which of his forty rhubarb hills to spade and divide. My Polish grandmother burned coal in a building with no running water and kept her geraniums going in coffee cans. These days, with room to spread out, she sorts and cleans seeds saved from the sweetest squash, the tallest hollyhocks. Ziploc bags of her favorites reach me by mail. In December, my mother argues with her flowers, moving her trellis here, no, there, and sowing her marigolds in the cracked window-wells, where somehow they will do their best for her again. And my father, in the arid subzero months when North Dakota is as barren and lifeless as an asteroid, roots hypothetical apple trees of a sturdier variety than those that succumbed to last year's drought, or invents new ways to foil the sweat bees that gut the crunchy little chestnut crabs for sugar.

LOUISE ERDRICH

47

It is hereditary. One year, late into the stasis of a February, I woke with the sure knowledge of how and where to trench my asparagus. On the heels of that thought came the conviction that the following June I'd sow a flowerbed, yet I'd never planted so much as a single seed in New Hampshire. It was a revelation to me that I knew about trenches, remembered the claws of three-year roots. But, like a long-buried race memory, in the end gardening was natural as day.

I have spent my whole life around people who can walk into the backyard and pull dinner from the ground, whose porches in October are stacked with Moregold squash, bins of tomatoes individually wrapped in torn newspapers, apples sorted into buckets. Even in March, my mother can select from her basement shelves an entire preserved harvest sampler, the summer surplus sealed tightly, the jars wiped clean, almost luminous in the underground gloom. I shouldn't have been surprised that a similar yen would overtake me, that I should picture myself cutting asparagus the way my father does and growing a patch of raspberries to be plundered by small hands. He owns an indestructible all-purpose hat that can be filled with fresh-picked beans or left for a day to shield a tender transplant suffering from sun-wilt. Now I have one, bought like his at a rummage sale.

My yearning to have summer in the winter has grown stronger year by year. Triggered after the solstice by the slow climb of light, fanned by the dependable arrival of seed catalogues on the twenty-sixth of December, the need becomes consolidated in the doldrums before New Year's Day, when my thoughts turn naturally to new beginnings. It is then that I begin the process of planting and revising my dream plot, my mind's ideal, my scentless winter garden. By rock-hard New Hampshire February, when the only colors in the landscape are the plumages of birds—seed-cracking grosbeaks, the ar-rogant crests of jays, the flames of the cardinals sinking and rising through the scrub alder—I have the outline of my scheme.

At night, when our children are asleep, and the reading at my elbow ranges from Acker to Svevo, I often turn instead to the stack of seed catalogues beneath my chair. I fold key pages, circle my choices with green Magic Marker. I decide that pampas grass is essential to the new design, a focal center of feathery plumes, and that the lemon-lily circle from a Minnesota friend must be moved, yet again, to bloom casually against a different boulder. The recurring fantasy, in which clumps of dried herbs adorn the kitchen, takes shape. This time I'll definitely plant tricolored sage. There is the question of which variety of climbing bean will best decorate the six-foot fence that once restrained our high-jumping Siberian husky. Should it be Kentucky Wonder, foot-long pole beans from Jung's, or once again the old-fashioned scarlet runner, which attracted ruby-throated hummingbirds and grew with such startling rapidity its shoots outdistanced the depredations of slugs?

There is that ubiquitous question of pests: which tactics? Last year, my beer bug-traps were lapped up by skunks, whose subsequent wild and odorous party kept the south side of the house off limits for a week. The latest slug-removal scheme, diatomaceous earth, kills less kindly than spirits, but I resolve this time I'll try it. My parents have advised me to wire cups of yeast and molasses to the apple trees, to attract voracious codling moths. I'll tape egg cases of the aphid-eating praying mantis to the posts of my fence, or release a quart or two of ladybugs, deliverable by UPS, guaranteed hungry upon arrival. And perhaps swooping purple martins, who devour hordes of mosquitoes, will take up residence next spring in the aviary apartment house we've provided.

48

All of this I do, undo, redo, week after week. But more than anything else, in deep winter, it is the idea of color that most occupies and inspires me. Color, like light, feeds the brain. The longing for it is a private and surpassing hunger. In the far north, hunters are sometimes attacked by a hiemal psychosis, the source of which is thought to be the absence of color in the landscape. Perhaps it is a mild version of this need that sends me to the drawing board with pictures of flowers, notes on their blooming seasons, and plans to successfully coordinate a kind of summer-long symphony.

Just as the salmon-pink Shirley poppies fade, there will be Missouri primrose, then the heavy spires of delphiniums, against which the magenta phlox will bud, the purple lythrum blaze. Down the borders of the flowerbed, among the stones, I'll replenish the orange and gold Icelandic poppies, their seeds brought two years ago from the Chateau Lake Louise. I'll keep the collection of wildly painted violas and perennial pansies, grown especially for me by a neighbor with a greenhouse. I plan the most dramatic palette combinations. The sunbursts of coreopsis with azure tufts of ageratum. I have never understood the attraction of Vita Sackville-West's all-white garden at Sissinghurst. After all this snow, who needs more *whiteness*?

Melville speculated in *Moby-Dick* that "whiteness is not so much a color as the visible absence of color, and at the same time the concrete of all colors." He considered the theory of natural philosophers, "that all other earthly hues—every stately or lovely emblazoning—the sweet tinges of sunset skies and woods; yea, and the gilded butterflies . . . all these are but subtle deceits, not actually inherent in substances, but only laid on from without; so that all deified Nature absolutely paints like the harlot."

It is, of course, light that produces color, white light of different wavelengths, frequency, and energy.

It has been estimated that human beings can visually distinguish some 10,000,000 different colors. No wonder the unrelieved whites and grays of winter, after two or three months, cause restlessness, mental fatigue, insomnia.

Waking in the dark, rising in the cold, sipping a cup of steeped chamomile buds, I review my splashy catalogues and revive myself with their exotic and enthusiastic claims. "From Ethiopia come white stars with mahogany eyes," "*Supermale* is so superior to other asparagus it almost defies comparison." Who can resist "a truly great 19th century rose . . . with a rich raspberry aroma?" Australian drumstick flowers, red hot pokers, lilies of Peru. The names themselves are almost intoxicating in their splendor and whimsy. There is a green-throated daylily named Thousand Voices, and its relatives: Tree Swallow, Parian China, Chicago Petticoats, and Eenie Weenie, a "vigorous, light yellow dwarf." White Lightning is a grandiflora rose. Song of Japanese Dancing Mice, a mauve ruffled iris. Double Persian buttercup, false dragonhead, japonica. Meadow sage, soapwort, and pincushion flower. Angel's trumpet datura, and Green Envy zinnias. Not to mention the fruits and vegetables, the radishes ranging from French breakfast to Easter egg to round black Spanish, or Sandwich Island mammoth salsify. Yolo Wonder peppers. Big Moon pumpkins that produce jack-o'-lanterns weighing over 100 pounds.

Pearly Gates morning glories. Heavenly blues. There is a ring of the biblical in old-time plants like Jacob's ladder, burning bush, Judas tree, and cosmos. I pick a whole bouquet of the demurely sexual—peacock Feather Nymph, Essex Witch, "a spicily-scented Dianthus with fine fringed petals," Climax marigolds, or the "rare and beautiful bleeding heart flower," Pantaloons. For the high-minded, there is the Chinese Scholar Tree, or Ivory Tower, a white wisteria discovered growing on the

49

campus of Princeton University. I may spend a half hour contemplating the tang of unknown fruits, like jostaberry, or wondering whether it would be possible to distill absinthe from the new Burpee's offering, *Artemisia absinthium,* wormwood, a silver-green perennial.

Within an hour, I'm sated, exhausted with the possibilities, and ready to sleep. Tomorrow, I'll fill the snow-sheeted yard, the field, Melville's "fixed trance of whiteness," with imagined masses of shade, abundant crab apple trees, pink and white blossoms studded with bees. In the view from my window I'll mentally clear new iris beds, sink ponds, build flagstone walks and arbors, or simply remember the gilded frieze of wild milkweed and goldenrod, the violet asters, August's profusion. All of these pictures vanquish the bitter monotony, and, in the end, exceed the yearly reality of what turns out to be my garden.

Full of the usual blights, mistakes, ruinous beetles and parasites, glorious for one week, bedraggled the next, my actual garden is always a mixed bag, falling far short of the imagined perfection. It is a chore, as well. Hard work. I'll by turns passionately weed and ignore it. The garden I tend does not in fact sustain me, although its fruits are bagged and labeled in the freezer.

Every year, the anticipation of summer becomes more necessary. The garden of the spirit is the place I go when the wind howls. This lush and fragrant expectation has a longer growing season than the plot of earth I hoe for three, at most four, temperate months of the year. Raised in the mind's eye, nurtured by the faithful composting of orange rinds and tea leaves and ideas, it is finally the winter garden that produces the true flowering, the saving vision.

50

Oh, not by sun and not by cloud
And not by whippoorwill, crying loud,
And not by the pricking of my thumbs
Do I know the way that the summer comes.
Yet here on this sea-gull-haunted strand,
Here is an omen I understand—
Sand:

Sand on the beaches,
    Sand at the door,
Sand that screeches
    On the new-swept floor;
In the shower, sand, for the foot to crunch on;
Sand in the sandwiches spread for luncheon;
Sand adhesive to son and sibling,
From wallet sifting, from pockets dribbling;
Sand by the beaker
    Nightly shed
From odious sneaker;
    Sand in bed;
Sahara always in my seaside shanty
Like the sand in the voice
Of J. Durante.

Winter is mittens, winter is gaiters,
Steaming on various radiators.
Autumn is leaves that bog the broom.
Spring is mud in the living room
Or skates in places one scarcely planned.
But what is summer, her seal and hand?
Sand:

PHYLLIS McGINLEY

Sand in the closets,
    Sand on the stair,
Desert deposits
    In the parlor chair;
Sand in the halls like the halls of ocean;
Sand in the soap and the suntan lotion;
Stirred in the porridge, tossed in the greens,
Poured from the bottoms of rolled-up jeans;
    In the elmy street,
        On the lawny acre;
    Glued to the seat
        Of the Studebaker;
Wrapped in the folds of the *Wall Street Journal;*
Damp sand, dry sand,
Sand eternal.

When I shake my garments at the Lord's command,
What will they brush from the Promised Land?
Sand.

SUMMER, FOR ME, WAS NEVER A TIME WHEN THE living was easy. In the absence of school, it was an ambiguous space that I had to fill with decision. Summer was my first attempt to entertain myself, to manage my own life, to plan.

It was almost the only leisure I had for thinking about myself. My face was flushed with thinking. In the French Quarter of New Orleans, where I was born, everything glared in the sun, nothing could be ignored. It seemed to me that summer was a time when life was turned inside out, when everyone came out into the street in order to decide what to do with themselves.

Standing on the sidewalk, confronting the day, I felt that the sun was ripening me, but for what? Like a wary animal, I listened to the whisper of the breeze, trying to hear what it was saying. In New Orleans, it carried the sound of insects, peddlers, train whistles, and blues. Especially blues. Summer was like a dance to an interminable blues.

Southern summers are infected by history.

ANATOLE BROYARD

55

The deep stillness in the middle of the afternoon is like a moment of observance, a ceremonial pause, to remind you of all the blood and effort that have soaked into the earth at your feet. You feel as if the dead have been planted there to fertilize the present. Southerners love their dead.

Summer in the south is one metaphor after another, like a profusion of blooms. One day a large snake came out of the sewer at the corner, showed himself to us, and then disappeared again. A fruit seller on a wagon cut a conical red plug from a watermelon and held it up with a knowing smile. I pulled at a ring embedded in the ground and a rusty spring shot dirt into my nose and eyes. I stood on an ant hill and red ants ran up my pants like fire. When I bit into a ripe fig from the tree in my backyard, I knew that there was more to the world than I could understand.

When the afternoon cooled, people in the French Quarter used to bring out chairs and sit on the sidewalk. My mother would powder her neck and face and move a fan in front of her as if she were absently waving at something deep in her head, behind her eyes. Everyone in the neighborhood was strung out on the sidewalk like wash on a line, as if to say, "Here we are, that's all there is, just us." And yet they didn't seem to mind.

One Sunday, dressed all in white, I was given a bouquet of flowers to lay on the altar in church. I refused to surrender them. That same summer I fell in love for the first time. The girl, whose name was Annette, was twelve years old, twice my age, and I made a necklace for her of four-o'clocks strung on a thread. Her boyfriend, who was also twelve, took pity on me. It was his custom, when Annette took a bath, to climb up onto the side of his house, which was across the driveway from hers, and observe her when the breeze stirred the curtains of her bathroom window. In the security of his superior age, he invited me to join him.

I wanted to. Oh, I wanted to. To this day, I dream of what I lost. My most precious possession at that time was a Sacred Heart medal, a fiercely anatomical representation, in lurid velvets, of Jesus' lifegiving organ, which was parted in the middle like a partly open book, as if for the inspection of the skeptical. I imagined Annette's beauty in her bath as something of that order and would have given anything to have seen it. But it meant sharing her with another, and so I never did.

There was a brooding madness, a sense of extremity, in New Orleans summers. Now that we have disarmed summer with air-conditioning, we forget the power of its impact. There was the time it drove old Mr. Salois, our next-door neighbor, to the boiling point. He was an eccentric widower who lived alone. His stinginess with money, speech, and gesture was legendary. Unlike most of the people on the street, who could speak English, Mr. Salois spoke only French. He was a more pronounced provincial Frenchman than any I have since met in literature.

A heavy rain had fallen, turning our unpaved street into a sea of mud, and, looking out of his window, Mr. Salois saw Marcel, a neighborhood boy of ten, splashing up and down, spattering himself with mud, in the middle of the street. I don't know what made him do it—he was not an unusual boy in any way—but his antics outraged the rational Frenchman in Mr. Salois.

He leaned precariously from his window and let out a stream of French at Marcel. It was more than I had heard him say in six years. He was practically screaming. Marcel's only reply was to stamp his foot in the mud and send it flying. Mr. Salois pulled back into his house, like a turtle pulling in its head. When he reappeared, he held a small nickel-plated pistol in his hand. Without another word, he fired a single shot into the air.

Summer was particularly hard on dogs, and, like Mr. Salois, they, too, often went mad in the heat of the afternoon. When this happened a cry would be relayed up the street: *Fou chien! Fou chien!* I was playing in front of my house one day when the cry went up. It must have been a weekend, for my father was home. He came quickly out of the house and carried me inside. Then he stood on the sidewalk looking up the street while I watched him from the window of our one-story house.

He held a hand ax in one hand. He must have brought it with him when he heard the cry, must have run to his shop in the backyard. How quick he was! A hand ax was like a hatchet with a longer handle. My father was a builder and had all sorts of tools.

A slim man of average height, he had more than average grace. He stood in a relaxed but alert attitude, at a right angle to me in my window so that I could see his face, which was wonderfully attentive, secretively concentrated.

The dog came racing up the street, foaming at the mouth, a large white mongrel the size of a German shepherd. The street was deserted except for my father, dreamlike in its emptiness. Like me, everyone else was at their windows. In those days, dogs in New Orleans were not inoculated, and rabies, which we called hydrophobia, was a serious matter.

When the dog saw my father, it seemed to me that he was further enraged by this man's calm, his poise. Though he had been running hard, he appeared to accelerate. I felt a terrible fear for my father, and I wanted to cry out to him, but he looked so studious, so deeply interested in the dog, that I didn't dare disturb him.

The dog leapt; it seemed to fly up off the sidewalk. My father altered his attitude ever so slightly, like a soldier coming smoothly to attention. He raised the ax, a conductor lifting his baton. It was a delicate movement, made with his wrist and his forearm.

With a graceful and precise gesture, the sort of gesture a Frenchman makes to emphasize a point, he brought down the ax. It split the skull when the dog was only a yard away from my father and it fell at his feet like an ardent admirer. I sensed, even then, that my father had subdued the madness of summer. It was one of the things fathers did.

Now I see that it was only temporary. Though my father is gone, the madness of summer is not, for I still feel it. When July arrives with its shimmering afternoons, I wonder what I'm supposed to do about them. One summer, I went to France, as if I could find the French Quarter, which no longer exists for me, in the Lot, a *département* in the southwest, which the inhabitants call *le pays perdu*.

I didn't find it. What I found was that summer, for me, is a fever of the mind, a bloom of consciousness, a sweating of regret, a premonition of desire. Another summer, I sat on the beach at Martha's Vineyard and tried to find or lose myself in the space that stretched from me to the horizon. I thought about what Wallace Stevens called "the madness of space . . . its jocular procreations."

When summer comes, I don't know what I'm going to do. The question hums in my ear, like the sound inside a conch shell.

F OR THOSE OF US SPENDING THE SUMMER AT
home, the public library has become a kind of club-
house. We twelve-year-olds haunt the corridors, carrying staggering armloads of books, acknowledging
each other grimly as we pass. The building has no
air conditioner, and we are sweating under our la-
bors, but somehow we feel *purposeful* here in this
small suburban branch library, where the children's
librarian occasionally looks up at us from her heat
stupor, nodding in approval. The walls are lined
with brightly colored Snoopy and Charlie Brown
posters that urge us to READ ! ! ! but we don't
need any prompting. We are way beyond the point
of initiation; what we are into here is *volume.*

As members of our library's Summer Reading Club, our responsibilities are simple: over the
course of the season, we must read at least ten books.
Ten. We say the number with true disdain. Ten is
nothing; ten is what we will have ripped through
before the first week in July, before the hottest days

59

MEG WOLITZER

have even started. Each of us is aiming for many, many more than ten.

How to explain this new appetite that arrives with summer? It's as though we spend the rest of the year refueling, and only when school ends are we able to rise up from our separate homes and convene in these muted library halls. Certainly during the school year we don't have *time* to read this much, between homework and after-school projects, but it's clearly more than a question of time.

And it's more than the fact that there are rewards involved, that at the end of the summer a huge party will be thrown in our honor. A magician performs, doves fly from his silk hat, and we clap as we're supposed to, but none of us is focusing on his magic. Instead we're glancing down at the Summer Reading Club newsletter we've been handed, a stapled-together leaflet that lists each club member by name and the titles of the books he or she has read. The book lists are long and single-spaced; most of us have read a disturbingly large number of books. We compare prowess, but we also take note of titles, with fondness or dislike or intrigue: *From the Mixed-Up Files of Mrs. Basil E. Frankweiler; It's Like This, Cat; My Darling, My Hamburger*. We are sitting in the darkness with a magician onstage producing doves and ropes of colored scarves, but all of us are distracted. We're lost in plots, characters, populated worlds that we've plowed through during the hottest days of summer. We all know that there is something magical about the amount of books we've read, something nearly miraculous about the sudden voracity that's been implanted in each of us. But it hasn't been implanted there merely by idleness or the promise of reward. The reason is bigger than that, and all of us know it, but since we're only twelve years old we can't yet name it.

* * *

Summers later, I've come to learn that there is something in the nature of summer itself—something contained in the shape and sensibility of those long, inert, months—that makes people want to read. As a twelve-year-old I learned to absorb large doses of ideas and images, and I never lost that ability. But I also never lost my sense of summer as the ideal season for reading. Although summer no longer means vacation time to me, at the beginning of June I still begin to fantasize about books.

Summer reading has a leisurely reputation, way up there with other genteel activities such as croquet and badminton and wildflower gathering. The act of reading has historically been considered a privilege, and summer reading is *privilege* taken to an extreme. Just the image of a reader in summer brings to mind something sensual and luxurious. We picture the reader outdoors only, arranged in some bucolic setting: forest or beach or yard. One stock image is that of a woman stretched out on a hammock surrounded by greenery, clutching a worn copy of *Middlemarch*.

No matter how we picture the summer reader, he or she is always seen *reclining*. This brings to mind the inevitable comparison of summer reading with bedtime reading. Throughout the summer, as before bed, it's often difficult to stay fully conscious. The body is in a state of repose, and the reader has to choose between the passive pleasure of sleep or the active pleasure of reading. At bedtime, reading may hold its own for a while, but sleep invariably wins.

In the summer, however, it's possible to do little else but read; it's possible to use a beautiful landscape merely as a backdrop. One's body becomes so comfortable that it doesn't need much attention. Responsibilities seem remote, and for once permission has been given to simply *lie* there.

For years, no matter where I spent the summer, I always gave myself this permission. If I went away, I took a suitcase of books with me, or else made sure I had access to someone else's books. One summer I stayed in a rented beach house, and spent many weeks reading through the owner's slightly damp collection. Another summer a college friend and I went to Europe, and whichever country we were in, we always tried to dig up English-language books. We ferreted around in the backs of general stores in small towns in Italy and Greece, sometimes triumphantly coming up with the most surprising titles: Dorothy Sayers's *Gaudy Night,* excavated from a bin in Corinth! John Cheever's *Wapshot Chronicles,* found on a bottom shelf in Brindisi! We read day and night on trains all over Europe. By the time the summer was over, we had polished off a wide variety of titles. I imagined I could continue at this clip forever, barreling each summer through novels and biographies and essays. It did not occur to me that at some point things might change.

During the summer after college graduation, I was living temporarily in my parents' house. As always, I had geared myself up for another summer packed with books; it was all I'd ever known, the only way I'd ever spent a summer. But this summer was already different in that the books themselves had changed. The items I now wanted to read, and the ones that had been recommended by friends, were richer, longer, *harder* than ever before. My summer reading list looked like the syllabus of a "Great Books from the Beginning of Civilization until This Very Minute" course at an experimental college: Shakespeare (including the histories); and then a smattering of Nietzsche and Melanie Klein; *The Confessions* of Saint Augustine; *History* by Elsa Morante; *Villette* by Charlotte Brontë; and finally, Robert Musil's classic, *The Man Without Qualities,* which a friend had thrust into my hands with an urgency that startled me. I deter-

mined to plow singlemindedly through all of these works; I would steep myself in them, and at the end of the summer I would feel the thrill of accomplishment. This was a solitary venture; there was no one around with whom to compare lists or trade volumes on trains. The desire to read had to come from elsewhere: from the siren-call of summer itself.

And summer *did* call. Each afternoon I went out into the yard and planted myself on a chaise longue, Saint Augustine's *Confessions* open in my lap. This book was a perfect choice—shining, stirring prose from another time and place. Because summer days are long, I was never quite sure of what time it was. I would look up from Saint Augustine, completely disoriented, thinking: One o'clock? Three o'clock? Five? I felt as though I could read forever and the sun would never set and no authority figure would ever order me to "put that book away."

And then I started *The Man Without Qualities*. I began Musil's massive novel in the middle of July, and managed to work my way through the first few chapters of dense, difficult prose until finally I could read no farther. I just wasn't up to it. I felt the struggle and the heat. All I wanted was to close my eyes, to take a rest. But I kept on trying, transporting the book everywhere—into the yard, back into the house, and even with me to visit friends in New York City, where the book itself had an odd effect on strangers. It *attracted* them.

"Oh," said a young man in the summer garden at the Whitney Museum, approaching the table where I sat mopping my forehead, the book lying shut in front of me. "You're reading Musil. I wrote my dissertation on him!"

I nodded and averted my eyes, murmuring something lame about the greatness of Musil. But I realized then that I had become *slack;* I was reading merely to get to the other side—of the book, and of the summer. This was a far cry from the grim determination of my twelve-year-old self, for whom the desire to read expanded to fill an entire season.

When I got home I slipped the book back into its place on the shelf, feeling enormously guilty, as though my failure would somehow be reported in a stapled-together newsletter at the local library. Nor did I fare so well with most of my other choices. I read in fits and starts, shuffling through the pile of books feeling overwhelmed and yet unable to stop. I never considered going more slowly, spending extended time on a book, finding an appropriate rhythm. By the last week of the summer I had managed to get through just a few of the items on my list. The rest were left with bookmarks wedged in the middle, or else splayed open on the coffee table or beside the bed. Two books were sheepishly returned, unread, to the library weeks after their due date, and the fines were huge. But it somehow seemed right that I should literally *pay* for my unwillingness, my inability, to read.

I paid in other ways as well. The unread books continued to haunt me, hovering nearby like ghosts who've felt cheated of equal time. I thought of *The Man Without Qualities,* and how fitting it was that I'd abandoned it. For if we don't read, then certainly we are left without many qualities. Summer remains summer: blank and hot, something to be gotten through, instead of transforming into the liveliest season of the year, when for once the body lies still but the mind works overtime.

Now when summer approaches I've got an entirely new game plan. I still think about what I might like to read, but I no longer take too many recommendations from friends. Instead I make a solitary journey to the local library to join the browsers, who stand with heads cocked, scouting for books beneath a fleet of whirring fans. These days I really do *browse* first before choosing a book; I stand for a long time and hope that some title or author's name will provoke me. If it does, then I pick up the book and look at the opening pages. Perhaps it isn't entirely fair to judge a book this way, but for now it's the best way I know. I stand and read a little way in, trying to imagine myself surrounded by greenery, keeping company with this book for hours at a time. Is this prose I want to lie down with? I ask. Is this a voice I want to hear murmuring in my ear throughout the longest days of summer? Will it make for good company? And if I suspect it will, then I check the book out. I've been choosing just a few books each summer—a few substantial, appealing books that have tended not to disappoint me: Russian novels; the Victorians; books that speak in southern accents.

Recently, waiting in line to check out my summer choices, I found myself standing behind a group of twelve-year-olds, all of whom were carrying impressive armloads of books. I peered over their shoulders and read the titles and names of authors I remembered from my own childhood. I did a quick spine-count; the boy in front of me was carrying fifteen books, and the girl in front of him had eighteen. The girl had apparently gone beyond her card limit, and I watched as the librarian apologetically made her put a few back.

Then I looked down at my own books, and felt a momentary wave of mortification. *Five* books. Not eighteen, not fifteen, not even *ten*. If these twelve-year-olds looked back at me they would most likely curl their lips in disdain. *Oh, that's what happens,* they would think. *You stop wanting to read. You become a little dumber, a little slower.* For certainly I must have looked that way, fully grown and standing with only five books, when there were so many more I might have chosen from this huge building that housed nothing *but* books. At twelve these kids were testing their limits, flexing muscles they didn't know they had. They were moving very, very fast, learning to feel at home among words. Only later in their lives would they start to slow down and understand the importance of pausing over a significant phrase or idea. Only later would they discover that the quality of a summer spent with books depends, finally, on the particular books one has selected.

When it was my turn in line, the librarian passed my selections under the white light of her photocopying machine and stamped the date, and within seconds I was checked out. She didn't make me put any books back; she didn't smile down at me and say, "Well, *you're* certainly an ambitious reader." Instead, checkout was a dizzyingly quick procedure. Standing with my five meager books, I felt a strong urge to explain to the group of kids that I also used to read fifteen books in no time at all. But the twelve-year-olds were dumping landslides of books into knapsacks and getting ready to leave, and all I could do was follow them out through the turnstiles, armed for another summer.

63

One summer night
I could not sleep and went outside.

I stood awhile in the somber air.

The musk of trees swept over me.
Down into nothing went the dark windows,
the stone flowers, the wasted breath,
whatever I'd carried with me over the years.

It seemed like hours I stood watching
my life fall into the dark.
And then I lay down
and the grass bent over me
and the wind of summer began.

I could not remember the sound of winter.
I could not remember the sound that wished to be winter
I thought of the earthworm turning among roots,
the owl's eyes waiting beneath his lids,
the mouse's bones glowing under his skin.

I looked up.
The green enormous rooms of leaves
swayed in the wind and shone
as if each kept a moon within.

I seemed so far from everything, so far from sleep.
The lawn shivered around me like water.
I could not imagine
a dreamless deep or a light that would not break.

MARK STRAND

I turned and turned in the smoke of my skin.
I floated among the bones of heaven.
Some sparrows had begun to sing.
A few leaves spun over the lawn.

I walked back into the house
and while the sun hooded the roof with light
I lay in bed. I closed my eyes
and did not move. All day

whatever I'd carried with me over the years
would burn and fall away,
burn and fall away.

OUR SUMMER OF LOVE

(An Authentic Memoir behind which the author stands exactly as a reputable automobile maker stands behind his car; The Power Train I guarantee for The Whole Trip; Simple Maintenance, tiny inaccuracies due to Normal Wear, misunderstandings due to negligence on your part— you pick up the bill.)

Here's how it happened:

I was standing on the steps of the Algonquin Trust; do I have to say that I am changing the *names?* Do you expect me to use the real names? I can barely face the existence of the real names. I like a little stage-naming; we all did. Let's start with me standing outside the Algonquin Trust, which we will establish as the Ultimate Decline and Fall Institution, the one that makes you feel like *shit,* because if you participate in it you're dead and if you don't participate in it you're dead, so when they ask you, "What is your *expertise?*" you say to them, "Measuring tiny differences in levels of possible deadness"; at which point, it is determined that you don't get to participate, even though you sense that *they* sense that telling the truth is the only road to happiness, and you are extremely sad at this point because you *had* determined (using your expertise, which was and is an extraordinary one, well suited to tiny calibration jobs) that it would be *slightly less bad* to participate than not to.

GEORGE TROW

67

So, I am standing on the steps of the Algonquin Trust. I had lunched with my father, who had told me in the politest way that I couldn't work there. Then I, politely, but not politely enough from my point of view because I worshipped the ground he walked on because he treated me so cruelly, and that was the spirit of the century, I thought, so he was, in a way, giving me the best possible education even if no payoff, or no anything. So, standing there, I can remember thinking about my body. I was a big guy, in a way, and I felt it, but couldn't focus on it, exactly, since the smallest tiniest bug eating dust at the Algonquin Trust seemed to have more *standing* than I had, but I was thinking about my body, seeing it, seeing it function, and she came up to me and said, "I love you," and then, "Really."

She was older than me. I was shocked. First of all, there are, in all civilized countries, certain rules and regulations; people of different ages don't talk to one another; or perhaps they do. I don't know, and I didn't know then. *Are* we a civilized country? *Do* people of different ages talk together? She produced this feeling of uncertainty in my mind. At the same time her tone was so . . . *forceful*. She said, "I love you" in a way a man standing on the county courthouse steps in Exeter, New Hampshire, had said, "Vote for Kennedy." I had not been able to vote for Kennedy. I felt under pressure to accept this woman's love.

So it was quite a week. She lived upstairs, up a long flight of wooden stairs in an old brick building. Downstairs they repaired boilers. They were all in love with her. She walked down the stairs to let me in—clomp clomp clomp in wooden shoes, or pad, pad, pad in bare feet, and those boilermakers would stop work. Her name was Dorothy. As to the boilermakers, they made a grinding noise, and then it would stop, and, as I went back upstairs, I felt that the eyes of the world were on me. Great feeling, man.

So, at the end of the week, I went to see my father. My father is writing his memoirs. He has three secretaries. One of my father's secretaries reads other people's memoirs; the second secretary filters what this first secretary finds out; the last, final, secretary gets to see my father. I mean, this is the situation *at this minute*. I know why these layers of secretarial interfacing are necessary: no one person will know for sure what my father is plagiarizing from the lives of great men. Secretary Number One is the only one I see now. I sit in her office and experience the memoirs of great men like a sound-and-light show designed to reduce tourists to some awareness of their peasant status. This is what it is like to visit my father now: you are surrounded by reminiscences: *War in Europe, Cripabel: The Secret Door to D-Day. My Life in the Desert,* etc. There is an idea in all this that all decent people are retired and are busy remembering. Active people are somehow wrong. In the old days he had only one secretary, but he had a job.

So what I said, June 21, 1967, was "What are my chances of getting a job?"

"Zero," he said.

When I came out, *she* was there. This is the right time to describe her: cotton dress really clinging to a brick shithouse, little pattern of posies and small flowers on the cotton dress that made you want to pounce on her, and a little straw hat. She went around like that. It drove the city crazy.

So we started a little shop, just a secret one, and that is how we met Earl. He was our first customer, and then we closed up. We were and are in love with Earl. He was driving a baker's van, possibly stolen, with the smell of fresh bread still in it. Earl, why not be blunt, is as mad as a hatter. Right now he is wailing at the moon. He has this wiry body that is almost circular: that is, he doubles back on himself sometimes. Sometimes it is hard to participate with Earl—he is racing around trying to bite his own tail. But every once in a while he stops and sings. He sang this song:

> *Our Life*
> What you know you can have
> Your life in full bloom
> Forest or scene of pale gold
> Our killers are coming
> That noise is their feet
> But we hear inside them
> A beautiful beat
> The mission of loves is
> Trying to hold
> A measure of sense
> Out on drums of pure gold
> Beat *here* on our drums of pure gold

Earl has gold eyes.

He took us to Des Moines. That's where he had grown up. We came into town, passed the state capitol, all shiny and gold and splendid; then we took a left. We rolled up in front of a hotel named for a president. This was a thing we learned during the Summer of Love: hotels named for presidents were *permissive*. Earl knew it all along. The older the better.

We drank a cocktail and Earl sang his song to us that night. We had two rooms with a connecting door. I was supposed to share one room with Dorothy, and Earl was going to have the other. It didn't work out that way. Dorothy was in one room and I was in the other and Earl ran back and forth between the two of us, trying to keep us happy. He would have sex with Dorothy and then he would come in and console me. He consoled me by explaining his song: the importance of every moment. "Our killers" were "hour killers." The stupid things people do to keep from being alive. I was impressed. Dorothy told me later that listening to Earl console me was like listening to a high sound like a wind or the voice of a perfect boy child. I could hardly wait for him to finish making love to Dorothy so he could explain more of the song to me. Dorothy said later that she was in an almost unendurable state; she could not stand to be away from him; however, when he was with her she found herself longing to hear the sound of his voice as he talked to me.

And the next day he left. We lost Earl, so it seemed.

On the road: we sneaked into those *back* towns, by which I mean those small Ur-towns you find stuck onto old cities like an appendix. *The blues*. Your shoes get hotter in this part of city life. We were on the other side of the Mississippi when we met a shaman named Mike. Arms extended, long sexy fingers in watery motion—he chanted nursery rhymes he said predated the Hopi. In general he claimed to know and to be in tune with Indians who were cool before the Indians most people know were cool. We got into a lot of trouble with Mike, especially with Indians. He never slept. I never saw him shut an eye. We rode in a '53 Chrysler he said was part of his grandfather's estate. At night, we pulled off to the side of the road, and Dorothy and I curled up in the back seat. The first night we were feeling a little weird about going to sleep with this lunatic with watery hands *not sleeping* in the front seat. I kept one eye open and then I fell asleep. My head was resting on Dotty's breasts, and I could feel the comfortable prickle of that old wool upholstery those Chryslers used to have—you know? It was all wool, I think, *rich,* and then I felt a voice inside me say *keep still,* and I did, and I felt Mike's hand pass a fraction of an inch above my head. It moved with incredible sureness, and with incredible speed, and it moved just above us, all over us, but never disturbing us. When it was over I looked up. Mike's head was grinning just above mine. "Old Mayan blessing," he said.

I got up just before sunrise and found him at the top of a hill overlooking the highway. He had made a little fire of sticks. "This is how my people greet the sun," he said. At other times he claimed to be an Orthodox Jew; in any case, I always drove the car on Saturdays; he would sit morose and glum, refusing to talk as though even the process of *being driven* violated his scruples. There is no point in not saying how Mike ended up. He has a small, very nearly perfect country house in Ireland, in the West Country. He has a fine collection of horns in the entrance hall, which is of singular charm: a rather magical room, much photographed, the proportions of which lend a light gravity to any social intercourse taking place there. The walls run up not quite two stories; the width is such that one feels held in place by a peculiarly benign pressure; although one knows one is free to move, one doesn't usually move; one stays still just as I did that night in the Chrysler. Outside is a Daimler which Mike says was part of his grandfather's estate. The horns in the hall always remind me of that morning on the hill when he looked into the fire on top of the hill. Well, there was a little something *in* the fire (Mike now serves punches and nogs which are the delight of his neighbors), and when I looked up I saw my friend grow and shed a series of horns; he was an antelope, and then he was Mike again; he was an elk; he was, most remarkably, a moose; he was never a buffalo that I can recall.

But it wasn't all fun. In a bar in Rapid City, he faced off with two Sioux. They were sleepy types who drank and drank until their eyes melted. They were muddy men with molten eyes. Mike was impossible. He talked about the money he was going to inherit, and made sneering references to sweat lodges. He was throwing colored powder all over the place—the place looked like a pastel fairyland, and then all at once it *was* a pastel fairyland, because there was a little something *in* the col-ored powders, and for a moment we all saw the world as Mike saw it: dressed up. The barman looked like an elephant, but he was dressed in a caftan studded with jewels; he had grass growing out of his face, and, looking closely, I could see little tiny lawnmowers at work to try to keep up with it, and little tiny men pushing them. The bar itself was a dam, like the Grand Coulee Dam, but there was a river flowing on top. What a beautiful stream! I couldn't take my eyes off the way it glittered and flowed. I probably missed a lot of other things, but I'm glad I kept my eyes on that glorious, beautiful river.

But I don't think the Sioux were impressed. Either they were immune to Mike's spell, or they had seen it before or—whatever, they just stood there, stolid, like a certain kind of businessperson. Mike was just desperate. I think he'd shot his bolt with that one—it was his Fourth of July, and it just didn't have any effect on them, none. So he ran right up to them, and took off his headband, as though *that* had significance. Let me describe the Sioux. One had white hair and was old, the other was black-haired. Both were fat. They had belts on with big trucks on the buckles. Remember them? You had a Kenworth steaming down your belly. The jukebox was playing some corny song, loud. Mike is screaming:

Nouveaux Riches!
Nouveaux Riches!

It made us want to get to San Francisco.

We began to swim way beyond the spar. Dorothy became extreme in matters of dress, and I—well, I took drugs. Only certain drugs, and only in a certain way—or so I thought. I was a connoisseur of the psychoactive; I stood over my scene and directed myself. I used my energy in such a way that I kept just the distance I wanted between me and other people—and I wanted a roomful of other people. I *danced*. I ate and I smoked, and all the time a certain energy was slowly being released in me.

"Damn, this is fun" was something I said a lot.

I looked around at the people I was with and I loved all of them and forgave them anything. I remember one long-faced man with dark circles under his eyes. Only the most negative energy could bring any desire for life into his face.

"That's part of it," I thought.

One day, I hit upon a recipe so good that I had vision after vision. I was walking along a road with golden bushes along one side, and handsome people began floating past me. It ended, and I said, "Good. That was perfect." And I went for a walk. I don't know if you remember what it was like to walk in the Haight in those days, but first of all, it was an old part of town, so you had old houses and so on, and then there would be gaps in the oldness caused by modern Americana, and then there were secret things. You'd pause next to a little door, the window of which was covered up by a multicolored piece of cloth, and you'd hear words not associated with old cities or modern Americana. I paused in front of one such door and heard a stream of words—it reminded me of Earl.

All of a sudden I wanted *more*. And I was sick to death of my insistence on *perfection*—just the right recipe, etc. I went to my dealer and got more, but it cost more. "It's the regular price," he said—exactly twice as much.

I looked around the room and everyone was engaged in a private dilemma. I went to the next room and had a vision of myself behind bars. I went back on the street; I didn't feel that bad, actually, I just knew that that was over.

And there was Earl, just like that. He was smiling, the big irresistible smile; Dorothy was with him—dressed way down. And they were in a car—a new Ford convertible. "Thought we'd find you here," Earl said.

During the next month, we played. Earl *was* the Summer of Love; that is, he summed it up. We looked at him, and he looked at the sun. We're outside a house on Page Street, or we are watching beautiful Hell's Angels motoring up the street to bury their dead. But we are always with Earl.

Earl stole cars. In America, it's hard to get to exactly the right amount of criminality, but Earl hit it right on the head with his lovely and industrious series of auto thefts. And he did it all for us. We were his God-given audience, as for a man working on a delicate glaze, standing over a hot fire. The summer fired *him* and he went after hot metal. The cars were always physically scalding. He never stole a car that had been standing in the shade or out of a garage. Always they had been in the hot sun, on some street, by some curb, waiting to meet him.

And then it was over. Amphetamines hit and the world was full of a thousand *parody* Earls. It was impossible. One day we went and bought a car—an old Chevy—and drove back to the East Coast to the Chesapeake Bay. Earl, right now, is, as I say, howling at the moon. Dorothy is wearing a cotton dress. And me, well I'm not at the Algonquin Trust. The trust, by the way, a very conservative institution in my day, made a *lot* of bad guesses about the oil business and isn't doing as well as we are. We're having a simple fish chowder, corn fritters, and poetry later. Can I shuck you an oyster?

I T IS A HUMAN PROVIDENCE THAT SCATTERS THE
holidays around so conveniently on the calendar.
The American summer has three days to mark its
phases—Memorial Day to signal its beginning, the
Fourth of July to mark the start of high summer,
and Labor Day to bring it to a gentle close. Of these
three, the first and third were invented and bestowed
upon the year by governmental fiat, and even the
Fourth is somewhat arbitrary. The Continental
Congress actually declared that "these United Col-
onies are, and of right ought to be Free and Inde-
pendent States" on July 2, 1776, and on the Fourth
merely voted to adopt the Declaration of Independence, which was publicly read in the yard of
the Pennsylvania statehouse in Philadelphia on July
eighth. It was not copied onto parchment and
signed by the delegates in attendance until August
second, and the last of the fifty-six signatories,
Thomas McKean of Delaware, did not affix his name
before 1777. The first anniversary of the Fourth of
July was celebrated that year in Philadelphia, with

JOHN UPDIKE

parades and oratory and fireworks and the ringing of bells, and the custom spread and has lasted. This most American of holidays serves to remind us, if we care, that our founding fathers, wearing wigs and jabots and lace-trimmed frockcoats, met and debated in a fearful sweat, and delicately and artfully stitched together our national fabric amid the muggy, buggy heat of a Philadelphia summer before air-conditioning and pesticides.

The northern Europeans who came here encountered hotter summers than they had known, and they were slow to compromise their costumes. For most of the nineteenth century, the middle class kept buttoned up and voluminously swathed in dark colors, and only the underprivileged enjoyed the privilege of dressing light. The Fourth of July still reminds us of that end-of-the-century loosening up—the arrival of straw hats and linen dresses, the resort to wide-porched summer hotels and sandy cliffs climbed by flights of wooden stairs, the discovery of the American summer as another continent, a land of ice and ice cream and baseball and beach picnics and outdoor concerts, of freedom felt in the body itself. We have brought forth a new world of nearly naked red men and brown women camping out and cooking out by seaside and lakeside. Sea and lake and mountain are where King Summer reigns, and the Fourth of July fireworks are his announcement of possession.

Yet fireworks have a sadness. They are expensive, somewhat dangerous, and soon over. Quickly subsiding into their final shreds and sparks, they impose our passion and mortality on the night sky. Though the Fourth marks the beginning of true summer warmth, already the long June evenings are drawing in, and by the end of the month the shimmering days have been perceptibly nipped shorter. The holiday has an undertow of perfect ripeness; it reaches its climax in the dark, not long before bedtime—in contrast to Easter and Christmas, whose glad tidings arrive in the morning, and Thanksgiving, which sluggishly crests in midafternoon. Slightly melancholy,

too, seems the Fourth's great show of red, white, and blue, hearkening back to a primitive patriotism that can only make us feel a bit guilty and inadequate, as Washington's Birthday used to before it was unceremoniously lumped into Presidents' Day—a holiday without a savor, a wintry excuse for a three-day weekend.

Bonfires, perhaps, more than fireworks capture the basic flavor of the Fourth. The initial event had the acrid taste of political defiance, the crackling of the violent cleansing that a revolution intends. The men whose prim and flossy signatures are aligned on the Declaration of Independence were risking their necks, and for eight years men of many nationalities died so that one more nation could be born. Our Revolution seems, in the attic of our shared imagery, a kind of popgun war, with chorus lines of redcoats and Minutemen; even the tatters of Washington's troops at Valley Forge and his icy crossing of the Delaware feel stylized and mock-heroic. Bonfires, which in some towns are still heaped up building-high on the main square, remind us, as Bastille Day and Guy Fawkes Day remind the citizens of other sovereignties, that conflagrations and constitutions keep close company, and that established statehood rests upon triumphant violence. It is grimly appropriate that every year, as fireworks misfire and canoes overturn, the Fourth of July is marked with a few more American deaths. Independence is risky. Strangely, high summer's only other significant national anniversary is V-J Day, celebrating Japan's surrender to our atomic bombs.

One's own memories of the Fourth tend to blend, much as summer days blend one into the next. My father, in the firefly-rife backyard of my first home, lights a bundle of little firecrackers and darts dramatically back, and we all stand around in an awed circle, at what we hope is a safe distance, as the device twists and jumps and shouts its furious, frustrated noise. It wants to kill us, and can't. I hold a sparkler at arm's length, marveling that its sparks do not burn. Then there is something we children call a "snake," which combustively turns itself into a coil of gray ash. How one acquires such things is at least as fascinating as their ignition: they are illegal in Pennsylvania and have been smuggled in from other, more permissive states; the illicit traffic in fireworks is as signal a feature of our national life as the different-colored license plates, the drinking ages that go up and down as state borders are crossed, and, for real grown-ups, the patchwork of statutes controlling divorce and abortion. These discrepancies help make the United States a more interesting place to live in, and hint at what the original uniters were contending with.

Later, myself a father, I drove station wagons full of sleepyheads to towns and beaches and country clubs where firework displays, ever threatened by local regulations and limited budgets, were still put on. Once, off Edgartown dock, we watched fireworks in a dense fog—subtle tints appeared in the mist above us, and explosive noises tardily descended. At the Essex Country Club, in Manchester-by-the-Sea, a golf course was the site, and members, in summer tuxedos and full-length dresses, watched from within a roped-off enclave while we nonmembers huddled in the sand traps. In 1976, on the two hundredth anniversary of our independence—a beautiful day all across the country—my wife and I flew from Chicago, and under us, from Indiana to Massachusetts, fireworks silently expanded and vanished like small soft radiant dandelion polls. A few years later, she and I were part of the immense throng that observes July Fourth in Washington, D.C., filling the Mall from Lincoln's Monument to the Capitol; the fireworks, in the vicinity of the Washington Monument, seemed very far away, as most things are in this grandly diffuse city. Most recently, just last summer, returning to my own yard after wearying of a local display, I discovered that fireworks look biggest and most astonishing when seen above and through trees—like the moon (that old dud that won't quite wink out), they take impressiveness from a near horizon. These giant chrysanthemums and jellyfish seemed, thrusting and pulsing just above the silhouettes of my arbor vitae and hickory tree, visitations from space, from beyond our three shadowy dimensions.

Of course there is more to the Fourth of July than fireworks. There are, or used to be, parades and footraces, clambakes and corn-on-the-cob, doubleheaders and sunburn and dyspepsia and beer. Its virtue as a holiday is that one is not expected to give any gifts or eat any large bird; its disadvantage is its delayed climax. It goes on all day. An enormous novel once of some fame, Ross Lockridge's *Raintree County,* took place entirely (with flashbacks) on July Fourth, 1892. At some moment during the day one has the sensation of being in Kansas. July Fourth is as close to the center of the year as Topeka is to the geographical center of the forty-eight conterminous states. It is the unmoving pivot, a little frightening in its stillness, a stillness we hear between the bursts of firecrackers, the crashing advance and pebble-rattling retreat of waves, the roar of powerboats, the radios in the sand, the hiss of pop-tops being pulled. Not all our deliberate and defiant fun can quite hide the long day's dry American silence. The clouds are high wisps of icy cirrus; it's cold up there. The tops of your feet and tip of your nose hurt from too many ultraviolet rays, and even after a shower, sand keeps trickling down your neck. The grand set-piece finale, with its starlike spinning rockets and undulating red and white stripes and grimacing eagle outlined in phosphorus, rather fizzles, even though the Independence Day Observance Committee invested a cool thousand in it and the fireworks contractor (a Japanese company, as it happens) virtually guaranteed success. Like most birthday parties, the Fourth of July makes us a little wary, a touch cranky. We itch to get on with life. Let the summer begin.

2. When Time Was Time

MOST EVERY SUMMER WE WENT: MY PARENTS and assorted children, piling into the suitcase-jammed station wagon (pre-air-conditioned comfort, pre-disposable diaper, pre-Interstate highway) to make the arduous journey. From our home in piedmont North Carolina, Mount Vernon, Illinois—the town where my mother's parents lived—seemed a hard place to get to.

We left before dawn, the youngest often carried to the car in pajamas. My father, gabby with holiday spirit, wore a sports cap with upturned bill and clip-on sunglasses that he'd flip up from his monster horn-rims when he read road maps. Mother copiloted cheerfully beside him. Her job was to spot elusive route signs, to refold the maps that he shook loose, to scout out the cleanest-looking filling stations, and to peel my father sticks of chewing gum.

He chain-chewed Juicy Fruit, its perky jellybean fragrance lightening the predawn air. As my mother ceremoniously offered him the first stick of

MARIANNE GINGHER

the trip, his face turned rowdy and boyish. He inserted a key, mashed the gas pedal, hearkened to the drumroll of the Plymouth's engine—and we were off.

The first day we drove fourteen or fifteen hours on a two-lane road that roller-coasted through the Blue Ridge Mountains, the Great Smokies, and shot the Cumberland Gap into Tennessee. In Bristol we stopped for gasoline, Tru-Ades, butterscotch Life-Savers, more Juicy Fruit, and to use the rest rooms, if we hadn't already relieved ourselves in the mayonnaise jars my mother brought along.

On one memorable descent into Bristol, our brakes failed, and my father slunk the Plymouth in low gear all the way down the mountain, jerking the emergency brake like a joystick, heroically dragging one foot along the pavement, waving away with martyrlike grandeur the fresh stick of gum my mother unfurled.

Once the hazards of mountain driving were past, we sang the exuberant, swaggering songs of survivors: military airs, mostly. To commemorate our safe arrival into the flatlands of Tennessee, my mother sang "The Tennessee Waltz." Then my brothers begged my parents to sing "Bill Grogan's Goat"—even the gruesome verse in which the train engineer slits the poor goat's throat—and they merrily complied.

We chattered noisily about Daniel Boone and the pioneers who'd traveled this route by horseback, blazing the Wilderness Trail. We marveled at their courage and counted ourselves lucky to enjoy the relative speed and poshness of a modern concrete highway. Daddy pointed out historical markers, Civil War graveyards and battle sites. And if our attention drifted toward games of Counting Cows and License Plate Poker, he roused us with his cornball rendition of "Daddy's Whiskers":

One morning at the breakfast table,
Mommy had nothing to eat.
She grabbed old Daddy's whiskers

'Cause she thought they were Shredded Wheat!
They're always in the way,
The cows eat them for hay,
They hide the dirt on Daddy's shirt,
They're always in the way!

We enjoyed high spirits until lunchtime—because it hadn't gotten hot yet.

It was the day's rising heat that dictated where and when we finally stopped to eat. We ritually chose a Howard Johnson's for their pistachio ice cream (triangular-shaped scoops served in frosty metal compotiers) and because all Howard Johnson's were air-conditioned. In the turquoise chill of the restaurant, we were as happy as fish in an aquarium, languishing over our luncheon plates long after our meal was finished and the youngest of my brothers had grown fidgety. Beyond the cool pane of Howard Johnson's window glass, the parking lot shimmered like a pancake griddle. To stall for time, we children even ate the crusts from our sandwiches.

We climbed back into the Plymouth whimpering, fussing, picking fights. You could feel the heat of the asphalt soaking through the rubber soles of your P.F. Flyers, melting them down. The sun flattened the tops of our heads, heavy as an iron, and the interior of the unshaded Plymouth roared like a furnace. Our skin stuck to the upholstery; the baby was allowed to ride naked, without his diaper, if he promised to venture the mayonnaise jar.

We were finished with games, with pointing out Burma-Shave signs, with singing, with the esprit of pioneers. We scrunched away from each other, so that we wouldn't stick together, folded our arms, and sulked. If we were lucky, we slept. The only things that roused us from our brooding stupor were the farm-sluggish smells of the countryside: hog and chicken lots, mud-brothy creeks, dead animals ripening along the buggy, overlush roadside, smells you could taste in the back of your throat, that made you grind your teeth and wake up hollering for mercy.

We were covered in prickly heat rash. Once, when we stopped to buy ice cream near a town called French Lick, Tennessee, my brothers took their vanilla ice cream cones and painted big bull's-eyes on their bare stomachs for relief.

We were bound and determined to make London Hall, Kentucky, before nightfall. And if my father now drove with a vengeance, if he broke the speed limit, it was because he knew, blessedly assured by his motor club guidebook, that waiting for us at London Hall was a spanking new motel outfitted with air conditioners.

London Hall, London Hall, we chanted as the miles ticked off. Surely we were much too sweaty and rumpled to enter such a place. My mother brought out a comb and slicked us all up, for we envisioned a castle with turrets, cool as stone. *London Hall, London Hall:* we breathed the hallowed incantation in each others' ears, on each others' rash-peppered necks, on the moist, closed eyelids of those of us still lucky enough to be sleeping.

At the London Hall Motor Inn, my father checked us all into a room as square and plain and white as the interior of an ice-cream carton. It was furnished with two double beds, a foldaway cot, and a couple of end tables equipped with *Reader's Digests* and Bakelite ashtrays. But what we saw, when we opened the door, paled in comparison to what we felt: air that clattered, it was so cold, air that dropped upon your shoulders like a metal cape, that went straight for your melted bones and ordered them instantly into solid, sentinel form.

A few seconds of exposure and we'd all raised goose bumps the size of thumbtacks. We plunged into the room, bouncing from one bed to the other. My parpents bounced, too. My brothers snooped around, opening drawers, parting the shower curtain, tumbling on the carpet, which was as bright red and icy cold as cocktail sauce. The air conditioner blathered away full blast in one corner, chatty-sounding as a good host. Frost glistened invitingly on its vents, and we kids scraped the frost off with our fingernails and ate it, smacking our lips, fluttering our eyelids with pleasure. None of us admitted when the cold became unbearable, but of course it did, and soon enough we were donning bathing suits and heading for the steamiest swimming pool in history.

To lie floating on my back in the London Hall, Kentucky swimming pool, thawing myself out from the arctic motel room, felt nothing short of prodigal: cows bellowing in the pasture (the pool was located next to a stockyard), an inkling of moon slipping into view, my family splashing close by, and supper wholeheartedly abandoned in favor of snacks levered from machines. This must have been my earliest brush with decadence. It never occurred to me, as I drifted on my back and stared up into the muggy twilight, watching the slow tufting of small soft-looking summer stars, that we were little more than halfway to Mount Vernon.

Some summers my father couldn't take time away from his office to drive us, and so my mother dauntlessly shepherded us kids aboard the Southern Crescent railway for a circuitous journey that involved a tricky connection in Atlanta. We were not only to change trains in Atlanta but train stations, too, a Houdiniesque maneuver my mother, with her brood of babies, managed only through the kindness of many strangers. Once we left the Southern Crescent and boarded the B & O line, we ratcheted along in our compartment for about eighteen hours—first aiming north toward Cincinnati, then west to Fort Wayne.

I remember these excursions as the greatest adventures of my childhood. Oh, those risky clamorous leaps between the bucking cars as we made our way to dinner! The naughty thrill of finding out that when you flushed the little toilets, their contents emptied on the

84

track! And no sideshow extravagance could equal the daring with which the waiters in the dining car poured our milk. With one hand they'd decorously present an empty glass at child's-eye level. The other hand produced a carton of milk as if by a snap of fingers and, brandishing the carton high above the clattering table, took what looked to be improbable aim and poured. The milk purled down, a Niagara Falls of milk. We knew it was wet, that in seconds we'd be drinking it, and yet it seemed transformed into something solid as it swung between the waiter's hands, suspended like a rope of taffy or the whipped-out arc of a jumprope. The train swayed, but the milk looped steadily down the air. We barely had time to gasp before it filled its intended target. Not one drop spilled. Daredevil Milk, we called it, and gulped it greedily, the way Popeye gulped spinach. Of course we begged for second glasses, but my mother said one glass was enough. She claimed that the milk had an acrobatic influence, that they probably flavored it with Mexican jumping beans, and that one glass before bedtime made us tumbly enough.

After dinner, though it was barely dark, we retired to our roomette to wash hands and faces in the little birdbath sink and slip into beds the porters had made up. I snuggled into my upper berth, much too excited to sleep right away, content to lie there feeling cozy, listening to the click and chatter of train wheels, the whoosh of dark, silent farmland outside the shaded window, the plaintive ding-dang of crossings that quickly faded, absorbed into the nighttime otherness of towns we passed. Who knew where we were? Only the beast-of-burden train knew as it tunneled through the night. My sheets crackled with starch. I've never felt so well tended, dreamy with prospect, and as fearless about the unfamiliar since.

We arrived at sunrise—the train made a special stop for us at the crossroads of a dew-covered nowhere where my grandfather's big blue Imperial was parked beside a cornfield. Nearby stood my grandfather, wearing a jaunty straw hat, and my grandmother, rouged, in a swirly Sunday dress, a purse swinging on her arm.

As soon as we'd alighted from the train, my mother's stouthearted firmness relaxed, gave way to a kind of girlishness as she allowed herself to be a daughter again. We children were permitted to scamper, expected to devise our own amusements. So if we chose to spend a whole afternoon gouging tar out of a road and chewing it, nobody protested. You could goof off to your heart's content and nobody said a word, nobody ever asked you to account for your day. You could derive enormous pleasure simply from sitting on the front-porch glider all afternoon, watching cars cruise up and down North Twelfth Street, counting the convertibles. North Twelfth was paved with maroon-colored bricks, and the sound the traffic made was a rich lopping sound like beaters whirring cake batter.

Which might remind you to go pester Maggie, Granny's cook, about making a favorite dessert for supper and letting you help. All desserts were made from scratch and they were culinary spectacles: twelve-egg angel food cake with cups of boiled custard on the side for dunking, Coronation Butterscotch Pie, Granny's Graham Cracker Roll, Hundred Dollar Chocolate Cake, which is how much a woman had offered to pay the chef for the recipe. At breakfast and dinner we ate off Fiesta Ware, and my brothers and I always argued over who got the cobalt-blue plate.

Roam, goof off, dawdle, snoop. I liked pilfering my Uncle Dick's bedroom. He'd left home by the time we started making our pilgrimages, but his bedroom remained intact with oddball treasures. He'd ditched a first-rate collection of science fiction books and westerns and a stack of RCA Victor records, big 78 rpm platters with burgundy and silver labels. My favorite record was a song about a balky racehorse named Beetlebaum. I was terrified of the name: the monstrous bass thrum of the word "Beetlebaum" leaping off the record made my heart pound. It sounded like a reprimand. But whenever I got the chance to slip off to Uncle Dick's bedroom alone and put the record on, I did. It was a test of some sort.

My brothers liked exploring the back alley, where Dada burned trash in a huge ashcan. A bitter, licoricelike smell of smoke hovered in the air, whether there was a fire or not. Sometimes we pretended the ashes were snow and staged snowball fights with big, flaky handfuls. Beyond the alley was the Bunchmans' house and broad lawn (they had six redheaded children) and a crooked little ankle-deep creek loaded with crawdads and salamanders. Dada had strung a rope swing from the maple tree that arched over the porte cochere. He'd laid out a croquet court in the backyard amidst metal scalloped-back lawn chairs and a fringed canvas hammock my brothers were always flipping each other out of. There was a gravel driveway that you could comb for hours, hunting mica specimens. In the basement stood deep zinc wash sinks with black rubber hoses attached to the spigots, where we children were encouraged to bathe. We liked to stuff the hoses in our mouths and pretend we were deep-sea divers hunting pearls.

Sometimes Dada would take us out in the little motorboat that he'd built and painted himself. He'd let us mess with the tools in his garage workshop; once he helped us build a triangular birdhouse that we painted to resemble the Eiffel Tower. He taught us Parcheesi and told us stories of his oil-rigging days in Oklahoma and about the time he lost the tip-end of one of his fingers in a piece of machinery. He talked about his and Granny's elopement on his 1918 Harley-Davidson motorcycle when she was still engaged to another boy back in Danville, Kentucky. He pulled half-dollars out of our ears and *paid* my brothers for giving him back rubs. He called

my oldest brother "Knothead" and they became best pals—the bestowing of a nickname will do that. Best of all, he let us watch him dress his stump, and once he let young Knothead do the honors.

Dada's stump was where one of his feet should have been. He'd lost the foot to a gangrenous infection. There wasn't anything scary about the stump except that it signaled an absent foot; we considered it a fleshly *contraption*.

The stump was round and smooth and pink like a small bald head, and Dada rubbed it with baby oil to keep it from drying out. He talked softly when he rubbed it, as if the stump were asleep. He said it was numb; he said you could stick a pin in it and he wouldn't feel pain although he'd still bleed. After he oiled it, he dressed it in a special sock and a cup-shaped brace and attached it to one shoe.

He limped, of course, but it wasn't his stump that slowed him down. It was his lungs. He'd survived a terrible car crash when he was a young man. His chest had been crushed by the steering wheel, all his ribs broken, his lungs punctured, his jaw so shattered they'd had to wire it back together, and he hadn't been expected to live. He loved to talk about surviving that wreck, how the doctors had hovered over him with grave predictions. But he'd outfoxed them, he'd say to us, slapping his knee, his struggle amply rewarded, for here we all were, years later, worshipping him.

We stayed in Mount Vernon for three or four weeks—sometimes longer. My mother got a tan. She and her old high school friends spent time together, playing golf, going to luncheons given in her honor. Much of the time we kids simply hung around the house with Granny and Dada, never feeling the need of things to do, never bored. It was the treasure-trove otherness of my grandparents' house that we relished and basked in. A kind of wealth awaited us there. It was a time of

indiscriminate savoring, of not only detecting differences but plundering them for all their worth.

Dada read his newspaper, and for hours I could content myself watching him read. Unlike my father, Dada wetted a thumb to help him turn the pages. Now and then he would pause and adjust his reading glasses—there was a pleasant rhythm to this motion. He crossed his legs at the ankles, displaying the clownish jigsaw designs of his Argyles. Whenever he read something in the paper that he didn't like, he'd shout, "Land!"

After I'd watched Dada awhile, I'd mosey into Granny's bedroom to find her seated at her vanity, arranging her hair. "You need a girl your own age to play with or you'll be *bored,*" she'd say. When she said the word "bored" she bugged her eyes as if she'd swallowed poison. But I liked "bored." "Bored" gave me latitude to call all the shots. "Bored" let me be dreamy to my heart's content. "Why don't you call up Mary Nelle Waters?" she'd suggest. "She's a very nice girl, even though she wears dresses."

Inviting company to play was always a command performance, and I'd answer the doorbell, dragging my feet, a grim hostess indeed. Mary Nelle and I played until we had a falling-out, an inevitability because we were both strong-willed girls. She'd get around to laughing at my southern accent and calling me "Mushmouth" and I'd yell, "Damn Yankee!" at her because anyone who pronounced their *i*'s in a crisp, superior, bright-eyed way was a Yankee to a southern child. I could drawl out the word "Yankee" so blasphemously, so lip-curlingly snide that Mary Nelle Waters would cry with shame. Once she took her revenge by setting a paper sack containing a dead squirrel in one of the basement windows. She positioned it behind a curtain so that days passed before we finally located it.

Of the children Granny introduced me to, I liked Fayette and Rocky Roo the best. I loved their names;

they were feisty kids who went barefooted and liked to chew the skin off tar bubbles, too. They both looked like Huckleberry Finn. But aside from Fayette and Rocky Roo, I pleaded with my grandmother for solitude. "Can't I just *poke?*" I'd ask her. "It's *summertime.*" The word seemed a verbal talisman I might employ at the mention of a disagreeable invitation. She'd look at me critically, as if into a mirror, then her face let itself go loose and bright with recognition. "Yes," she'd say, "isn't summer wonderful all by itself?" She'd say this in a giggling, secretive way, bunching her shoulders, busying herself once again at her vanity, daubing her face with Charles of the Ritz Velvet Texture Lotion, which made me think of summer as a kind of vanishing cream one might slather over blemishes of inconvenience.

I'd watch her take a metal nail file and measure a precise amount of Chantilly powder onto the tip and sprinkle the powder inside her brassiere. It was the only scent she liked. If I asked her to, she'd take out her false teeth and let me examine them. She'd sing, "I Went to the Animal Fair" as many times as I liked. And with tireless, big-eyed expressiveness, she'd recite rhymes from her childhood:

> Onery, orry, ickery Ann,
> Philistan, Phalistan, Nicholas, Jan,
> Queevy, quavy, English Navy,
> Stinktum, stanktum, cherrico bunk!

She'd allow me to mess with her hearing aids and try on all her hats with veils. And her eyes would mist fondly as she told me about growing up in Kentucky and her home, Granite Hill, the estate near Danville that no longer belonged to the family. She told me lots about Nannie, her mother, and showed me the elegant tortoiseshell combs that had once anchored Nannie's braids. She brought out a fan made from black ostrich plumes and a ladylike parasol that Nannie had carried on her arm to tea parties. She, like my own mother, her daughter, had gone home every summer to visit until her parents died. She had taken three children alone in a '34 Chevrolet and driven a thousand miles down lumpy dirt roads that stretched tenuously between the oil fields in Oklahoma, where she'd lived, and the farm in Kentucky. Nothing, she said, would have stopped her.

It wasn't until I was an adult with children of my own, long after both Granny and Dada had died, that my mother told me the truth about them. I forget exactly how she told me—only that there was nothing vicious in her confession. Her truth sprung from a context that had everything to do with family continuity, but in one startling, innocence-unraveling moment, she revealed to me that my grandparents' marriage had been fraught with despair, that there had been times when Dada's rage had shattered the Fiesta Ware. Granny had taken her children back to Kentucky every summer to escape him.

"In today's world she'd have left him," my mother said. "But it was the Depression. What would she have done? Where would she have gone?"

"Home!" I said. "To Nannie in Kentucky."

"Impossible," my mother said. "Granny's father had taken a grim view of her elopement to begin with. As far as he was concerned, she'd made her bed and she could lie in it."

The mystery I now confronted was not so much the source of my grandparents' incompatibility, what devils my grandfather had wrestled with, or why my grandmother had stuck with him. The mystery that loomed largest of all was my mother's seemingly vibrant tolerance. As she talked about her childhood, it was clear that shadows of her parents' troubles hung over her still. Then, how was she able to return, summer after summer, to Mount Vernon to visit them? How had she been able to forgive her parents enough so that she could share her children with them?

Listening to her recall old griefs, I couldn't be swayed. The unhappy parents that belonged to my mother bore no resemblance to the grandparents I had known; I couldn't share my mother's disappointments. I felt eerily unrelated to her. Who was this man who'd been so stingy and glum, this weak and dreamy wife? How were they the same affable, vigorous people I'd clung to and loved, guardians of my happy childhood? Listening to my mother's revelations, I felt voluminous gratitude. That she had allowed me the romance of my grandparents seemed a brave and generous gift, those trips to Mount Vernon and the imperishable memories they brought to my life a kind of counterweight to the burdens she'd borne as a child. Love, despite its flaws and lapses, had been allowed to come full circle.

My mother's decision to take us to Mount Vernon was as much an exercise of her faith in possibility as a gesture toward reconciliation. Our unspoiled, unknowledgeable hearts made us go-betweens of an infectious goodwill. We were unencumbered by the past; watching her parents attend us, my mother must have felt a mixture of relief and wistfulness.

Maybe my grandparents were more receptive in the summertime than at any time during the year. Our visit was occasion for their release from whatever pinched routines they otherwise obeyed. We commanded their audience; we asked torrential questions; we raised up the ghosts of their pasts and walked fearlessly beside them; we begged them away from the confines of themselves. A breeze poured busily through their house all day, freshening the air with our comings and goings. Curtains twirled at the windows, and no door was ever locked.

When my own children return from a holiday spent with grandparents, they carry a boxful of treasure: seashell necklaces Papa has fashioned, the glistening hulls

of june bugs, sycamore balls, gnarled and squatty mushrooms, the tangible stars of early fallen maple leaves—all things bright and beautiful gathered on a walk in the wild woods with loved ones. They have seen a lizard for the first time. Their pockets bulge with bird feathers, chunks of milky quartz. Their faces bloom with satisfaction.

I think they look taller, looser, older somehow. Are they really as beautiful as they seem to be, or is their beauty a trick of happiness as they troop home with their spoils? For a moment, seeing them, I am my own mother watching my flush-faced play long ago in Mount Vernon.

I am my grandmother glimpsing my young mother's face brighten on the drive up the lane of one-hundred-year-old oak trees at Granite Hill. I am Nannie's pioneer-stock mother, shading her eyes, gazing into a field simmering with the ruckus of wildflowers where her children leap and chase and disappear like dreams. I am myself, ten years old, calling after my crazy brothers to Stop! Wait up! as we race to the swimming pool at the London Hall Motor Inn over which dazzles the fiery weather of dreams: stars of a billion summers yet to come, light of a billion summers past just now filtering to Earth.

91

SUMMER SERENADE

When the thunder stalks the sky,
When tickle-footed walks the fly,
When shirt is wet and throat is dry,
Look, my darling, that's July.

Though the grassy lawn be leather,
And prickly temper tug the tether,
Shall we postpone our love for weather?
If we must melt, let's melt together!

OGDEN NASH

ONE FRIDAY I WAS SITTING UP ON THE HILL behind my house with fifty thousand acres of untouched wilderness—forest, ponds, rounded mountains—at my back. I was watching a chipmunk. He stood up on his hind legs, bleach-white belly quivering, looking alertly round. A shadow passed; he dove for cover. Three or four minutes later he climbed out again; this time I moved, not much but enough that he squawked and disappeared. The game continued until I gave up and wandered down toward the house, pausing for a look in our pond. An unidentified duck swam up and down the far shore, sticking his red head under the surface in search of food. Longish bill, white chassis, slight crest—a merganser, perhaps. It required a long sit with the binoculars and the bird book. It may not have been a merganser; it may have been something else. "Think of our life in nature," said Thoreau. "Daily to be shown matter, to come in contact with it—rocks, trees, wind on our cheeks! The solid earth! The actual world! The *common sense! Contact!*

BILL McKIBBEN

Contact!" My point exactly. But one must admit that nature has a few drawbacks; there's little opportunity to spend money, and wildlife, despite the name, are deeply distrustful of loudly amplified rock-and-roll. Every once in a while I want a dose of the bad old days before I convinced myself that it was more satisfying to sit really still and wait for the porcupine to show up. Those days, maybe once a summer, my wife and I pile in the car and head an hour south to Lake George.

Lake George, which stretches forty miles north-to-south near New York's border with Vermont, is a venerable tourist haunt and a living history of the summers of my youth. Every year when my family would go to some pretty spot and hike up mountains, I would hurry us through lunch, pick a few obligatory berries, and march everyone back down the trail so that we could get to the nearest tourist town and spend some money. Hot dogs! Pinball! Action! I know my million-dollar beaches, my miracle miles, my fabulous boardwalks. And Lake George is among the best. Summertime is for kids going places with their parents. Lake George is suffused with that sense of inevitability, as if the various revolutions of the two decades between my birth and my majority hadn't happened and the world was the same reliable place where Dad drove and Mom read off the attractions from the AAA guide and I kicked Tom in the back seat.

What Williamsburg is to the colonial period, Lake George is to the late Eisenhower epoch. How venerable is this town? The big restaurants along the choice blocks of Canada Street feature specials like chicken à la king. (This is not some New American Cuisine chicken à la king. This chicken à la king has been chicken à la king all along. When the restaurant critic for the local daily rates the eateries, he says things like "Entrees come with a choice of potato, and my baker was one of the best I have eaten for months.") *And Lake George boasts at least 162 holes of miniature golf,* including two thirty-six-hole layouts and the world's oldest (self-professed) miniature golf course.

The oldest course, in a small downtown lot next to Mr. B's Subs, has suffered over the years. The invention of electricity has left many of its holes a little out of date (for example, the one where you swing the hanging log back and forth on a chain to create an obstacle). The green carpet is frayed, the seams make putting difficult, and no one sweeps away the pine needles between seasons. It always reminds me of another summer, when my brother and I turned our suburban backyard into a miniature golf course that drew children from two and three neighborhoods away. (Its profitability diminished when my mother, a liberal, made us slash the greens fee from a quarter to a penny.) We had this one hole, where you hit the ball into a wheelbarrow and then Tom turned the wheelbarrow around and trundled the ball about ten feet toward the hole and let it roll out, that beat anything on this course. Still, the sense of history here is almost palpable. On a misty day it would not surprise me to see, through the wispy clouds, ladies in bloomers and petticoats and corsets and veils and button shoes and straw hats and whatever else they wore bending over putts.

Lake George offers the visitor a choice of three amusement parks—Gaslight Village, Magic Forest, and Great Escape. I've visited all three over the years. Gaslight Village, though still operational, seems to be on the way out, facing a future as the parking lot for the planned convention center. The Forest and the Escape, however, really represent the ends of the attraction spectrum, an almost geological depiction of the progress in the notion of amusement. An enormous Uncle Sam stands in the parking lot of the Magic Forest. Inside its gates, the attractions include a replica of the Statue of Liberty, "Lake George's only diving horse," a year-round Santa Claus available for visits, and, of course, the Bird Show. "There is a good chance," the management promises, "you might have seen these birds on national TV." If you have ever turned on national TV and seen a macaw playing cards, a macaw subtracting, a macaw picking up the phone receiver, or a macaw riding a tiny scooter, a tiny bike, or a pair of tiny roller skates, these are the birds.

Great Escape is a different sort of operation, a generation or so ahead of Magic Forest but an attractive decade or two behind Six Flags or Disney World. Just for instance, one of the attractions sports a brand new sign that proclaims it to be "Mr. Chipper's Magical Mystery Ride." What it is is a Scrambler, instantly recognizable to anyone familiar with a county fair—the Scrambler is the Ur-ride, the one that no self-respecting or even self-loathing carnival would be without. When the fair came to my hometown, a few of the rides would change each year. One year we got the Zipper, where you were strapped into a sarcophaguslike cabin that went up in the air and turned upside down, and one night we counted six people throwing up on it. But there was always the fried-dough stand, and always the Scrambler, and they always set up next to each other, so as you slammed around in the metal cars you'd come in and out of the smell of the sweet grease. Anyway, at Great Escape the Scrambler squats inside a decaying geodesic-dome building, so that it revolves in the pitch dark except for a strobe light and a "light show" that looks like a homework project for the Haight-Ashbury free kindergarten. Fun, though.

All the favorite attractions are there. At the bumper cars, a benign-looking mom drives carefully around all possible trouble, smiling cheerfully if she is bumped. If the cars had turn signals, she would use hers. (Once, caught in a vacation traffic jam, we were being passed by a line of lawless cars in the breakdown lane. Finally, in deep frustration, my mother cranked down her window, leaned out, shook her fist—and yelled, "Un-pleasant!" at a startled driver.) Great Escape also has a 180-degree theater, one of those marvels that have perhaps seen their very best days but still linger pleasantly. The scratchy print opens with the air force Thunderbirds flying maneuvers over the desert and *you are in the cockpit*. Then the action switches to New York City and an awesome sweeping view of Times Square and the theaters along Forty-second Street before they were "revitalized" into office towers. (In the movie, *Deep Throat* is still showing at the porn house on the corner.) It's a pretty great show. Outside the theater, some goats in a pen are ostensibly reenacting the Billy Goats Gruff. There's one of those machines that will sell you feed pellets for a quarter, but the goat has forced a hole in the fence and as soon as you put your coin in he clamps his mouth to the slot where the feed spills out, eliminating the middleman.

Dinner for us, too. Mama Riso? Michael Anthony's (Fettucine Cagiucco)? Trattoria Siciliana? Luigi's? Ciro's (Fettucine Alfredo with Fruits of the Sea)? La Roma? Paolinos? Lazio's? Pagnott's? Giuseppes? Mario's (Osso Bucco)? This is a scungilli town, though there's also a Bavarian House ("Breakfast at the House of 3 Eggs") and a Hofbrauhaus, and of course the Tiki Resort Inn with the Waikiki Supper Club featuring the Hawaiian Revue (for your late night entertainment, it's "Naughty Hattie," formerly "Hurricane Hattie," a "keyboard comedienne, a luau of laughs"). Essentially, a lot of solid food—restaurants here still boast about their relish trays. Us, we go to Art's Lobster Shack, for steamers, the bibs, the works. We sit on the upstairs deck and watch the families wander by—Mom, Pop, a daughter, two boys with brush cuts, or Mom, Pop, a boy with a brush cut and two daughters. Much cotton candy. This town is a sociologist's nightmare, the nuclear family still uncracked. More than the Scrambler, I suppose, this is what I come

to see. How odd to be nostalgic for that ordered world of intact families, "traditional" arrangements. It never occurred to me, growing up in it, that there was anything else.

Every once in a while the booming foghorn of one of the sternwheelers—the *Ticonderoga* or the *Mohican* or the *Minnehaha*—sounds in the medium distance, reminding everyone that there is a lake down there. Time has sullied the Jewel of the Adirondacks, Queen of Lakes. Sometimes the authorities have to close the Million-Dollar Beach to swimmers because the fecal coliform count gets too high. But business does not seem to suffer much. Unlike, say, Niagara Falls, which is surrounded by a very similar tourist colony, Lake George itself is a vestigial organ. Entrepreneurs rent a large number of devices—jet skis, para sails, paddleboats—that require a body of water for their operation, but these seem to appeal to a minority. It's not as extreme as, say, South of the Border, that highway exit in the Carolinas with seventeen gift shops and the hundred-and-fifty-foot-tall sombrero-shaped observation tower where for a dollar you get a terrific view of Interstate 95. But you can definitely do Lake George without getting wet. (One thing you can do is go to the wax museums. "Foolish Mortals, This is the House of Frankenstein," reads the placard outside one. "Be warned, this is not just another wax museum!" Up the street, the Movieworld Wax Museum dates Lake George as perfectly as any carbon test or tree-ring count. Who's the big draw? Dr. Zhivago. For the hip, there's the Fonz.)

Like any resort community, Lake George would be incomplete without a certain whiff of youthful vice, some mild sin for those difficult in-between years when you're too old to stroll the boardwalk with your parents and too young to have kids of your own. The hot spot in town is D.J.'s Nite Club, where Tuesday night is always Ladies' Hot Legs Contest Night (and Thursday is Mens' Hot Chest Night, with over $200 in cash and prizes). That's about as bad as it gets, although there was a flap once about the Scanty Shanty, a naughty lingerie shop on a side street. (The mayor told the press he had been personally shown the clothing involved, and hoped "to relieve the minds of citizens whose morality had been offended.") Mostly, though, the nightlife runs to Johnny Milanese ("Manilow to Mandrell") at the Roaring Brook or Nelson Sardelli at the Georgian or the "psychic dinner show" in nearby Glens Falls, featuring medium Anne Fisher.

Alienated youth, therefore, tend to migrate to the edges of town, and to Skateland in particular, which offers roller skating and a water slide but mainly a go-kart track that stays open under the lights till midnight. In the fevered imagination of my youth, go-kart tracks were the place for bad complexions and worse attitudes, miniature golf for juvenile delinquents, motorized billiards. I always wondered what kind of parents took their kids to the go-kart track. Not my kind, thankfully, or else the nice illicit tingle I feel on arrival would have vanished. Actually, Skateland is not exactly the inner circle of hell. Everyone *does* wear black T-shirts with the names of heavy-metal bands—Metallica, especially, the last time I checked. But they pretty much all obey the rules, except the one about staying twenty feet apart from the other karts, and if you break that, you just have to make a short pitstop is all. A go-kart travels at about fifteen miles per hour on the straightaways, and yet the proximity (six inches) to the pavement and the roar and the shake from the engine make it feel like about a hundred and eighty, magic of a high order. I have my doubts about whether cars were a worthwhile invention, but go-karts—noisy, greasy, a little dangerous, and only $2.50—go-karts rule!

It costs $3.75 for a nightcap round of miniature golf, more than double the price at the world's oldest course in the center of town. But this was Sir Goony

99

Golf ("It's the Gooniest!"), most technically advanced of all the town's many links. (We play them all, though. Each has one or two classic holes—the Paul Bunyan, the backside of the horse, the big hat, the London Bridge, the German beer stein, the Empire State Building, the Liberty Bell, the giant orange, and so on.) At Goony Golf, the greens are true and fast, though the overall pace can be a little slow, when certain families fail to obey the six-strokes-maximum-per-hole rule (and utterly ignore the two-strokes-on-any-ramp rule). The nineteenth hole, of course, offers a chance at a free game; I miss, but am filled with the memory of a mosquito-ridden night in my childhood when my mother, after patiently playing an entire round on some humid course with her avid sons, quite by accident knocked her ball straight into the clown's nose and had to play another round. That is what a place like Lake George is best at—it's a childhood preserved in amber and yet freshly available to the next generation. This course is essentially the same as the ones I played on in my youth, and the next generation of min-iature golf courses, even if they involve striking the ball into laser-driven time warps or nuclear-powered black holes, will still be close enough. In a world of constant flux and motion . . . but I think you get the point.

Time to head home. We drive through town once more, past Waterslide World with the twin kamikazi slides and the bumper-boat lagoon, past the Log Jam Restaurant ("Visiting Lake George without dining at the Log Jam is like going to Paris and not seeing the Eiffel Tower"), past the Mohican Motel and the Samoset, past the Christmas Shop and Wagars Candy Factory with the homemade turtles, past the store with the tattoos you can remove with baby oil, past the Surfrider Motel with its giant sign of a diving woman in a red swimsuit and bathing cap of a particular and not so distant era, past the Rickshaw Annex, where in his umpteenth season Chef Sik Kwan Lee is still setting fire to the pu-pu platters. And then we head into the dark once more, and the woods, and the mountains. It's been a nice day—the time, quite literally, of my life.

Around five o'clock on hot summer mornings in New York a breeze springs up from the south. It stays around just long enough to clean the air, then dies at sunrise. For an hour or so my bedroom is cool, cool enough for me to wake and fumble for the sheet I've tossed off during the night.

The breeze isn't just felt; it's heard and smelled. Ginkgo trees tap against the screens, and their curious scent—one that, until I realized what it was, had me looking suspiciously at my cats—seeps into the room. If I had air-conditioning I wouldn't know that breeze, so, in a sense, I wouldn't really know a city dawn. But because I don't, I have been gently wakened at what my family always called the best part of the day and sip my coffee in its gray light and dense silence.

A long time ago I lived in an apartment with old wiring and windows on an air shaft. Air-conditioning wasn't possible and neither was sleep, and I remember dark, hot walks along Second Avenue looking for an open ice-cream parlor and theaters

MARY CANTWELL

patronized for the climate, not the movie. Heat lingered into late September in that apartment—it had sunk into the walls—so when I moved it was with a resolution never to live like that again.

After that I had air conditioners. Usually there was only one, but for a while I had them blasting from both ends of a floor-through. The living room, which was where the currents met and married, was like a meat locker.

When I moved into my present apartment it was too late in the season to bother with installing an air conditioner. I would wait, I thought, until the spring. But spring came and I had other things to think about, and summer slipped in without my noticing, and then one August day I realized I was happy without that dull whine and that false weather—that I was hearing summer sounds I hadn't heard in years.

At night, for instance, I can hear the neighbors talking in their gardens just as I used to hear them on the porches of my childhood, but with a difference: there is a hum in New York, as if of machinery, and it is always present, even in a neighborhood like mine where there is no industry, little traffic, and few tall buildings. I can hear the occasional sough of winds through trees and the occasional bird, too, and during storms the rain and thunder seem to enter the rooms.

These are the country sounds I was raised on. A friend speaks with longing of the city sounds she cannot hear because her apartment is impossible without a machine in the window chilling the air and eating up money. The rest of the year she is companioned by the traffic, fighting drunks, and late-night restaurant-goers on lower Third Avenue, and they are to her—a native New Yorker—what whispering leaves and noisy sparrows are to me. But in summer she cannot hear them; though she is comfortable, she is lonely. That the sound of a honking horn is inferior to that of a honking bird is, after all, an arbitrary decision.

One sound that is beautiful in summer, as beautiful as that of a running brook, is that of a purring refrigerator. Mine is lined with bottled New York tap water, assorted diet colas, grapefruit juice, and, on rich and giddy days, Perrier. The freezer holds ice cream and ice cubes and not much else; opening it and facing that arctic air holds a thrill unknown to cooler heads.

How, though, would I manage in a room that is 90 degrees if I couldn't sweat? My unfortunate mother cannot—I suspect her mind forbids her body so ungenteel a display of humanity—and is given to swooning. But I am always dripping, not a beautiful sight, perhaps, but one grateful for its cooperative glands. My face is red and my hair sticks to my head. A shower is to me what the sea they bathed in was to those marching women in *A Town Like Alice*. The pleasure is heightened by the misery that precedes it, and when I towel-dry my hair and put on a cotton dress or nightgown just off the ironing board I feel as if freshly emerged from the egg.

Ironing in summer: it is a crazy thing to do, especially for someone who doesn't iron well at the best of times, but only cotton will do in the heat. So I press my old-fashioned nightgowns, my pillowcases (the sheets shift for themselves), and the rather peculiar robes I consider suitable wear for opening the front door. If the kitchen grows stifling, then how much cooler seem the other rooms.

The door is opened to very few. True, my ceilings are high and the windows face the direction of that dawn breeze, but I seldom have guests in summer. They wouldn't be happy, although I know they would be polite and would fan themselves as inconspicuously as they could with napkins or some such. They'd have to bat mosquitoes, too, or at least those few that have slid through the tiny holes the cats have made in the screens. So on those nights and weekends I am usually alone, the only illumination—because light is heat—from the television screen or the reading lamp beside my bed.

But there is one guest I recall. It was a Saturday afternoon, and I had lowered the canvas blind over the big window in the living room so that the light seemed subaqueous. "Oh," she said, "this looks like Venice." I was pleased and said so, though I have never been in Venice and what the room reminds me of is a dry-goods store in the Rhode Island town in which I grew up. It was huge and cavernous and shaded by deep awnings, and I was there a lot during the summer I was learning to knit, buying a yarn called Red Heart. Then I would walk home through elm-lined streets and spend the afternoon, an instruction book in front of me, trying to turn the heel of a sock.

I was very close to the seasons then because our summers were warm and our winters cold. Our springs were the kind about which bad poetry is written and our autumns those for which New England is famous. If it has been some years since I moved into this apartment and I am still without air-conditioning, it is because I want those seasons again—indoors as well as out. Spring I can have with supermarket daffodils and fall with dried flowers and winter whether I want it or not because there is insufficient caulking in the world to stopper the drafts that sneak through my walls and windows. Now I have summer too: especially in that five o'clock breeze.

HORSE-CHESTNUT TREES AND ROSES

Twenty-some years ago, I read Graham Stuart Thomas's
"Colour in the Winter Garden." I didn't plant
a winter garden, but the book led on to his
rose books: "The Old Shrub Roses," "Shrub Roses
of Today," and the one about climbers and ramblers.

By the corner of the arbor I planted the splendid
Nevada (a Spanish rose, Pedro Dot) and on the
arbor yellow Lawrence Johnston—
    I've never known
anyone who made a real success of that. Then
a small flowered rose (like a blackberry in flower),
whose name I forget, and then, oh loveliness, oh
glory, Mme. Alfred Carrière, white, with a faintest
blush of pink, and which will bloom even on a
north wall. I used to shave and gaze down into her—
morning kisses. The day Robert Kennedy died, a
green and evil worm crawled out of a bud. I killed
it, a gardening Sirhan Sirhan.

At the corner of the house Rosa Mutabilis fluttered
its single, changeable wings. My favorite, perhaps.

Then, in the border, along the south side of
the white house, Golden Wings (a patented rose—
did you know you can patent roses? Well, you can);
prickly, purplish Rose de Rescht; Souvenir
de la Malmaison (said to be named by
    a Russian Grand Duke in
honor of the Empress Joséphine, Empress of Rosarians);

JAMES SCHUYLER

Mabel Morrison, lifting her blowsy white blooms
to the living-room windows.

Then Georg Arends, whose silver-pink petals
uniquely fold into sharp points (or is Georg
my favorite?).

And darkly brooding Prince Camille de Rohan, on
which, out of a cloudless sky,
   a miraculous rain
once fell. (But I'm forgetting Gloire de Dijon,
Dean Hole's favorite rose.)

Then the smallest, most delicate, delectable
of all, Rose de Meaux. Alas, it pined away.

And elsewhere more: Rosa Gallica, the striped
and the pink, the Pembertons, Persian yellow,
and unforgettable cerise Zéphirine Drouhin.
And a gray rose, Reine des Violettes. Sweet-
brier, Mme. Pierre Oger, Variegata di Bologna.
And more, whose names escape me.

I went by there Sunday last and they're gone, all
gone, uprooted, supplanted by a hateful "foundation
planting" of dinky conifers, some pointed, some
squatty roundish. I put a curse on it and them.

On either side of the front walk there towered two
old horse-chestnut trees. I loved their sticky,
unfurling leaves, and when they bore their candles

it was magic, breath-catching, eye-delighting. Cut
down, cut down. What kind of man cuts down trees
that took all those years to grow? I do not
understand.

Oh, well, it's his house now, and I remove the
curse, but not without a hope that Rose de Rescht
and the rugosas gave him a good scratching. He
deserved it.

But oh dear: I forgot the five Old China Monthly
roses, and I always wish I'd planted Félicité
et Perpétue—it's their names I like. And
Climbing Lady Hillingdon.

(But the Garland grown as a fountain seemed
somehow beyond me.)

There are roses and roses, always more roses.
It's the horse-chestnut trees I mind.

Odious hateful vandal.

HORSE-CHESTNUT TREES AND ROSES JAMES SCHUYLER

WE GROW UP EXPERIENCING SUMMERS AS IN-termissions, and once we hit our teens it is during these breaks in our structured regimen that we initially taste the satisfaction of remuneration that is earned, not merely doled. Tasks defined as "work" are not only graded, they are compensated; they have a worth that is unarguable because it translates into hard currency. Wage labor—and in the beginning, this generally means a confining, repetitive chore for which we are quickly overqualified—paradoxically brings a sense of blooming freedom. At the outset, the complaint to a peer that your business supersedes your fun is oddly liberating—no matter what drudgery requires your attention, it is by its very nature essential, serious, adult.

At least that's how it seemed to me. I came from a line of people hard hit by the Great Depression. My mother and her sisters went to work early in their teens—my mother operated a kind of calculator known as a comptometer, while my aunts spent their days at a peanut factory and at Western

MICHAEL DORRIS

Union, respectively. My grandmother did piecework sewing. Their efforts, and the Democratic Party, saw them through, and to this day they never look back without appreciation for their later solvency. They take nothing for granted. Accomplishments are celebrated, possessions are valuable, in direct proportion to the labor entailed to acquire them; anything easily come by or bought on credit is suspect. When I was growing up we were far from wealthy, but what money we had was correlated to the hours some one of us had logged. My eagerness to contribute to, or at least not diminish, the coffer was countered by the arguments of those whose salaries kept me in school: my higher education was a sound group investment. The whole family was adamant that I have the opportunities they had missed and, no matter how much I objected, they stinted themselves to provide for me.

Summer jobs were therefore a relief, an opportunity to pull a share of the load. As soon as the days turned warm I began to peruse the Classifieds, and when the spring semester was done, I was ready to punch a clock. It even felt right. Work in June, July, and August had an almost biblical aspect: in the hot, canicular weather your brow sweats, just as God had ordained. Moreover, summer jobs had the luxury of being temporary. No matter how bizarre, how onerous, how off my supposed track, employment terminated with the falling leaves, and I was back on neutral ground. So, during each annual three-month leave from secondary school and later from the university, I compiled an eclectic résumé; lawn cutter, hair sweeper in a barber shop, lifeguard, delivery boy, temporary mail carrier, file clerk, youth program coordinator on my Montana reservation, ballroom dance instructor, theater party promoter, night-shift hospital records keeper, human adding machine in a Paris bank, encyclopedia salesman, newspaper stringer, recreation bus manager, salmon fisherman.

The stolid titles disguise the madness of some of these occupations. For instance, I seemed inevitably to be hired to trim the yards of the unconventional. One woman followed beside me, step by step, as I traversed her yard in ever tighter squares, and called my attention to every missed blade of grass. Another client never had the "change" to pay me, and so reimbursed my weekly pruning with an offering culled from his library. I could have done without the *Guide to Artificial Respiration* (1942) or the many well-worn copies of Reader's Digest Condensed Books, but sometimes the selection merited the wait. Like a rat lured repeatedly back to the danger of mild electric shock by the mystique of intermittent reinforcement, I kept mowing by day in hopes of turning pages all night.

The summer I was eighteen, a possibility arose for a rotation at the post office, and I grabbed it. There was something casually sophisticated about work that required a uniform, about having a federal ranking, even if it was GS-1 (Temp/Sub), and it was flattering to be entrusted with a leather bag containing who-knew-what important correspondence. Every day I was assigned a new beat, usually in a rough neighborhood avoided whenever possible by regular carriers, and I proved quite capable of complicating normally routine missions. The low point came on the first of August, when I diligently delivered four blocks' worth of welfare checks to the right numbers on the wrong streets. It is no fun to snatch unexpected wealth from the hands of those who have but moments previously opened their mailboxes and received a bonus.

After my first year of college, I lived with relatives on an Indian reservation in eastern Montana and filled the only post available: Coordinator of Tribal Youth Programs. I was seduced by the language of the announcement into assuming that there existed youth programs to coordinate. In fact, the youth consisted of a dozen bored,

disgruntled kids—most of them my cousins—who had nothing better to do each day than to show up at what was euphemistically called "the gym" and hate whatever "program" I had planned for them. The youth ranged in age from five to fifteen and seemed to have as their sole common ambition the determination to smoke cigarettes. This put them at immediate and ongoing odds with the coordinator, who on his first day naïvely encouraged them to sing the "doe, a deer, a female deer" song from *The Sound of Music.* They looked at me, that bleak morning, and I looked at them, each boy and girl equipped with a Pall Mall behind the ear, and we all knew it would be a long, struggle-charged battle. It was to be a contest of wills, the hearty and wholesome vs. prohibited vice. I stood for dodgeball, for collecting bugs in glass jars, for arts and crafts; they had pledged a preternatural allegiance to sloth. The odds were not in my favor, and each waking dawn I experienced the lightheadedness of anticipated exhaustion, that thrill of giddy dissociation in which nothing seems real or of great significance. I went with the flow and learned to inhale.

The next summer, I decided to find work in an urban setting for a change, and was hired as a general office assistant in the Elsa Hoppenfeld Theatre Party Agency, located above Sardi's restaurant in New York City. The agency consisted of Elsa Hoppenfeld herself, Rita Frank, her regular deputy, and me. Elsa was a gregarious Viennese woman who established contacts through personal charm, and she spent much of the time away from the building, courting trade. Rita was therefore both my immediate supervisor and constant companion; she had the most incredible fingernails I had ever seen—long, carefully shaped pegs lacquered in cruel primary colors and hard as stone—and an attitude about her that could only be described as zeal.

The goal of a theater party agent is to sell blocks of tickets to imminent Broadway productions. The likely buyers are charities, B'nai Briths, Hadassahs, and assorted other fund-raising organizations. We received commissions on volume, and so it was necessary to convince a prospect that a play—preferably an expensive musical—for which we had reserved the rights to seats would be a boffo smash hit.

The object of our greatest expectation that season was an extravaganza called *Chu Chem,* a saga that aspired to ride the coattails of *Fiddler on the Roof* into entertainment history. It starred the estimable Molly Picon and told the story of a family who had centuries ago gone from Israel to China during the diaspora, yet had, despite isolation in an alien environment, retained Orthodox culture and habits. The crux of the plot revolved around a man with several marriageable daughters and nary a kosher suitor within five thousand miles. For three months Rita and I waxed eloquent in singing the show's praises. We sat in our little office, behind facing desks, and every noon while she redid her nails I ordered out from a deli that offered such exotic (to me) delicacies as fried egg sandwiches, lox and cream cheese, pastrami, *tongue.* I developed of necessity and habit a telephone voice laced with a distinctly Yiddish accent. It could have been a great career. However, come November *Chu Chem* bombed. Its closing was such a financial catastrophe for all concerned that when the following January one Monsieur Dupont advertised on the placement board at my college, I decided to put an ocean between me and my former trusting clientele.

M. Dupont came to campus with the stated purpose of interviewing candidates for teller positions in a French bank. Successful applicants, required to be fluent in *français,* would be rewarded with three well-paid months and a rent-free apartment in Paris. I headed for the language lab and registered for an appointment.

The only French in the interview was "*Bon jour, ça va?*" after which M. Dupont switched into English and described the wonderful deal on charter air flights that would be available to those who got the nod. Round-trip to Amsterdam, via Reykjavik, leaving the day after exams and returning in mid-September, no changes or substitutions. I signed up on the spot. I was to be a *banquier,* with *pied-à-terre* in Montparnasse!

When I arrived with only $50 in traveler's checks in my pocket—the flight had cleaned me out, but who needed money, since my paycheck started right away—no one in Paris had ever heard of M. Dupont.

Alors.

I stood in the Gare du Nord and considered my options. There weren't any. I scanned a listing of Paris hotels and headed for the cheapest one: the Hotel Villedo, $10 a night. The place had an ambiance that I persuaded myself was antique, despite the red light above the sign. The only accommodation available was "the bridal suite," a steal at $20. The glass door to my room didn't lock, and there was a rather continual floor show, but at some point I must have dozed off. When I awoke the church bells were ringing, the sky was pink, and I felt renewed. No small setback was going to spoil my adventure. I stood and stretched, then walked to a mirror that hung above the sink next to the bed. I leaned forward to punctuate my resolve with a confident look in the eye.

The sink disengaged and fell to the floor. Water gushed. In panic I rummaged through my open suitcase, stuffed two pairs of underpants into the pipe to quell the flow, and before the dam broke, I was out the door. I barreled through the lobby of the first bank I passed, asked to see the director, and told the startled man my sad story. For some reason, whether from shock or pity, he hired me at $1.27 an hour to be a cross-checker of foreign currency transactions, and with two phone calls found me lodgings at a commercial school's dormitory.

From eight to five each weekday my duty was to sit in a windowless room with six impeccably dressed people, all of whom were totaling identical additions and subtractions. We were highly dignified with each other, very professional, no *tutoyer*ing. M. Saint presided, but the formidable Mademoiselle was the true power; she oversaw each of our columns and shook her head sadly at my American-shaped numbers.

My legacy from that summer, however, was more than an enduring penchant for crossed 7's. After I had worked for six weeks, M. Saint asked me during a coffee break why I didn't follow the example of other foreign students he had known and depart the office at noon in order to spend the afternoon touring the sights of Paris with the Alliance Française.

"Because," I replied in my halting French, "that costs money. I depend upon my full salary the same as any of you." M. Saint nodded gravely and said no more, but then on the next Friday he presented me with a white envelope along with my check.

"Do not open this until you have left the Société Général," he said ominously. I thought I was fired for the time I had mixed up krøner and guilders, and, once on the sidewalk, I steeled myself to read the worst. I was out of ideas, and felt the quiet panic of blankness.

"Dear Sir," I translated the perfect script. "You are a person of value. It is not correct that you should be in our beautiful city and not see it. Therefore we have amassed a modest sum to pay the tuition for a two-week afternoon program for you at the Alliance Française. Your wages will not suffer, for it is your assignment to appear each morning in this bureau and reacquaint us with the places you have visited. We shall see them afresh through your eyes." The letter had thirty signatures, from the director to the janitor, and stuffed inside the envelope was a sheaf of franc notes in various denominations.

I rushed back to the tiny office. M. Saint and Mademoiselle had waited, and accepted my gratitude with their usual controlled smiles and precise handshakes. But they had blown their Gallic cover, and for the next ten days and then through all the days until I went home in September, our branch was awash with sightseeing paraphernalia. Everyone had advice, favorite haunts, criticisms of the Alliance's choices or explanations. Paris passed through the bank's granite walls as sweetly as a June breeze through a window screen, and ever afterward the lilt of overheard French, a photograph of *Sacré Coeur* or the Louvre, even a monthly bank statement, recalls to me that best, finally most instructive, of all my summer job summers.

117

At midsummer before dawn an orange light returns to the mountains
Like a great weight and the small birds cry out
And bear it up

W. S. MERWIN

119

THERE IS A PHOTOGRAPH TAKEN OF ME IN THE
summer I learned to shuffle cards. I practiced at a
collapsible table in a square-sided aluminum trailer.
At first each card felt as unresponsive as a slice of
fresh bread. By the end of vacation the entire deck
riffled backward and forward between my hands. It
seems an odd thing to have done, to have spent
hours introducing randomness to a finite set. But I
come from people, mainly on my father's side, for
whom card games are human translations of a divine
colloquy, a colloquy that always starts at random.

In the photograph, I am standing in front
of the trailer, which looks more like lead than aluminum. Behind our pink Buick you can see the lake
where my family is vacationing. This is Iowa or
Minnesota. Though trees border the lake, it does
not look like a very amusing body of water. It looks
like a spot where farmland was incontinent. Still,
we had fun there. I learned to shuffle cards. And in
the photograph, I am holding up a long stringer of
fish whose species are lost to my memory. They

could be bullheads, walleye, crappies, bluegill, perch, bass, or pike. I caught them all. I have a big smile and my arm is tired from holding them up.

I fished assiduously as a child. I fished in a creek that ran through the town cemetery, in a creek that gave me creosote burns from climbing around a country bridge, in a creek where I cut open my foot on a rusty can just—I recall—as one of those famous bottle-green storms was bearing down on our midwestern town. I fished in puddles left by summer flooding, where there could not possibly have been any fish. But mostly I fished with my dad on bountiful northern lakes. He is an excellent angler and he taught me well. Despite assiduity—and despite many photographs like the one I have mentioned—I can't remember a single fish I caught.

Sometimes instead of taking the trailer we rented a cabin—Cross Lake, Minnesota, was one such place—with room enough to invite my maternal grandparents. They were hymn-playing, not card-playing people; they conducted their colloquy directly with the Lord, though I don't want to exaggerate the strictures of their faith. At Cross Lake my grandmother, who was a very old-fashioned-looking woman, raised her dress knee-high to wade barefoot in the little fillip that that humble water gives the land, and my grandfather, who always wore overalls and would have repainted our rented cabin if we had let him, waded too. There is a photograph of the two of them, life-preservered to the ears, grinning into the breeze a ten-horse outboard motor kicks up when attached to a stodgy rowboat. My mom took that picture. She too was heavily life-preservered, bundled in kapok because she didn't like to swim. In the shallows at the bathing beach on our home lake (a two-hundred-acre affair) she perfected a walking dive that turned, halfway, into a graceless panic that kept her shoulders, neck, and head from getting wet.

I was first given an adult liberty on one of the lakes where we vacationed. I was told I could take the boat (and its motor, therein the liberty) out on my own to fish. The only restrictions concerned bottle-green storms and swimmers: I was to avoid both. Anyone who thinks that I intended to fish has forgotten the exhilaration of piloting a craft alone for the first time. I had two plans. The first was to run out to the center of the lake and drift over the deepest water, watching the curtaining shafts of sunlight pierce to the limits of clarity. There wasn't much in that plan because the lake wasn't very clear. The second plan was to run all the way across the lake, beach the boat, and walk up into the forest far enough to pretend that I was the first explorer to gain the shore of that inland sea. There wasn't much in that plan either. The other side of the lake was full of wading grandparents.

So I fished. And soon I was glad not to fish alone anymore. That is how fishing works. Your dad takes you. It requires no homework or chores. It can't affect your allowance. Laziness is the sport itself. You pee in the woods. You lunch in the boat. Luck is all. You get home late. Summer is perfect.

Dad and I took a round plaid cooler and a thermos of coffee with us. We sought weedbeds and rocky points and midlake shoals. Once, we tossed our pop cans overboard, thinking they would sink. Instead they floated, and for the rest of the day we caught a fish every time we trolled between them. It became quite a joke with us. A floating pop can would heave into view, like a channel marker on the Mississippi, and we would laugh. Sometimes my dad caught a fish. Sometimes I felt a shudder on my line and began to reel in. After a minute or two the fish roiled the surface just off the bow. I reached down, lifted it up, and this is the part I can't remember.

How many hundreds of times must I have experienced that moment as a boy? I reached down and held in my hand a miracle of compression and elongation, as miraculous in its way as the roundness of the earth. It had scales or a black leathery skin. It had barbs or spines or teeth to avoid. It was copper-green or cleverly striped or so brilliantly dappled in the unmoistened light of air that its eye became a reflective pool in a miniature landscape of incomprehensible beauty. This description is not constructed from memory. It is imagination, aided by photographs. Take me literally. I cannot remember the moment—repeated, as I say, many hundreds of times—in which I paused and looked down at the fish in my hand before returning it to the lake if it was too small to eat or adding it to our stringer, which hung from an oarlock.

I recall in ridiculous detail learning how to shuffle: the growing suppleness of the deck, how badly the feathering of one half-pack into another could go awry—causing a small explosion that hurled cards across the trailer—how I ranked the suits in perfect order just to watch them grow deranged over time. And yet those memorable moments when the most important mystery in the lake came into view have slipped away without a trace. A fish's colors fade rapidly when it's removed from water. You have one live instant in which to fix it with your gaze, to memorize the pattern and subtlety of its hues. In my experience, it cannot be done.

I think I know the reason. It comes from trying to stare the present in its unblinking, mirrored eye. The present is the object of peripheral vision, which allows us to go about the business of looking directly into the future without crashing into card tables. The instant in which you hold a fish in your hand is like the fish itself after it has been returned to the lake: it has come and gone and you are left wondering what it was you held. I think that most of us cannot look at the present without going blind. That's what happened all those times I held a fish in my hand just above the undulating surface of its home. I thought, "I am really going to see this fish," and at that moment I went blind. It is amazing, once you get the hang of it, how easy it is to shuffle without ever really looking at the cards.

Do not think that I was some boy phenomenologist who went fishing for the ineluctable mystery of it. My dad fished, so I fished, and what he taught me led slowly to astonishment. He did other things that astonished me. He could drive from our house to far-off lakes or to my grandparents' house, a distance of over one hundred miles, without consulting a map. I recognized many of the points we passed on the way, but I had no idea how to connect them, nor did I realize how few alternative routes there were in a state like Iowa. Perhaps when I grew up I would be able to remember long, complex routes without effort. Perhaps I would be able to play long, complex games like bridge. Perhaps I would be able to hold a fish in my hand without going blind.

Though I fished, I also swam, and it was swimming that gave fishing much of its appeal. I felt at home in the water, unlike the adults I knew, whose prominently veined, phosphorescent legs looked like leech bait. I could imagine the lair of the largemouth bass or the northern pike—a tiger in a bamboo forest—from having swum with my eyes open underwater. I could mimic the finning weightlessness of a sunfish and feel its neutral gravity in my limbs. And yet, in almost any lake we visited, there were depths I couldn't plumb and weeds I couldn't penetrate because of fear. These are excellent places for fish to hide, but I didn't want to hide: I wanted to see. I wanted the water to be flooded with light. Even the smallest lake can seem infinite when you find yourself trapped in the weeds.

As a swimmer I needed less than infinity. I needed a concrete public pool with a chain-link fence around it, a fence that in our small town served as the outer limit of a Little League diamond. At the peak of summer, the water was clear, the concrete deck was vaporously hot, and the pool was filled with kids my age, including deeply tanned girls wearing modest pale bikinis. I swam in the visual element. In early evening, when the pool was quiet, its attractions grew. If, as often

happened to me, you were playing right field and a ball was hit through your inaccurate hands, you might have to chase it all the way to the pool fence. Behind you lay humiliation, ridicule, and a two-run error. Before you lay the pool, its opals and turquoises deepening in the shadows where a particular friend might still be swimming, her long hair streaming behind her, a vision of innocent lubricity. It might occur to you to turn and heave the ball wildly in the direction of the white uniforms in the distance, to turn back and remove your own white uniform, to climb the fence and dive into the water. Then and only then might you wish that a pool were as infinite in concealment as a lake—that you might find a recess in the weeds where broken light would fall upon the two of you until your camouflage was perfect.

That is the sort of fantasy I used to have as I drifted over weedbeds with my dad at the helm of our rowboat. From above, the weeds looked inoffensive, like Swiss chard or overgrown asparagus reaching upward from the lake bottom. My line could be seen nicking the water not far away. Dad and I could talk our talk and say our say without uttering a word about anything but the weather and the technicalities of our sport. If you were doing a certain kind of fishing at that particular time in history, it was probably OK to toss a couple of pop cans overboard. (You wouldn't do it now.) And if you happened to catch fish whenever you trolled between those cans, then that might be evidence of some kind of order—not order on a Miltonic level perhaps, but commensurate to the late fifties in Iowa or Minnesota. Despite the frenzy in the minnow pail and the bits of sandwich lettuce floating in the bilge, by the end of the day a sense of harmony had filled the boat.

Running home, we watched the shoreline pivot slowly until it presented us with a familiar scene, a dock, a line of trees, a lantern hanging near the trailer door.

My mom, who had put on a sundress and fixed her hair, could certainly be gracious to a couple of returning anglers like my dad and me. I held up the stringer of fish, and she carried on as if I had single-handedly herded a flock of wild turkeys out of the November woods to save our starving settlement. A snapshot was taken. You could see the fish when I put them on the cutting board. My little brothers and sister gathered around to do just that. One of them always touched a fish's eye just to find out how it felt.

The death of fish I caught never bothered me. In the late fifties in Iowa or Minnesota, boy was put on earth to catch and eat fish, to play a rotten right field, and to swim like a tadpole in trunks. It was the fish's eye that got to me, that aqueous bulb on the end of an internalized nerve stalk. Under water it was focused: in air and in death, who knows? It was an eye designed to see only the present—I noticed it could not close—and the present had been my lure wobbling past on the end of a nearly invisible line. I, who could lay such calculated plans to catch a fish, weighing means and ends, buying lures, tying knots, making casts, looking into the future, could never really see the fish I caught while color still flushed its scales. The fish—whose only future was its present— no doubt saw me perfectly, and the image was etched on its brain forever.

After a short grace, the fillets, dredged in flour and quickly fried, always tasted buttery. There was egg salad or fresh peas or sweet corn or potato chips on the side. We ate outdoors on a picnic table covered with a plastic checkered cloth. When we kids had dried the supper dishes, my dad got out the cards. The game began by shuffling them into randomness, and as it progressed, the order of the deck increased. You're never too young to play cards.

THE TIME: July 1962

THE SCENE: A screened porch, evening

THE CHARACTERS:

STEVE (just graduated from high school)

RONNIE (his sister, home from her senior year in
college)

DAD

STEVE: Hey, Dad, didn't we used to have a couple bowling balls?

DAD: What do you want with bowling balls in this heat.

RONNIE: Maybe they're in the garage.

DAD: Don't be silly.

STEVE: Come on, Dad, where are they?

DAD: Don't go in the garage now. What do you want bowling balls for at this time of night.

STEVE: Ronnie has to bowl.

DAD: Aw, what are you talking about.

RONNIE: We're just going bowling.

VERONICA GENG

DAD: What do you mean, bowling. Do you know what time it is?

STEVE: It's only nine o'clock.

DAD: Nine o'—Jesus, what's the matter with you? Your mother's already asleep.

RONNIE: Gee, then I guess we can't bowl in the house. We'll have to go to the bowling alley.

DAD: Nine o'clock at night people don't go bowling. Look at it, it's dark out.

RONNIE: I thought the car had headlights.

DAD: You don't even have bowling shoes. What are you gonna do, bowl in those? You can't bowl in sneakers, you gotta have shoes.

STEVE: Look, Dad, they rent the shoes.

DAD: *Rent?* What, you're gonna wear somebody else's shoes?

STEVE: Everybody does that. They put powder in them.

DAD: What do you know about powder? You're a powder expert now.

RONNIE: Fine, then we'll buy some shoes.

DAD: Oh, you're gonna buy a pair of shoes now for one game.

STEVE: Listen, you rent the shoes, they put powder in them, and you wear them. And you bowl with them. They have these nifty little—

DAD: Nifty. Nifty. Where the hell did you learn to talk anyway?

RONNIE: Dad, leave him alone. This is getting to be a hassle.

STEVE: It's no hassle, Ron.

DAD: Hassle. What is it with you two? You got a hassle, nifty, go bowling.

STEVE: Dad—

DAD: What do you want to go bowling for? All of a sudden you've got this big interest in bowling now all of a sudden.

STEVE: Dad, look, Ronnie couldn't pass her grades in college because of her phys ed credit, so now she has to bowl because she didn't want to go in the water and swim.

DAD: What do you mean, she didn't want to—

RONNIE: Look, Steve, just forget about it.

STEVE: Ron, are you jumping on *me* now?

DAD: How are you two going bowling? What are you gonna use for money?

STEVE: Ronnie, you have money, don't you?

RONNIE: Let's just forget it.

STEVE: No, now I'm getting interested. Come on, Dad, want to go bowling with us?

DAD: What, *now?*

RONNIE: Forget about it.

DAD: Aw, for Christ sake, you don't go bowling at this hour.

STEVE: Come on, Dad, just bowl a few frames with us. You and Mommy used to bowl all the time, remember?

DAD: You don't know what you're talking about. Your mother doesn't bowl at midnight.

RONNIE: Come on, Steve, I can't stand here all night arguing about the proper times to bowl.

STEVE: Dad, come on. You can wolf down an order of french fries.

DAD: I'm not hungry.

RONNIE: You're sitting there with candy bars.

STEVE: So he eats candy bars—so what? Leave him alone.

RONNIE: It's not healthy.

STEVE: Yeah, Dad, come on over to the alley and work up an appetite for some fries.

DAD: Jesus Christ, do you know how much a bowling ball weighs? How is Ronnie gonna go bowling? She looks like a good meal of corned beef and cabbage would stand her on her feet.

RONNIE: Look, all I want to do is graduate from college.

STEVE: Dad, leave her alone. She's upset enough that she doesn't want to put her head under water.

DAD: What's that got to do with anything?

STEVE: You know, it's a swimming credit she couldn't get.

DAD: Swimming. You know what it is, swimming?

RONNIE: No, Dad, what is it?

DAD: Swimming—all swimming is, is relaxing. In the water. That's all it is. Swimming is a relaxing. You put your head in, you relax, that's it. Otherwise you sink like a stone. Tense up in the water and you can forget about it.

RONNIE: Oh, so, Dad, wait a minute, when's the last time I saw *you* swimming? You go out there and wade.

STEVE: Come on, Ronnie, don't pick on him.

RONNIE: You *wade* in there, in your shorts—

DAD: Get out of here. You're gonna tell me about swimming? You've been in college too long, that's what your problem is. Then you come here and tell me about bowling and swimming.

RONNIE: This is just really upsetting me. If I don't fulfill this credit—oh, forget it. Forget about it. I'm not graduating from college. Just forget about it. We're not going bowling.

DAD: Oh, so you're not graduating from college now, huh? Now it's my fault you're not graduating from college because you don't have bowling shoes.

STEVE: Dad, forget the bowling shoes. They have millions of 'em in the alley.

128

SUMMER SESSION VERONICA GENG

DAD: Oh, so you know all about bowling. Where's your bowling ball?

STEVE: They have balls all over the place.

DAD: What, at this time of night?

RONNIE: They don't take the balls away just because it gets dark outside.

STEVE: Really, she has to bowl to graduate from Penn. She was supposed to pass her swimming test, but she can't swim.

DAD: Of course she can swim.

STEVE: She can't swim. She's afraid to swim.

DAD: Where in the world did you get that idea?

STEVE: Dad, look, have you ever once seen her swim?

DAD: You're crazy.

STEVE: You know how she just stands there in the shallow end and then lounges around on a towel.

DAD: She could swim fine if she wasn't too goddamn hoity-toity to swim.

STEVE: Dad, I'm telling you, she had a traumatic experience in Atlantic City that time when we were kids. She got knocked down by a wave. So now she won't put her head underwater.

DAD: Where the hell do you get this stuff?

RONNIE: Forget about all that. They said I could graduate without swimming. All I have to do is bowl a certain number of frames over the summer and send them the score sheets.

DAD: That's the silliest thing I've heard yet. They're gonna let you go bowling when you're supposed to swim?

RONNIE: They couldn't care less what I do. So I'm not swimming.

DAD: You better start swimming in a hurry, because you're not gonna be able to bowl. You couldn't bowl if your life depended on it.

STEVE: Dad, anybody can bowl.

DAD: And that's where you're wrong. Swimming, yes. As long as you don't tense up. But with bowling, it's a horse of a different color.

STEVE: Dad, if she can't bowl I'll teach her. It's no big thing. All she has to do is keep hurling the ball down the alley and boom!—sooner or later she'll hit something.

DAD: She'll hit something, all right.

RONNIE: They didn't say I had to bowl *well*.

DAD: What, now you want to have a traumatic bowling experience? You have to prepare for these things, you can't just get up there and—

STEVE: Bowling is a Zen thing. It's all in the—not actually in the mind but in the nonmind. Like an animal, or a fish.

DAD: Fish breathe in the water.

STEVE: That's what I'm saying.

DAD: Look, people cannot breathe water. People and animals—they have lungs, not gills.

STEVE: Will you stop? Of course people don't have gills. Of course they don't. What do you think, I'm stupid?

DAD: Are you calling me stupid?

RONNIE: Steve, look, leave him alone. Forget about it.

DAD: 'Cause if you're calling me stupid, you can forget about the bowling.

RONNIE: I don't care. This is upsetting me now.

DAD: *You're* upset?

RONNIE: Yes. This is just upsetting me. Forget the whole thing. Forget college. I'll go to the Sorbonne.

DAD: She'll go to the Sorbonne. Listen to this. What are you gonna study there, French water sports?

STEVE: Dad, are you coming bowling with us or not? That's all we want to know.

DAD: If you're so smart, what are you planning to do for money? You know how much it costs to go bowling?

RONNIE: It's only a couple of dollars. Just give Steve a couple of dollars and we'll go. I don't need anything.

DAD: Give *Steve* a couple of—Jesus Christ, you want me to give him money to go bowling? He's only a kid! It's dark out there. You're being silly now. You want to go bowling, first of all you need *shoes,* and then you need money. And you're gonna take this kid in the middle of the night—

RONNIE: It's not the middle of the night at nine-thirty.

DAD: You don't listen to reason. You know how hard your mother and I worked to send you to college, and now all it comes down to is bowling in the middle of the night?

RONNIE: Look, it's not—

STEVE: Ronnie, let me tell him. All you're doing is pissing him off.

RONNIE: What are you, my lawyer, now?

DAD: All this happens because you don't want to put your head underwater? That's what this is all about? I thought I told you about swimming.

STEVE: Dad, will you back off the swimming thing?

DAD: No, wait a minute, let me tell her about swimming. You reach down to the bottom of the pool, and you keep your head straight, and you breathe. When you're in the water, you breathe. That's it.

RONNIE: That sounds terrific on paper—

DAD: What do you mean, on paper? What are you talking about? Where does this kid get this from? I'm talking about swimming, she's talking about paper.

STEVE: Dad, will you—

RONNIE: Steve, no, wait a minute, I want to hear what Daddy has to say about swimming. He's telling us all about swimming now.

DAD: Look, don't get smart.

RONNIE: No, I want to hear this. I want to hear about swimming. *That's why I can't swim! Because you never taught us to swim!*

DAD: Oh, you want to hear *me* now. I thought two minutes ago you wanted to go bowling.

RONNIE: Fine. Forget it, I'm not staying here with this. I'm packing. I'll be upstairs packing.

STEVE: Ron, look, forget about packing, we're going bowling.

DAD: Bowling, packing, swimming . . .

STEVE: Dad, stop.

DAD: All I'm telling you is, you don't fight the water. Otherwise, if you fight the water—you never fight the water. Never ever. You let the water support you, because if you're afraid to let it support you, you just go right to the bottom. The bottom will draw you like a magnet. Gravity takes you right to the bottom and you can't breathe and that's it.

STEVE: Dad, this is the same thing I'm saying about bowling. It's a gravity thing. The alley creates its own momentum, and you just go with it. It happens *for* you. And the gutters—the gutters create fear in a bowler. They're there as a fear thing. If you tense up, the ball will leap into the gutter. Whereas the pins actually draw the ball to them. It's an attraction of bodies—like planets. It's perfectly natural. If you relax, the ball goes for a strike.

RONNIE: Yeah, but only in the middle of the night, when it's really dark out. You turn on the car headlights, you breathe, keep your head down, plenty of powder, a few candy bars just to make sure you keep your strength up, and boom!—the next thing you know you're graduating from the Sorbonne with a degree in packing.

DAD: I swear I don't know where you kids learned to talk this way. You want to go bowling, go bowling. But I'm telling you, they're not gonna let you wear those shoes.

131

D ead dog. This Fourth,
This Independence Day,
Gun shot with cannon-lead
Explodes—
Erodes to emptiness. Dog's dead.
Dropped down in ocean lawns, it deeply drowns;
The town lies still, its skin untouched, serene,
No rhetoric ignites the churchyard green,
At dawn, no ladyfingers crack cool airs with popping smokes,
At dusk, no high cathedral-bulwark built on fire provokes
An audience to sobs of Ahs and Ohs! And so it goes:
The loud and bragging cannon, tamped with torts
As Independence self-aborts.
The Old Cause falters,
Steel Celebrations flake to rust.
The grand lust lingers.
But, with match unstruck,
Mad boys stay stuck in bed,
Turned ancient in a night
Because no sublime nonsense stirs their bones with fame.
No devil-crackers scour graffitied walls with flame.
No games of rockets soar,
No war's lost dead ghost by
All Blue and Gray on sunbaked streets.
The dumb Mayor greets all sights eyes sealed, mouth mute,
No flute nor fife, no moon-drummed summer-brass
        burned bright,
Who'll light the Mayor's fuse to hear him
Charge up Bunker Hill for half the night?
No one.
No cavalcade of cars,

133

RAY BRADBURY

The rich in robes, straw hats,
Time's autocrats, its dear dull patriots
Are bound, flag-furled
And buried deep.
Their small world lost and forfeit to New Law.
The things they dreamed from 1812, and said,
Are shunted, turned from, spurned, and scattered, dead.
No boys at dawn bounce forth to fire—
Announce the Day.
At noon, alive, they're winding-sheeted still.
And hear! No Taps from shade-side slope of tomb-strewn hill.
Parades, long spent, hide in the City Hall's car shed.
The Civil monuments stand lean and chill, unread
By young or old; only the ancient blind
On rare occasions rake trembling touch,
To find
The lost war's names,
The winning shouts,
The losing shames.
But both are buried now
Where dry grass
Burns in starched parades
Where only shades and shadows rustle noons
And no fife fire-flaunts fine cannonades or hum-drums tunes,
No Lincoln on the White House porch to tell the band
        to look away, look away Dixieland.
No Johnny Comes Marching Home,
No Tenting Tonight on the Old Camp Ground,
And nowhere found
A trampling of the Vintage where the Grapes of Wrath
        were Stored.

ALL HOLIDAYS, BE DEAD RAY BRADBURY

All's bored.
No South. No North. No July Fourth. No Independence Hall.
What's the meaning of it all?
Our souls are bled.
Where is the graveyard chart to spell,
To tell the living from the dead?

ALL HOLIDAYS, BE DEAD RAY BRADBURY

136

THE SUMMER OF LOVE WAS ONLY A YEAR OLD and Woodstock was only a year away when the five of us, known collectively as The Agents, rock and roll band with unlimited potential—that is, no established audience to speak of—decided to turn professional. We rehearsed for months in a basement storage room of the apartment building we all lived in, Matty (Apt. 3-N) and Ronnie (4-R) on guitars, Barry (2-R) on the drums, Richie (5-P) on the organ, and I (6-S), on the sax, wailing away the hits of the day—woodshedding, as real musicians like to say. In a room full of rusted baby strollers and kitchen appliances and abandoned bicycle parts, we honed our act and aimed for the upcoming Battle of the Bands contest at the local Y. But we were thinking past that when we decided upon "Journey to the Center of Your Mind" as the audition tune. We were thinking past first prize—a single recording contract with ABC-Paramount Records.

None of us had figured on coming in second.

STANLEY MIESES

None of The Agents could have imagined the conclusion of the Battle of the Bands contest when Cousin Brucie, the famous deejay and special celebrity judge, swept past our bandstand and anointed our rivals, The Deep Six. It was a slow-motion horror show for our band—the way Cousin Brucie paraded his frozen smile past us; how his eyes found the middle distance as he rounded in front of our platform and kept going; how the spotlight he had in tow graced us and then an instant later put us in shadows; how the words hung in the air with extra echo and reverb when that deejay voice announced the first-prize winners; all of which was capped by *cheers for the other guys*. Our reward for second place—an all travel-expenses-reimbursed nonholiday summer weekend tour of three minor Catskill hotels. I went home and considered studying for my SATs.

It took some convincing, but we decided to accept the second prize. Mostly it was levelheaded Ronnie who convinced us to be professionals, and Matty, who as always, thought it would be a great way to meet girls from out of the neighborhood. But when Julius Fu entered the picture and volunteered to serve as our tour accountant and roadie, then it seemed churlish and defeatist not to try it out. Julius Fu, nicknamed for his peculiar haircut (Caesar's) and moustache (Manchu's), already had solid credentials in the financial world for the brilliant way he could divide the check for eight at the Riverdale Diner *in his head*. And at seventeen he already knew he wasn't clever enough to be a schemer, unlike any of the guys in the building, and he was a welcome presence despite his terminal squareness.

An assistant to Cousin Brucie at the radio station gave us our assignments—Friday night at the Grand Mountain Hotel "teenage lounge"; Saturday night at the Karmel Hotel; and Sunday afternoon at the East Pond "youth lounge." We were to receive $20 for the first two shows and $10 for the third, and we had to negotiate our own transportation, keep receipts for everything, and take them to the station for reimbursement upon our return. Being New York City sixteen-year-olds, we didn't own cars, or even have access to a car, so we had to negotiate with the first hotel contact to be picked up at the local Short Line bus station, and with the subsequent two employers to fetch us as well, which we did from a local pay phone Barry'd rigged up so we could make free calls. Once all the travel arrangements were set, and a vote was taken to offer a one dollar share per man of the bounty to Fu, we ganged up on our parents. My parents handled the news as if I'd said I was running away to a hippie commune. My argument to them, I recall, contained the buzzwords "freedom" and "civil rights," and I didn't at all pick up on their concern that my clarinet and their sweat equity in my classical-music-school training would be left in the dust. I divided them and conquered. To my worried father I made a private promise that going "on the road" with a rock band was not a serious career choice and thus would not interfere with his dream of law school for his son. I told my mother that it would look bad for her son if he was the only boy forbidden to go. And so my parents allowed me to be a free Agent for a weekend.

Over the next two weeks, we thrashed out a playlist of songs we arranged for our first tour outside of our home zip code. The consensus was that summertime demanded fewer ballads and more up-tempo rockers, especially since the third leg of our tour was a Sunday afternoon appearance. So we dropped the Dave Clark Five's "Because" (but kept the only other ballad we knew well enough, Jimi Hendrix's "Hey Joe," since it was our lead guitarist's romantic showcase number) and added "Tequila," an instrumental I'd been lobbying for so I could finally play a saxophone part intended for the saxophone. We agreed on a final playlist that began with our signature song, "Secret Agent Man," followed by the

138

Young Rascals' "Good Lovin'" and their version of "Mustang Sally," "You Keep Me Hangin' On" (the Vanilla Fudge version), "Tequila," "Midnight Hour," "Hey Joe," and our rousing finisher, "Journey to the Center of Your Mind." Twenty minutes or so of perfection, with a reprise of "Secret Agent Man" scheduled as the encore, should lightning really strike us for once.

On a dismally hot Friday afternoon in July, we pulled together our instrument cases, our tiny Vox amps (like the Beatles', an important bonding detail), our friends, Matty's latest girlfriend (Matty was the only member of our group to be so fortunate), and the send-off made us dewy-eyed again, and we talked ourselves into thinking that after this weekend nothing would ever be the same again, that somehow this odd turn would lead us to the lighted path of fame and fortune. At the same time I had the realization that the next generation's voice in the wilderness wasn't likely to be heard howling teenaged rebellion in a Jewish resort area in the mountains of upstate New York.

We loaded the equipment onto Julius Fu and departed for the Port Authority bus station, prepared to scale the Catskill Mountains. First stop: the small town of Kerhonkson, New York. Other than an understanding that we were first going to play the "teenage lounge" at the Grand Mountain Hotel, not one of The Agents had a secure picture of what the job was going to be like. We got a better sense of it when we were met at the bus station by the assistant to the hotel's social director, an old man wearing a snap-brim cap, a Ban-Lon shirt-jac, Bermuda shorts that reached his kneecaps, and sandals with calf-high stretch socks.

"So you're Secret Agents," he said with a quizzical air and a strong Eastern European accent, as we stumbled off the bus. "I'm Izzy Faber. Call me Izzy. What are those boxes?" he asked. Fu was unloading the amplifiers. "You can't use them," he said.

"Do you have a house PA?" asked Ronnie.

"No electric," said Izzy. "It's Shabbas. The Sabbath. You're Jewish boys, no? You won the contest from the YMHA, yes? So you play the guitars normally."

"But we play rock and roll, Mr. Faber," we protested. "We play electric guitars. Didn't anyone tell you?"

"It's Shabbas. Didn't anyone tell *you?*"

The ride in Izzy's station wagon to the hotel grounds was long and silent. We passed verdant, lush lawns, rolling, soft hills, a big blue-and-purple sky nearing sunset. Inside Izzy's ramshackle Ford station wagon, it was not so beautiful. Izzy finally reached the hotel grounds, and he swerved dramatically onto the circular driveway in front of the main building. He turned off the ignition and waited for the engine rattle to quit before addressing us. "I'm sorry, boys, I know you're disappointed, but look what a big success Theodore Bikel is with a guitar and no screaming. You'll see. The show must go on," he said, wrapping the quotes around it like a noose.

After the guests at the Grand Mountain Hotel had eaten dinner and recited and sung a lengthy post-dinner grace, the show did go on—in a plywood-paneled recreation room that had been cleared of Ping-Pong and bumper-pool tables and was lined with metal folding chairs. Izzy reappeared in front of the assembled group and served as the unamplified emcee.

"Boys and girls, this is a rock and roll group Cousin Brucie the famous deejay thinks is just what the Pepsi Generation wants to hear, only tonight they're not going to hear them so good. Here are the Secret Agents." The gig, as we desperately wanted to regard it, was attended by a number of preteens and toddlers, who made their presence felt. There were maybe twenty-five sons and daughters of the hotel's clientele, who found the occasion ripe for relieving themselves of a little rancor for having been dragged to their parent's kosher retreat,

139

only to find themselves entertained by a group of disorganized boys strumming unplugged electric guitars, over which the sound of bar-mitzvah-quality saxophone and all of us singing without the mercy of microphones must have been unbearable. We didn't have a chance. But we did play our encore number—only because we rushed through our playlist at breakneck speed and felt obliged to fill out our twenty minutes, which we did, if you count what felt like eighteen solid minutes of gleeful booing. At the end of the show, we packed up, and in a sullen single file we were led into the kitchen, where Fu was handed a sealed envelope by a black man in a soiled apron. Acknowledging Fu, Izzy said, "This is for all of you," adding that we should not open the envelope until after sundown Saturday night, in accordance with the Sabbath observance; but in the privacy of our overnight room next to the dishwashers', the five of us and Fu couldn't resist our first roadshow payday, so Ronnie carefully opened the envelope and discovered not twenty but twenty-five single dollar bills, and Izzy's business card. Fu was exultant, and he counted them out three or four times. The five of us wanted to commit suicide, and here Fu was contemplating a career. We turned on him cruelly until he threw his five dollars on the floor. No one would touch it; in the morning Fu picked up the money, the amps, and the overnight bags and dropped them in Izzy's station wagon and sat there stewing while someone placed a telephone call to the Karmel Hotel and arranged for our bus to be met in Kiamesha Lake.

The Karmel was not, thank God, an observant hotel. It was *kosher-style,* said the beefy-faced man who introduced himself as Carl when he picked us up in *his* station wagon, a mid-sixties model DeSoto with push-button transmission. The Karmel had big-name nightclub entertainers on the weekends, he told us, listing a number of people with names that sounded like the names of entertainers. We relaxed. This place had electricity. Show business history. "The Capris played here, and so did The Jesters," said Carl. "And now you guys. Are you any good? I hope so. I gotta tell you, I wish you didn't wear your hair like fairies."

At the Karmel, the setup was indeed more professional. They had an on-premises nightclub called the Club Oasis, which had a sound system that would let us use our amplifiers, house microphones, and a real stage ringed by tiers of tables, so that you could play down, up, and side-to-side. It also had a neon sign out front, and I don't think that the group ever experienced a higher state of well-being than at the moment the neon lit up and cast a pale pink glow over the cardboard signs tacked onto the portal posts: "Teenage Lounge To-Night From NYC The Agents 8PM Showtime." At that hour the club was perfectly lit, tested for sound, poised for an evening of professional entertainment, and absolutely empty. By nine o'clock, only three people had wandered in, and they informed us that our appearance had coincided with Teenage Go-Kart Night at an amusement park in the next town. They were dispatched to find Carl. Carl returned, more amused than apologetic, and shrugged it off. "I tell you what. You hang around, and I'll let you play a couple of numbers tonight before the big show." The big show, featuring a supposedly famous "blue" comedian, was the show the hotel weekenders lived for, what they cut their summer Saturday workday in half and spent the rest in a two-hour mountains-bound traffic jam for, what they spent their day preparing their hair for, what they dragged their jewelry across state lines for. And although The Agents really lived in the moment when we believed that playing for an adult audience of show business aficionados could be an epiphany we'd relive forever, the reality was—and we observed it very quickly when we stepped out onstage—that here was a crowd that was not going to be amused by the raucous scratchings of a bunch of fairies their children's age. In a moment of crystal-clear show business savvy, we agreed to play "Tequila" and get the hell out of there. We'd never experienced such expert rapid-fire heckling, nor had we ever found ourselves surrendering the stage to guys at tables turning around to their friends sitting at other tables and shouting insults about us, joined by the emcee, who had an open microphone throughout the song. Our exit was followed by a comment from the oily-haired master of ceremonies, which, though we couldn't make it out, brought a wave of laughter that echoed all the way out the door and poisoned the clean night air.

"That's it, we're going home tomorrow. This sucks," said Ronnie. We all agreed.

It only took another minute or so to come to the irrevocable conclusion that we would break up as a band, as friends, as neighbors, go to different colleges in different towns, marry strangers, and never phone or write to each other.

The next morning Carl pulled up in his DeSoto and we piled in, only to discover en route that he had planned to offer us a kind of reparation for our suffering by driving us directly to our final stop at the East Pond Bungalow Colony. How or why he remembered this bit of information upon our arrival escapes me, since he couldn't remember Teenage Go-Kart Night, but now he was compounding the pain by making it impossible for us to pack it in. We arrived at East Pond, and the only one making a move out of the car was Carl. "Isn't this right?" he roared. He drew the attention of a man who looked like a puffy Jack Klugman, sitting in a white Adirondack chair on the porch of a large wooden barnlike structure at the center of an encampment of smaller cabins.

"You're the boys from so-and-so," said Jack Klugman, mentioning the name of the radio station assistant. "Where've you been? You're supposed play in fifteen minutes." It was quarter to eleven in the morning.

"I thought we were supposed to play this afternoon," said Ronnie. "We were told around three."

"These people are here for a weekend," he said, "and some of them leave to beat the traffic in the afternoon. Don't worry; there are plenty of kids who're waiting for you. Plenty. Bring all your stuff to the casino." He pointed to another barnlike building next to the main office. To Carl, whom he had greeted familiarly, he said, "You hear these kids? Any good?"

"Oh yeah," said Carl, "The kids love this long-haired stuff."

There *were* plenty of kids waiting for us. Plenty around the ages of eight to ten, a sure sign that their older siblings wouldn't be caught dead in the same place. The bungalow colony, which didn't seem that large, had produced an audience of about twenty-five kids, and maybe ten more young, square-looking parents of the youngest kids. And though The Agents were a committed rock and roll band, we found our will utterly eroded, so that when we were asked to conduct sing-alongs of "Michael, Row the Boat Ashore" and "Kumbaya," with the addition of some guy from the bungalow colony on acoustic guitar, we didn't object. But when we finished, the guy with the acoustic guitar left, and lo and behold, with him went all of the younger children. For a moment we didn't know what to do. Then a couple of teenage kids who had been loitering around the entranceway, unbeknownst to us, wandered in and helped us locate the electrical outlets in the room, we plugged in our Voxes, and a single microphone, and heralded our arrival with a solid keening jolt of audio feedback before launching into "Secret Agent Man" with a fury. We followed the playlist and the kids followed us, and a few cut loose and began to dance during "Mustang Sally." By the time we hit the Amboy Dukes' high-voltage opening to "Journey to the Center of Your Mind," the audience had swelled to forty—believe me, we counted them—and they were ours, clapping in time and singing the chorus of the song out loud like drunks at a baseball game. Lots of guys who said they were from Brooklyn and Queens came over and shook our hands and asked us about what else we played and who we listened to, and Matty got into a deep conversation with a girl who went to Art and Design High School downtown. Ronnie signed an autograph for a shy little girl, and then everyone slowly filtered out the door and back to their parents' cabins, to pack up and head back to a weekday summer in the city.

Soon, we too were on the road again, on the Short Line back to New York City, exchanging single dollar bills to even out our weekend's take, and handslaps for a job well done. Eventually, we got around to discussing a few ideas for the band's future, plans that would take us well into August.

143

144

My Summer Day

A deeply troubled friend whom we've invited for a therapeutic country weekend is alternately laughing and weeping in an upstairs guest room. The vegetable garden is ominous with produce that will be unusable if not picked before dusk—beans approaching the size of small carrots, foot-long clubs of aggressive squashes. My children have reached that gregarious age (thirteen, fourteen) when they must be driven daily to swim with different friends whose houses are forty minutes' distance apart. For the third time this fortnight, a few ebullient, self-invited guests have arrived for an overnight stay ("We'll be driving by Cornwall on the way to the Cape"), and I've become an authority on the variety of ingredients—squid, pine nuts, fennel root—that can enliven that most serviceable Invasion Time fare, cold pasta.

The toilet that services most of the upstairs rooms has broken down; all local plumbers are on vacation; an acquaintance who is a breeder of

FRANCINE DU PLESSIX GRAY

poodles by profession, and has volunteered to fix the plumbing, arrives quite drunk at noon and grows drunker as he proceeds to remove the toilet from its base, leaving us with the added problem of how to remove his prostrate body from the bathroom floor. I am a fortnight late on the deadline for some article, a lapse of punctuality that punctually occurs between June and September. My conscience is further plagued by many unacknowledged manuscripts ("You might remember me from that writing workshop five years ago") whose authors demand an immediate reading of their novels-in-progress. A monkey being boarded by my children for the summer has escaped from her filthy cage and is jabbering at me from the heights of a neighboring tree. "Tennis, anyone?" a cheerful guest calls out at 6 P.M. I could strangle him. By this time I'm briefly immersed in a hot bath, trying to recover enough strength to put the finishing touches on home-grown sorrel soup, cold pasta, and homemade sherbet for ten; sobbing, "I hate summer, I hate summer"; filled with that seasonal anxiety familiar to most contemporary women, which cries out, "Time is devouring me; I shall never be any of the seventeen people I am trying to be."

And yet we are not exclusively miserable at the end of such a summer day. Having picked, cooked, driven, solaced, welcomed, provided cheer for some eight hours, and done "our own work" for some ten minutes, we are also filled with a certain crude, elemental joy. I, for one, might even be deliriously happy. This ambivalence is familiar, for I knew two kinds of summer as a child: half of the season was spent with French relatives who celebrated summer, and the other half with Russian relatives who flooded it with tears.

SUMMERS PAST

My aunt Simone was an indefatigable redhead with a violent need to shelter, counsel, nurture, share—a variety of atypical French impulses caused by an unfulfilled yearning for ten children of her own. She was a

guardian angel of my childhood, and it is her bountiful nature that inspired, with perhaps disastrous results, my own seasonal impulse for earth-mothering. Her house in Picardy was filled from June to September with every young transient whom she found reason to take under her wing, she never ceased to grow, pick, store, prepare. I followed her daily to a capacious vegetable garden tended by two farmers called Cain and Abel, to orchards replete with peaches, apricots, pears, quinces, prunes, currants, and every sort of berry, to the dusty fruit-fragrant cellar in which she stored her abundance. I accompanied my jovial uncle to the banks of the Somme River, watched him catch trout, which Aunt Simone would serve within the hour, *au bleu,* for lunch. I reveled in her teeming kitchen's smells—leek and sorrel soup, succulent *boudins* bursting with lard under their tight crisp skins, tall vats of raspberry jam simmering on the stove toward which Aunt Simone's plump strong arms lifted me so I could skim off their fragrant foam.

As the frailest, favorite child I was put to sleep in a cot at the foot of my aunt and uncle's bed when their hospitality ran to riot. I listened with wonder to their whispering of endearments—how much I love you, my life, my treasure—first intimations that there could be such a thing as a long and happy marriage. And fell asleep to the litany of summer's bounty woven into their tender murmurs: this year's crop of quince will yield at least fifty pots of marmalade, Abel's asparagus is the best of the decade, did you take a look at the peaches. . . .

That was July. Then came August with the Russians—ah, my dears, what a difference. In August I was a single child among three aging relatives whose nurturing instincts were solely centered, every summer, on the culture of regret. The month was spent in a tiny wooden cottage built by my great-grand-uncle Kuzmin; he had duplicated with remarkable fidelity, upon a melancholy plain of the Gironde, one of the glumly dark, low-ceilinged *izbas* of the Russian countryside. It was there that we were invited to share memories of his disconsolate past: wandering through Europe during the Russian Revolution, he had married a German circus acrobat, had spent his meager savings on buying her a riding academy; she had fled with a trapezist.

My second companion in this dim dwelling was Uncle Kuzmin's sister, my great-grandmother. Babulichka was a woman of stupendous fortitude during the winter. But her equally abundant virtues of delicacy and tact impelled her every summer to adopt her brother's lachrymal disposition. And so—endless and nostalgic recitations of loves ruined, possessions lost, time past and unrecapturable; of the samovars and Fabergés left behind thirty years before in Saint Petersburg, the dachas in Lesnoe and town houses on Nevsky Prospekt abandoned to the mercy of the Bolshevik monsters.

The disconsolate trio was made complete by Great-Aunt Sandra, another treasure of my childhood, a sad-eyed beauty in her late forties who had been a promising opera singer in prerevolutionary Russia, and had several times shared the stage with Chaliapin. Memories of her as beloved as those of Aunt Simone, but bittersweet—the flutter of faded silks and mended laces, smells of belladonna, rosewater, steaming kasha, the rough edge of the cameo brooch that I fingered as she soothed me to sleep with a Russian lullaby. On August evenings, under the melancholy eyes of a few icons Uncle Kuzmin had rescued from Russia, we sat at a table by the light of a green-glassed kerosene lamp. Babulichka and her brother punctuated their reminiscences with games of cards and chess. Aunt Sandra played recordings of her past operatic performances on an ancient crank-up Victrola. She had never recaptured, in exile, the budding glory of her Russian career, her voice had begun to wane. And once or twice each summer, as she played a recording of her beloved *Die Walküre,* she ventured to follow, in her voluminous mezzo, her own past rendering of Brünnhilde's war refrain. "Hoyotoho-ho, hoyotoho-ho," Aunt

Sandra sang, but only for eight or ten refrains, for her voice would soon dissolve into a medley of sobs accompanied by single, heroic tremolo notes . . . Uncle Kuzmin hiccuping slowly in his grief, Great-Grandmother enfolding her large daughter in her arms, *"Dushinka, golubchik,* why these tears, you have had such a fine career. . . ."

Ah yes, *have* had. That was the leitmotif of my Russian August. Aunt Sandra's fading mezzo, crescendo of summer abundance sung to the diminuendo of time's ravage, my own hoyotoho became the cry of a war goddess all right, with this substantial difference from Wagner's: she was the summer goddess of destroying time, the double-faced deity who is both life-giver and devourer, who returns yearly with her bounty and simultaneously warns us of our eventual return to dust.

Poets

These most accurate sensors of the collective psyche tend to take a Russian, disconsolate view of summer. Name me one masterpiece whose euphoria for July or August is equal to Wordsworth's for his April daffodils, or Keats's for the mellow fruitfulness of autumn. Poets have tended to deplore summer's transience rather than praise its beauty: "[its] lease hath all too short a date." They use it to scan our years, measure the threat of advancing age. "Three score summers have I seen," "after many a summer dies the swan." Its beauty strikes poets as fickle, deceptive. "Eternal summer gilds them yet" (Byron on the isles of Greece), "but all, except their sun, is set." Little of springtime's elation in summer verses ("Spring, the sweet spring, is the year's pleasant king") none of the guileless bounty of autumn, which comes "jovial on, crowned with the sickle and the wheaten sheaf."

The first stanza of Yeats's "Sailing to Byzantium" is about a country of perpetual summer where nature has run amok to threaten all civility and social order, where

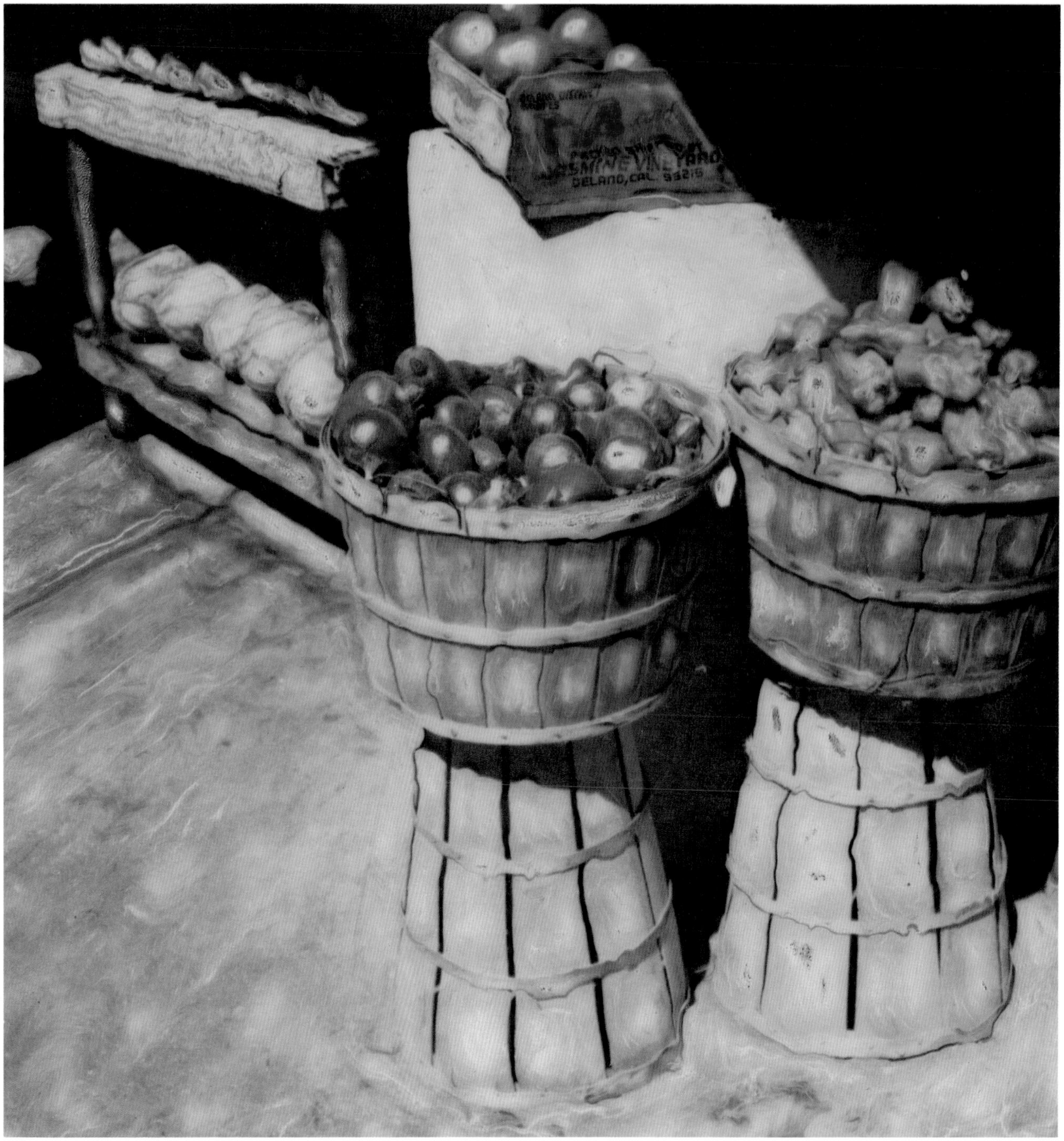
DELANO, CAL. 93215

"Caught in that sensual music all neglect/Monuments of unaging intellect."

As for Pushkin, he is downright derogatory about our season: "Oh glorious summer! I would have loved you if it weren't for the heat, the dust, the mosquitoes, the flies."

I have a theory about poets' distrust of summer. It is in this most rapacious of seasons that the ambivalence facing all writers becomes most poignant: our desire to drench in the world for inspiration, our simultaneous fear that this contact will drown our powers; our contradictory need for participation and withdrawal, for summer's frenzied elation and winter's quietude; a choice in which most writers would choose winter, what Thoreau called "life near the bone where it is sweetest."

The dilemma transcends poetry, reaches every one of us: vernal, orgiastic need to be engulfed in the Cosmic Whole (or the Lover); simultaneous desire to preserve, undiminished, the wintry fortress of Self.

"Beautiful Summer"

Brainwashed by the joys of Aunt Simone's Arcadian Julys, by the perilous association of rural plenitude with marital bliss, I grew up, from the age of ten, saying that I wished to marry a gentleman farmer. My imagination grew fervid with prospects of cultivating perfect roses, of rooms filled with dogs and children, of guest-filled tables groaning under my exquisite food.

"A gentleman farmer!" exclaimed my friends (those who knew me best). "You'll go crazy!" I married one. My friends were almost right.

For I immediately set out, upon moving to the country over three decades ago, to re-create the smells and tastes of Aunt Simone's gardens, kitchen, larders. I planted salsify, Belgian endive, fennel, Jerusalem artichokes, white asparagus, all manner of fare ill-suited to our more arduous New England climes. But there were no more Cains and Abels to cultivate a garden; there was, at best, a hapless occasional teenager who barely knew the difference between parsley and rhubarb; my husband, a kind but puritanical man who looks on any method of lessening work as vaguely sinful, prohibited mulch with the sternness of Jonathan Edwards banning Sunday debauchery. And within a few weeks my first and long-desired garden loomed before me brown and grim and bare as a grave. Hoyotoho the foot-high weeds shouted at me, hoyotoho they continued throughout the summer, threatening to choke the few prosaic crops—beans, carrots, squash—that had deigned to grow. By mid-August my Slavic temperament had quite overcome my French one. I dug through the garden sobbing about the ravages of time on my life, dutifully storing into the tyrannical freezer thirty quarts of peas, baby corn, and puréed pumpkin, putting up fifty jars of rose geranium jelly . . . a simple leap from those early years to the August evening that finds me loathing summer, loony friend giggling upstairs, self-invited guests on the rampage, immense unusable zucchini shipped out as lewd jokes to horny friends.

Summer Recaptured

My favorite summer days are spent alone by the side of an ancient, cracking, primitively kept-up swimming pool, on the same spot where over a quarter of a century ago I sat pregnant with each of my two children; where I later saw them take their first steps, admired the sweetness of their naked bodies, heard them speak some of their first words. They are now tall men in their twenties, who speak of things far beyond my understanding, such as microeconomics, and the eighteen-inch pine saplings planted two decades ago tower thirty feet above me.

On a late August day I seek refuge here to regather the energies dispersed by the Valkyries of summer, look forward to the potential sweetness of the few decades

149

that remain ahead, accept with increasing serenity that most difficult message of summer—the irreversibility of time.

Toward afternoon's end I walk to the vegetable garden to pick a dinner (garden safely contained now to a quarter of its former size, sanely mulched a half-foot deep with hay). Relief of the earth's forthcoming sleep, barely audible hoyotoho of slowed, late growth. I look with particular affection at those tenacious crops that scorn summer's fickle, frenzied brevity—the parsley that will survive many frosts, the obstinate succulence of beets and carrots that will yield into Thanksgiving week. I already start replanning next spring's garden (fewer tomatoes, lettuce rows closer together), marveling at the elemental drive that still urges us to this detestable, satisfying task. The subconscious mind tolerates many contradictions, and few aspects of reality are more replete with them than summer. . . . On the way back to the house I think back to certain days of the past season that were surely some of the year's happiest, that were, perhaps, a life's perfect day.

Gathering dew-burdened peonies and Japanese irises shortly after dawn for a huge bouquet.

Taking a walk on the nearby Appalachian Trail with four or five friends; splendor of the Cathedral Pines near Cornwall inspiring one of us to sing Schubert lieder (which are mostly about spring and autumn).

Rapacious pleasure of finding a crop of wild mushrooms in the woods. Bringing them home, many hands in the kitchen to help out with a marvelous dinner.

As many generations as possible at the table, ranging from late infancy to the hoary seventies, my own children, inviting many friends. Fruition, abundance, procreation, tribe, the joy at all that teeming growth and venerable age seated at the table. . . . Summer, I say to myself when recalling such a day, there's nothing like it; and tomorrow is September first.

151

152

SUNGLASSES

On an olive beach, neath a turquoise sky
And a limeade sun, by a lurid sea,
While the beryl clouds went blithely by,
We ensconced ourselves, my love and me.

O her verdant hair, and her aqua smile!
O my soul, afloat in an emerald bliss
That retained its tint all the watery while,
And her copper skin, all verdigris!

153

JOHN UPDIKE

W

HEN I WAS A LITTLE KID, OF COURSE, I WAS brown all summer. That's because I was free as a bird—nothing to do but catch bugs all day—and didn't care what color I was. Whatever didn't wash off handily at night was the tone I took.

Puberty ended all that. As we know, puberty alienates the skin from the mind and both skin and mind from the young person involved. If I had it to do over I would go through puberty again, but I would do it where no one could see me.

Spring vacation when I was fourteen I traveled sourly with my parents—the last people anyone would choose to go through puberty with—to Daytona, Florida. On the beach I met a strange girl, named Lu, from Racine, Wisconsin. She spelled it out for me, in a provocative tone of voice: L-U. I had never met anyone named Lu or from Wisconsin, and I had certainly never met a girl who was cute by popular standards (by any standards—her hair was bouncy and the color of lightly buttered toast) and yet would be the one who approached me on

ROY BLOUNT, JR.

the beach—*because she saw me reading an anthology of stories of horror and the macabre*. There must have been something wrong with a girl who had perky-but-full lips and also admired the stories of H. P. Lovecraft ("The Call of Cthulhu," "The Rats in the Walls"), but to my way of thinking at the time, borderline schizophrenia was the only thing that seemed to pull everything together. When I met her there on the beach she was more or less my color. I turned my back for a moment and when I looked again she was already the hue of an Almond Joy.

I didn't want Lu to sink deeper and deeper into sepia without me. And, hey, I was only a couple of years removed from brown boyhood. So I abandoned myself to the sun. Chuckled when Lu wondered, in a provocative tone of voice, whether I wasn't rushing it. Did take certain precautions, like keeping my arms akimbo so as not to run the risk of white stripes down the sides.

The next morning I woke up (to use a word that often appeared in stories of horror and the macabre) *eldritch:* a pulsing salmon-pink, with tiny white blisters all over. Since my first instinct at that time was to be ashamed of being seen in any condition, I was not about to return to the beach, even for Lu, especially for Lu, looking like I'd been covered in garish chintz.

Lu surely found other fish to fry—her father was a big dairy magnate, she refused to eat ice cream for that reason, and she had been to seven high schools. When I got back to my school, my new color had nearly all scaled away. What traces remained did not move anyone to ask me, "Mmm, where'd you get all that tan?" However, a naturally platinum-haired senior majorette, whom I had never had any pretensions to being on the same level of reality with, stopped me in the hall. "Who do you go to?" she said.

For a wild moment I thought she had said, "Who do you go *with?*" I was astounded to find that I was larger than she was physically. I answered, "Whuph?"

"Your dermatologist," she said. She thought I had been undergoing dry-ice treatments.

Officially my complexion is "ruddy." It says so on my draft card, which was issued in October 1959. In the fall and winter months, when other Caucasians tend toward the peaked, I look healthy, at least by 11 A.M. But often in the summer, by comparison to more seasonal people, I pale. And showing my draft card does no good. In summer, sometimes, my draft card looks tan next to me.

It would be one thing if I were a roofer, but the kind of work I do—this, for instance—doesn't get me out into the sun *regularly*. I travel, type, talk. On a given Fourth of July I may have Juned where it isn't sunny, as in departure lounges. I may have spent June *losing* a tan of some interest.

The last real tan I had was one March. I got it in Africa, riding camels. A camel-riding tan is an honest tan, especially if it has been achieved despite eighteen-power sunblock.

Sunblock is a great invention for people who want to make it clear that their purpose in life is nothing so superficial as getting tan. If you happen to get tan while putting all your effort into (a) learning to imitate the cry of a camel (an amalgam of moose gargling diesel fuel, club man being goosed by steward, and outboard motor in too-shallow water), and (b) not getting burned so badly that you end up looking stranger than the camel, then fine. If someone, say a senior majorette, should ask you where you got such a tan, you can say, "Hm? Oh, let's see. Zanzibar?" Getting tan has not been your pursuit.

However. A cool, incidental tan may well be a head, arms, and knee-to-ankle tan—which should be enough for decent people, but then you turn up in a bathing suit somewhere and you look like one of those 1940s shoes. In fact your tan may begin halfway down

156

your forehead, because you have been wearing a practical hat, a hat appropriate to camel-riding, say.

There are only so many things you can do, as an adult, in a bathing suit. In fact there is only one thing you can do in a bathing suit without being largely covered, like the earth itself, by water. That one thing is sunning.

I hate to be just . . . sunning. Sunned against is more like it. Lying smeared with lotion on sand in the hot sun is like being rolled in cornmeal and dropped into a hot pan of Crisco, only less dramatic. "Soaking up the rays," sunners call it. I would rather soak up gravy, thereby replenishing, not depleting, the body's essential oils. (I say that, but of course I've had to lose my innocence about gravy, had to learn the malignity of it, as we all have, in these health-conscious times. We have to live more naturally and wholesomely, stop eating the things we love.)

One spring in my late twenties I was in Florida, covering the baseball training camps. I was new to sportswriting and hadn't made many sporting friends or started to drink much yet. I was in Florida for a month, and I had to do something. For some reason I decided to take another shot at tanning. I applied myself systematically. Anointed my limbs. Held to a schedule. Within a week I possessed, for the first time since age twelve, a good deep hamburger-bun glow over every mentionable part.

A consummation, but also a responsibility. It isn't easy to cover spring training and maintain your tan, too, what with the games being played in prime sunning time. Driving to ballparks, I would roll my left sleeve up awkwardly high and hold my arm and shoulder out the car window at various angles, to catch the sun all around. The police pulled me over and accused me of giving intentionally farcical hand signals. I didn't care. I got so transcolored after a while that in the light of my motel bathroom I was orange. After that nothing was enough.

I developed new fears. One day I went to Flamingo, Florida, in the Everglades, and sat on a dock watching pelicans and eating a po'boy sandwich. Observing. Getting outside myself. Pelicans are like snowflakes, in that no two of them are alike. But no given pelican is like any snowflake, either.

Suddenly a blackbird, which I hadn't been watching, swooped down and literally grabbed my sandwich from my hand, with his feet.

The po'boy was too heavy for him to fly very high with, so I ran after him a few steps and grabbed it back, scarcely damaged. I had paid eighty-five cents for it, which would be a couple of dollars today. I liked it. I was still hungry. Ignoring the blackbird's cries, I started eating the po'boy again.

But then I began to worry. I might catch some kind of rare tropical disease from a South Florida blackbird's feet. Who knew what the symptoms might be? What if my tan fell off!

My last day in Florida, I overbaked. I turned a peculiar, sizzling shade of rust. I sat in my hotel room fascinated by the color of my own stomach. What had I become? Fiery chills ran through my thighs. At length I slept, and tossed, and dreamed that I had fallen off a speeding bicycle and was skidding over concrete.

But as I flew north, burnt sienna, I was under the impression that it had all been worth it. I went straight from airport to office.

No one said anything.

I dropped hints.

No one took them.

Finally I worked my tan into an editorial conference. When someone said, "That's a good line," I sprang up, tore open my shirt, tugged at the top of my pants and said, "Speaking of lines. . . ."

There it was, visual proof. The line where my bathing suit had left off and the rich dark gold began.

Only no one seemed impressed, favorably. I looked down. It was gone.

Airport X-ray machines, I now believe, neutralize tan in some cases.

"Oh," someone said, grudgingly, at last. "You got a little color."

You can "get a little color" drinking! Which is what I worked on that year as the spring gave way to summer. I found I had a knack for it. Years went by. Drinking is more active than sunning, and it makes you feel no worse in the morning than sunning does. And it recalls your innocence.

The girls that I caught bugs with back in the old days were so easy to talk to. No, not easy, fun. Because that was when summer was summer, you were out of school, you didn't have to do anything most of the time (back when time was *time*), the pavement was hot but your feet were tough, and the air was sultry but you were out moving, creating a breeze, and you could treat yourself to an unhealthy soft drink of some kind and it would be sweet, refreshing, exactly what you wanted.

And the bugs were for the taking. Bumblebees to trap between jar lid and jar, roly-polies to roll up into hard gray BB-sized balls lined with little curled legs, lightning bugs to snatch in midflash and get that funny smell on your fingers, grasshoppers in your fist like vaguely pulsing stem-wads and then you'd open it and feel them ping off. You wouldn't torment bugs, but you wouldn't care how they felt, either; if they died they died, the sun shone on them and you alike.

Drinking was like that to some extent. The way I did it. But it's changed. Lately I have so many forms to fill out. And I don't feel as fluid as I used to in my joints. My very children are borderline adults. And I need to take niggling conscious measures to shore up my everyday health. And I tend to wake up before I want to. And money is so much more of a *consideration* than it used to be. And I find drinking gets irksome. Who has time for it anymore? Not even reporters. A campaign-trail press veteran was quoted as saying of his new, young colleagues, "They don't even drink at *night*."

O temperance! O mores! You start thinking about why you are drinking, and how much of it you ought to be doing, and it gets to be too much like sunning. So I am drinking less and less, and the days get longer and the nights earlier, and I suppose as a matter of course I will be spending more time wholesomely in the sun.

The last remark surprises me. But it could well be true. On television I saw an international fashion model being interviewed. She looked a little hard, you know, but ravishing. She said tan was passé. What she was at pains to maintain now, she said, was just "a blush." Which is what I have long maintained by way of natural embarrassment. Now, if tan has become unseemly, my life can be expected to adapt. I've noticed of a noon that I was outdoors mowing the lawn in nothing but athletic shorts. By the time I am elderly I may be back to running after bugs (Nabokov did it), brown as a berry.

158

159

3· Between Wild and Sheltered

TODAY I CAN SEE ON THE MAP THAT SAINT Ignace, in upper Michigan, where I spent my childhood summers, is farther north than Montreal, which accounts for my recollection that to get there from central Illinois was a matter of an endless journey to a remote, primeval no-man's-land. Here my family had a log house, which had been built by a great-uncle decades before, and here we would spend the three months of summer. I felt for this house the special love that almost everyone, I've since discovered, feels for a summer house—a love quite different from the feelings people have for the houses we grow up in. Perhaps a summer house is where you discover that you are you, and that is something that cannot happen in an ordinary place.

In those days, one reached the northern shore of the Great Lakes by ferry across the isthmus that connects Lake Michigan to Lake Huron—the Straits of Mackinaw. The very word "straits" must have added to our sense of difficulty and adventure in getting there. The waters of this body were often

DIANE JOHNSON

rough, and sometimes the crossings would be canceled. When you embarked you could not see the opposite shore, and the deep call of the vessel's horns gave a sense of an ocean ahead.

My little brother and I would feel sick, excited fear, arriving each early summer, to see what natural disasters would have befallen the house in winter when we weren't there. The snow of northern Michigan might have reached the eaves and pushed the windows in. Certainly the plaster chinks between the logs would have fallen out and have to be replaced by my father, who also would repaint the logs with creosote against the termites, scenting our hair and clothes for days with piny stink. Screens had to be put up, the chimney cleaned. The winter would have washed things up on the shore in front of the house—sometimes logs or the corpses of fish quite strangely near the porch, suggesting how the icy waves had risen to strike the door of the empty house.

It was the view of my parents that life in summer must be lived as simply as possible, in order to enjoy a virtuous sense of rustication and proximity to nature. This is a conventional enough belief, connected, I suppose, to the belief that sending poor children to camp, to live in uncomfortable tents in the country, improves their character and may even deter them from lives of crime. Whether my parents' theories were born to justify the discomforts of our cabin, or the discomforts had fostered the theories, I never found out. Certainly we had none of the ordinary amenities of wintertime urban civilization—our cabin for years had no indoor plumbing and no running water except what you pumped at the sink. We slept on a screened-in porch, or in a hot little room under the eaves, the windows open equally to lake breezes and mosquitoes. The peeled logs of the walls and pine floorboards under bare feet gave us splinters. We had electricity—a tiny bulb by the outhouse that attracted june bugs, so that a small child obliged to creep out there

in the night would inevitably step on their crunchy corpses. (This outhouse was eventually deemed too spartan even for us, and a real bathroom was installed, but I believe the early experience has given me what small measure of adaptability I possess.) We had kerosene lamps, too, in case the electricity failed, as it sometimes did in the black summer storms that swept across the Great Lakes, making whitecaps on a violent sea.

The summer house was free of the strange convention of his and hers by which the father is sent out each morning—the house was as much my father's as my mother's—to chink up, bring wood into, and hammer loose shingles on the roof, like a pioneer householder. Far from being carefree, our simple Michigan life, I now realize, must have been, especially for my mother, a demanding succession of primitive rituals to do with water-gathering, fire-tending, and protecting her young from wildlife, for in this part of the country there were bears, skunks, mosquitoes, spiders, leeches, porcupine, chiggers, snakes, wolves, and bats.

With some of these members of animal creation we shared the house itself. Once a skunk came to live beneath the floorboards, a problem delicate to resolve. The bats that wheeled out of hiding at dusk, however, would by late evening return to their shelter, the eaves of the sleeping porch where the children's beds were. The mosquitoes continued their whining circles overhead. In the distance, the cries of wild animals.

My parents evidently loved to play at this frontier idyll, and busy themselves with nesting and security. But it was the sense of menace that my brother and I loved. Personifications of Summer in classical painting suggest how enduring is the impression of this season as safe, garlanded, unclothed, carefree, and benign. To us it seemed the opposite, a season of ubiquitous, rather delicious, peril. We had to be anointed against the mosquitoes and burrowing chiggers, pulled indoors when the bats began to swoop, warned against the mother bears that were sure to be lurking near the blueberries, be ever on the lookout for porcupines and skunks, against whom we would need to protect our dog Tarby, if not ourselves. How we dreaded the shiny, slimy leeches lurking in the shallow water—bloodsuckers waiting to attach themselves to our skinny limbs. There was the constant danger of polio and drowning. Even the scratchy berry brambles might hurt us, and down by the water grew a malevolent skunk cabbage that entrapped poor insects to a sticky death and could get even you with its odious scent if you happened to brush against it.

So of course I loved our summer house, with its danger and discomforts, more than I loved our "real" house, scene of schoolwork, regulation, orderly life. The philosopher Bachelard speaks of the way many of our ideas and recollections are attached to specific rooms and places to which we will return in memory all our lives. "The house is one of the greatest powers of integration for the thoughts, memories and dreams of mankind." But he is talking about the primordial birth house, and he sees it as a refuge and shelter. Its imagery is therefore that of the winter house, which protects with warmth and light against the darkness and cold, both real and spiritual, of the world. "We comfort ourselves by reliving memories of protection."

To me the summer house is strangely the opposite thing, a house which forces us into the world on our own resources. Equally dear, it is not a shelter but a jumping-off place benignly promising that our explorations and solitary wanderings won't bring us to grief. It is weathering the perils of summer that reassures us that we will be able to survive the more serious wintry perils later on.

There is a theory of memory that says that you remember more of the things that happen when you were happy than when you were not. The happiness of our summer house was conveyed in the lightened mood of the adults, the warm sense of idle days, the growly voices of my father and his brothers playing piquet on the porch. We had happy pastimes—fishing, swimming, berrying (wild strawberries in June when we got to Michigan, and blueberries later in the summer). All these were things we did together, a family.

But more important was the sense of being there alone. If the summer house evokes a memory of ideal life, perhaps it was because in summer one was not in school, was unsupervised, could hide in nooks, could enter into the oddness of things, enjoy the secret life of the house with no one to tend—or seem to tend—us. Turned loose to wander in the woods, it seemed to us that no one worried beyond telling us about the bark growing on the north side of trees.

Reading is the most solitary essential pastime to which all summer houses are peculiarly dedicated. You can read all the things you meant to, or never would get around to. You can read trash and long classics. In our cabin I read *War and Peace,* but also stories of other children's summers—*Diddie, Dumps and Tot,* or *The Five Little Peppers,* and (no doubt a different summer) racy historical novels sent to my mother by the Literary Guild and thrown into her suitcase for her summer reading. Now, in summer I read the quite surprising thrillers friends leave in my Tahoe house, or books of poems I never quite have time to muse about in winter.

Another luxury is not reading at all. It is the boredom of summer that seems in retrospect the most precious and formative thing—the most important part of a summer house is that it is a place to be bored in. To the organized city child, these hours of messing about by oneself must be the crucial ones in which we discover ourselves, develop a point of view, learn to rely on ourselves as reliable observers, establish in our own minds that we are we. The perfect summer house has therefore

165

to have deep corners and retreats, and it should have access to wilderness places to wander and mess around and be alone in. In our cabin I had a little room upstairs under the eaves, with a mezzanine that gave a view of the grownups downstairs. In the evenings, if there was a fire, the sheets of heat wafted stiflingly up. On hot days, the sun heating the creosote stifled with the smell of pitch and a certain dusty smell of the old curtains. Here I would drowse and dream and do nothing, or make worlds of paper dolls, or weave on my Indian bead loom.

In the winter world of the real house, sober furniture is dedicated to its uses: you sit on an upholstered chair, eat at a mahogany table. In a summer house, caprice reigns. The chairs are made of birch logs, and the chandelier is made of coffee tins painted bronze by my great-aunt Lottie. The same decorative impulse that dictates the fanciful antler constructions of Adirondack houses is behind the things we made of birch bark and twigs we gathered in the woods. In a rented summer house, one drapes the alien chairs in costumes, as at a masquerade party, for the summer house is in every way part of a masquerade of happiness and harmony, and the fun of being someone else.

In fact the whole summer life is a disguise. You pretend to some other condition entirely. My husband, a Californian, spent his summers on Catalina Island. There, on the Pacific rim, and before the Second World War, the fancy was to be Japanese. They had straw mats and screens and paper lanterns. In our Michigan house we pretended to be Indians, perhaps in the same contrite, propitiatory spirit that hunters wear horns and pretend to be deer. And of course we wanted the beautiful Indian rugs, the handsome baskets, and gods'-eyed figures that our Indian game allowed us. We wore buckskin moccasins made by the local Indians, and the house even had a pseudo-Indian name—Playwickee. This now seems embarrassing to remember.

Indians were the first ethnic group of which a child from downstate Illinois might be aware. We rode our bicycles in a park, in the park was a little museum, and in the museum real scalps, tattered and seedy, hung from the lodgepoles, reminding us of the frightening recent past. In Michigan, the Indians fishing near our cabin or stretched along the pier in the village were fat and amiable and wore plaid shirts. We knew that Mr. Barker, a friend of my father's who ran a nearby lodge, was mostly Sioux. It seemed to my brother and me that our father was privileged, enormously select, to be taken fishing with a real Indian, and we expected he would come back with mysterious outdoor lore. We felt not sympathy but chagrin when once he nearly drowned, sinking in his waders like a city slicker. But he did learn, somewhere, to strip the bark from birch trees, and he made us a teepee, a little summer house of our own, to hide away in.

I suppose, nowadays, few people can have a house in total isolation, but a summer house must seem isolated, gazing out at water or into a forest and pretending to ignore its neighbors, to preserve the sense of transaction between wild and sheltered. Our cabin had neighbors to either side—I remember Mrs. Barrater, she whose hair turned mysteriously brown, when it had been white. From taking Vitamin B-12 shots, she said. Haha, said my parents. But her house was almost invisible in pine trees, and we had a vast, unpeopled forest behind, with logging roads and CCC trails, and a castle rock where some tragic Indian legend had been enacted.

At the end of summer, the rituals are of battening down. Back go the shutters. The rugs are rolled and the lawn chairs stacked on the porch under sheets of oilcloth and a piece of old sail. Now the grasshopper must become the ant, for even in late August, the whiff of winter in the air, which comes all at once, in a day, warns of desolation and snow. And school. And new clothes. Worldly

167

city notions beguiled us, yet we hated to leave the house alone, "left like a shell on a sandhill to fill with dry salt grains now that life had left it," as Virginia Woolf wrote of that moment in *To the Lighthouse* when the family goes away. We worried what would happen to Playwickee without us.

Of course it was not the house we worried for, but for ourselves, that we might not return. And of course, one summer, we did not. Something happened. Time passed, we grew, moved, our aunts died, the house was sold, we have other houses by other lakes. But a few years ago, a cousin passing through Saint Ignace walked around our cabin, for it was there still, and said that the log furniture is the same, the tin lamps the same. We found this image of permanence reassuring; for we ourselves are not the same.

168

170

Stepping into the temperatures of the stream,
I felt the bed,
the intricate temperatures
quickening and in some sense giving rise to the slate bed,
which I doubt would have been as hospitable
with as many resting places if the water had not made the rock
passable, a concourse that let us walk easily;
in fact, there were a few of us walking downstream.
I guess what excited me most was
the license to enter and merely be there,
and then I enjoyed letting it go on and on like tap water,
the permissive current letting me stretch out
or arrange the bed so that several temperatures
passed through my body at once.

Something as unapproachable as maturity
put in layman's terms but not scaled down
or vitiated is what I believe I became part of
when I entered the stream. And it was the same
as I had imagined by looking. And for a while
I enjoyed the fast, ingratiating current
and the slate, which was becoming passive
with many resting places and companions.

Like a figure whose awkward weight you see entering
a courtyard, closer to the activity than it has ever been,
I stepped into the stream
and onto the clarified plan.
What I enjoyed most was being able to enter
the thoroughfare and arrive
into the present for sure as another object
sheared by fast moving warm water.

MARJORIE WELISH

171

WHEN THE THUNDERBIRDS ARRIVED AT CAMP Grayfeather, Ellen, Chen-cheu, and I were waiting for them, lounging on the splintery steps of the recreation hall. Behind us, a big fly with a weary August note to its buzz banged against the screen door. In front of us, under a level evening sun, the straw-colored Delaware countryside—pointedly referred to as "Wyeth Territory" in the camp catalogue—rolled off from our own wooded hillside toward the bluish haze that was Maryland. It was a Tuesday and just after dinner, the tranquil period in a camp day, when the woods are filled with the soft clanging of bells announcing evening activities and the air still holds a whiff of tuna casserole. After dinner was supposed to be journal-writing time for the three dozen or so fourteen-year-olds who made up the rank and file at Grayfeather, but Chen-cheu, Ellen, and I had slipped out of our tent in order to witness the coming of the Thunderbirds. It was an event we were awaiting with the same kind of horrified delight as that with which biblical adolescents,

ANDREA LEE

as deep in glandular boredom as we ourselves were, must have greeted a plague of locusts. The Thunderbirds were a black teenage gang, one of many that battled in the close brick streets of Wilmington, and, through some obscure adult arrangement, they were coming to spend a week with us at camp.

"Do you think they'll have knives, Sarah?" Chen-cheu asked me, rubbing an array of chigger bites on her ankle.

Chen-cheu was the camp beauty, a Chinese-American girl from Oberlin, Ohio, whose solid-cheeked, suntanned face had an almost frightening exotic loveliness above her muscular swimmer's shoulders. She had, however, a calm, practical personality that belied her thrilling looks, and she talked with a flat midwestern accent, as if she'd been brought up in a soddy.

"Nah," I said. "Gangs use guns these days."

In fact, my only knowledge of the habits of gangs came from seeing the movie *West Side Story,* but, like the other black kids at Grayfeather, most of us the overprotected or dreadfully spoiled products of comfortable suburban childhoods, I had been affecting an intimate knowledge of street life ever since I'd heard about the Thunderbirds.

"Maybe we'll end up massacred," said Ellen, in a hopeful voice, unwrapping a stick of gum.

Ellen was always chewing gum, though it was against camp rules; she had come to Grayfeather with about a thousand packages of Wrigley's hidden in her trunk, and even, to the derision of her bunkmates, made little chains of the wrappers. She chewed so much that her father, a Reform rabbi in Baltimore, once made her walk around a shopping mall with a wad of gum stuck to her forehead. She and Chen-cheu and I had been close friends all summer—a brisk female triumvirate who liked to think of ourselves as Maid Marians, both lawless and seductive. (In reality, it was only Chen-cheu who provided the physical charms, since Ellen and I were peaky,

bookworm types.) The three of us made a point of being on the spot whenever anything interesting or scandalous happened at the camp, and the arrival of the Thunderbirds was certainly the most riveting event of the summer.

They were not the first visitors we'd had at Grayfeather: already we'd played host to a morose quartet of Peruvian flute players and a troop of impossibly pink-cheeked Icelandic scouts. The Thunderbirds represented, however, the most ambitious attempt to incarnate the camp motto, which was "Adventures in Understanding." As Ellen once remarked, instead of being a tennis camp or a weight-loss camp, Grayfeather was an integration camp. The campers—most of whose fathers were professors, like Chen-cheu's, or clergymen, like mine—had been carefully selected to form a motley collection of colors and religions, so that our massed assemblies at meals, chapel, and campfires looked like illustrations for UNICEF posters.

It was at chapel the previous Sunday that Ned Woolworth, the camp director, had announced the coming of the Thunderbirds. "During the next week, you'll be more than just kids relating to kids," he said, strolling up and down between the rows of split-log benches, scanning our dubious fourteen-year-old faces with his benign, abstracted gaze, his big, gnarled knees (his nickname was Monster Legs) working below his khaki shorts. Woolworth was tall and looked like Teddy Roosevelt, and had an astonishing talent for not knowing things. He ignored the generally unenthusiastic silence, as his campers coldly pondered the ramifications of doubling up in tents with their comrades-to-be, and passed over the muttered lamentations of the camp misfit, a Nigerian diplomat's son named Femi. He read us a few lines from *The Prophet,* and then told us we would be like ambassadors, bridging a gap that society had created. It appeared that the staff had already written and gotten permission from all of our parents.

*   *   *

The arrival of the Thunderbirds at Grayfeather was signaled by a grinding of gears and a confused yelling from far down the dirt road that led through six miles of woods to the camp. As Ellen, Chen-cheu, and I poked each other in excitement, a battered yellow school bus, covered with a tangle of long-stemmed graffiti, rattled into the clearing and swerved into the dusty parking lot beside the rec hall. The bus ground its gears once more, shuddered, and seemed to expire. The doors flew open and the Thunderbirds poured down the steps into the evening sunlight.

"They're so *small!*" Ellen whispered to me.

There were ten boys and seven girls (the girls forming, as we later found out, a sort of women's auxiliary of the Thunderbirds)—brown-skinned teenagers with mature faces and bodies and stunted, childish legs that gave the boys, with their well-developed shoulders and short thighs, the look of bantam cocks.

One of the boys came up to Chen-cheu, Ellen, and me and stood rocking on his heels. "Hello, ladies," he said. "My name is Marvin Jones."

He wore tight black pants and a green T-shirt that was printed with the words "KING FUNK," and he had an astonishing Afro pompadour that bobbed like a cresting wave over his mobile, trickster's face. Above his left eye, he had dyed a platinum streak in his hair, and down one brown cheek ran a deep scar. Looking at him, I had the feeling that something unbelievable was happening in front of me.

"Hello," said Chen-cheu, Ellen, and I in a faint chorus.

In a minute, Ned Woolworth and the rest of the staff were there organizing things. The sleepy little camp clearing, with its square of sun-bleached turf and its cluster of low, green-painted buildings, seemed suddenly frantic and overcrowded. Radios weren't allowed at Grayfeather, but one of the Thunderbirds had brought a big portable receiver that filled the air with a Motown beat.

Martha and the Vandellas were singing, their shrill, sweet voices crackling with static, and the Thunderbirds were bouncing to the beat while they eyed the camp, shoved each other, picked up their abbreviated luggage, and shouted back and forth. Meanwhile, the rest of the Grayfeather campers had slipped unobtrusively, even furtively, out of the woods, like an indigenous tribe showing itself to explorers; they settled on the steps and porches of the rec hall, to swing their feet and observe. Little Nick Silver, a math whiz from Toughkenamon, Pennsylvania, who at a precocious twelve years old was the youngest kid at camp, sat down next to me. "You have *got* to be joking," he whispered. "They'll eat us for breakfast!"

With the Thunderbirds had come a counselor from the social agency that had sponsored their visit: a tall, sallow white man with thinning curly hair and a weary, skeptical way of regarding the woods, the camp buildings, the evening sky, and his charges. He talked with Ned Woolworth for a few minutes and then climbed back inside the battered school bus, turning around only once to smile sardonically at the Thunderbirds. "See you later, guys," he called out. "Behave yourselves." The Thunderbirds responded with a kind of roar, and then the school bus started up with another wrench of gears and rattled off through the trees.

Once the newcomers had filed down the path into the woods, to put their bags away in the tents, one of the counselors rang the evening-activities bell. "We'll have introductions at campfire," she announced. "Be friendly!"

We campers simply looked at one another. With the Thunderbirds gone from the clearing, a powerful current of noise and energy had suddenly been shut off. Bats flitted across the darkening sky, and a breeze from the lake carried a smell of damp leaf mold. While the others were lining up, I went over to inspect a far corner of the dining hall, where I'd seen a group of the Thunderbirds clustering. There, scratched deeply into the green paint, was a miniature version of the same long-stemmed, weirdly elegant graffiti that had covered the school bus, and that I had seen spray-painted on decrepit buildings on trips to the city. It read: "T BIRDZRULE."

Marvin Jones was the leader of the Thunderbirds. At the get-acquainted campfire, it was his command that galvanized his troops into standing up and stepping forward, one by one, to give their names. (L. T. La-Wanda. Doze. Brother Willy.) He himself stood by in the firelight with a crazy tremor running through his body, wearing a rubber-lipped showman's smirk, like a black Mick Jagger. (Stretch. Dewey. Belinda. Guy.) In the bright circle of hot moving light that baked our faces and knees and left our backs chilled with the damp breath of the big pine grove behind us, we campers studied the Thunderbirds and they studied us. Both groups had the same peculiar expression: not hostility but a wary reservation of judgment. As bits of ash danced like a swarm of glowing insects in the draft of a fire—a big log-cabin fire, built especially for the occasion by the woodcrafts class—Ned Woolworth, his cheerful, freckled wife, Hannah, and the rest of the staff guided us all through a number of cheers and folk songs.

Most of the counselors looked eager and uneasy. The near-instantaneous grapevine among the campers had already reported that the Thunderbirds had gotten into trouble immediately after their arrival, as they walked down the path to the boys' tents. Marvin Jones and two others had shinnied up a tall, skinny tree—one of the birches, unusual in that area, and beloved by the nature counselors—swinging on it and pulling it down with their combined weight until it seemed likely to break. When one of the counselors asked them to stop, Marvin Jones, laughing crazily and hanging on to the birch, responded, "This is the *woods,* man! Ain't *no* law against climbing no tree in the woods!"

That night, the Thunderbird girls who had been assigned to share our tent refused to undress until the light was turned out. There were three of them: a pair of tiny, frail-boned twins named Cookie and June, who had large almond-shaped eyes, hair done identically in an intricately braided puff over each ear, and small breasts in sharp, pointed brassieres that stuck out like Dixie Cups through the clinging nylon of their blouses, and Belinda, a stocky girl who looked twenty years old and had a slight squint, straightened hair bleached a bright orange-red in the front, and a loud, unbridled tongue (I had heard Belinda laughing and cursing above the others when they got off the bus). She was subdued now, as were Cookie and June, the three of them sitting bolt upright on the tightly stretched army blankets of the cots that had been set up for them, muttering replies to the kindly chitchat of our counselor, Molly. Molly was from Jamaica—a student with an anxious, plump face and a delightful habit of shaking her head at her campers and exclaiming, "Girls, you are becoming hardened in your ways!"

The three Thunderbird girls responded to Molly with a sudden opacity of gaze, glances among themselves, and abrupt fits of shy giggling. We campers were stricken with shyness ourselves: there was none of our usual roughhousing, or bedtime ballets in our underwear. Instead, we undressed quickly in our bunks, turning away from each other, painfully conscious of the contrast between the lavishly equipped trunks from which we drew our pajamas and the small vinyl bags that our guests had brought. Once Molly had turned off the single yellow bulb that illuminated the tent and had strolled off up the path to a staff meeting at the rec hall, the tent was unnaturally silent.

I arranged myself on my lumpy top bunk as I always did—with the sheet over my head to keep off mosquitoes—and breathed in the scent of slightly mildewed canvas from the rolled sides of the tent. From the

bunk beneath me, Chen-cheu, an instant and sound sleeper, gave an adenoidal snore, and I could hear little clicks and rustlings that meant that the Thunderbird girls were undressing. There was a cool breeze blowing with a steady rushing sound in the trees, and I wondered what the girls from the city were thinking as they listened, perhaps for the first time in their lives, to the noises of the wild night. Never had I been so aware of the woods as a living place around me. Over the stubborn saw of the crickets, I heard two hoots from a white-faced owl that lived in a tree near our tent, and a gradually intensifying gray light in the direction of the lake meant the moon was rising. In my mind, the moon mingled with the yellow school bus that had brought the Thunderbirds, and then suddenly I found myself sliding quickly out of the vision, knowing that I'd been asleep.

What had awakened me was a soft voice. It was the new girl June, calling out to her sister in a whisper. "Cookie—Cookie—are you up? I hear a noise."

There was a creak as Cookie got up and crept over to her sister's cot. I leaned my head out slightly from my bunk, and in the dim moonlight caught a glimpse of the tiny girl, her hair greased and braided for the night, dressed in her underwear. It hadn't occurred to me until then that perhaps the Thunderbird girls didn't have pajamas. "Hush, girl," whispered Cookie to her sister, sitting lightly down on the cot. "Hush up! You want these bitches to hear you?"

"But there's a noise," whimpered June.

"Hush up, girl. It's just trees, that's all. Just trees."

There was silence, and when after a few minutes I edged my head out of the bunk to have another look I saw that Cookie had lain down on her sister's cot, and that the two girls were sleeping with their heads close together on the pillow.

*   *   *

At breakfast, Ned Woolworth announced to a chorus of groans from the campers that instead of swimming or canoeing or tennis we would divide up into small groups for what he called rap sessions. My group included Ellen; Jackie Murdock, a camper notorious throughout Grayfeather for his prolonged belches at mealtimes; a round-faced Thunderbird named Ricky; and a skinnier Thunderbird named Les, who wore a peculiar rust-colored bowler hat. There was also Marvin Jones, the Thunderbird leader, who wore an army fatigue jacket, open to show his gleaming bronze chest, and sat slumped, wiggling his feet, an expression of exaggerated forbearance on his face. The six of us met with a counselor in a grove of pin oaks near the chapel. It was one of those clear, dry, autumnal days that occasionally leap ahead of their time into the middle of August. The sky was a sharp blue, crisp moving shadows checkered the ground, and in the eyes of all the kids sitting there was a skittish, inattentive look, as if they might dash off suddenly into the breezy woods.

A green acorn plopped down near Ricky, the Thunderbird sitting beside Ellen. "Wha's that?" he asked her, pointing.

"That's an acorn," said Ellen scornfully, tossing back her red hair. "Didn't you ever see an acorn before?"

"No, Sweet Thighs," said Ricky, giving her a lascivious, cherubic smile that showed a broken front tooth. He picked up the acorn and put it carefully in his pocket.

The counselor clapped her hands. She was a diving coach, with a pugnacious, sunburned face and a blunt, bossy way of talking. "This morning, we're going to discuss friendship," she said. "We all have friends, so let's talk about them—who they are, and what they mean to us—"

"I don't have friends," interrupted Marvin Jones.

"What?" said the counselor.

"I said I don't have friends," said Marvin Jones,

looking at her seriously, the platinum streak in his hair glittering in the sunlight. "Yeah, that's right, Miss. I mean, shit—scuse me, Miss—I got my *men*. Spike is my *man*. Ricky is my *man*. And L. T., that dude with the sunglasses and the 'Free Africa' T-shirt, he's my *main* man. I mean, them dudes will cut for me. But they don't be no *friends*. And then we got the Thunderbird Queens—I mean our ladies."

"*They're* not your friends, of course," said the counselor acidly.

"No. Like I said, we don't have no friends. We got enemies, though—the Twelfth and Diamond Street gang. You ever hear of them?"

"No."

"Well, that's good, 'cause the T-birds are on top. Wait a minute—I'll show you something."

He gave a curt, imperious nod to Ricky and the other Thunderbird beside him, and an odd tension seemed to seize all three of them. The woods seemed very quiet for a minute, and all at once, synchronized, they stood up, snapping their fingers. In high, plaintive voices, they broke into words and rhythms that were not quite a song, not quite a chant: "What the word/Thunderbird . . ."

It was a strange mixture: a little bit of Motown, a bit of the interlocking verses all kids use to choose sides for games, a bit of the bouncy silliness of football and basketball cheers, all bound together quite naturally with swearwords—words that we Grayfeather campers all knew and used enthusiastically among ourselves, in spite of what parents and teachers and counselors had to say. The Thunderbird song could have been ridiculous, but instead it was thrilling, carrying with it, to those of us who sat listening, all the resonance of a dangerous young life in the city. It was clear that the song was not intended as an entertainment for us but was presented as a kind of credential, like the letters scratched into the paint of the rec hall. Ellen and I punched each other excitedly in

the ribs, and tried to remember every word. When the song was finished, Marvin Jones and the two other Thunderbirds flopped down abruptly at the base of a tree, their faces full of restrained pride.

"That was great, fellows," said the counselor. She was trying to seem cordial, but it was clear that she was uncomfortable, almost angry, about what had just happened. "Let's see if you can do a little more talking now, so that we can get to know you."

Marvin Jones picked up a twig from the ground and tapped the toes of his sneakers with it—one, two, three. "Lady, you just got to know us," he said.

Down at the lake that afternoon, Jimmy Terkel, the boating counselor, gave a briefing on canoeing to an assembled group of campers and Thunderbirds. Jimmy Terkel was a dark, soft-spoken young man, who loved the little irregular lake, with its cedar water and clustering lilies; all summer he had made canoeing into an austere rite, embarking on solitary voyages at dawn or sunset, an angular silhouette at the far corner of the water. The afternoon had grown overcast, and as Jimmy Terkel talked about water safety and demonstrated the proper way to dip and feather a paddle—the lecture was chiefly for the newcomers, since the campers had been handling canoes all summer—swarms of audacious gnats made forays at our eyes and ears.

Suddenly, in the middle of the talk, Marvin Jones strode over to one of the aluminum canoes on the shore and began to push it toward the water. "I want to go for a ride, Mister," he said politely to Jimmy Terkel. "I know how to do this. I see it all the time on TV."

Three other Thunderbirds grabbed paddles and rushed over to the canoe, pushing it through the shallows to deeper water, and tilting it dangerously when they all climbed in, about fifteen yards from shore.

"That's too many in a boat, fellows!" called Jimmy Terkel, coming forward.

The gunwales of the overloaded canoe were riding about six inches above the surface of the lake, and the boat shipped water as the passengers thrashed about trying to position themselves; miraculously, the canoe did not capsize. There was an argument between two of the Thunderbirds ("You on my *arm,* man!"), and then the canoe took off with an irregular splayed motion, as Marvin Jones and a second Thunderbird paddled with great splashing thrusts.

"Oh, *no!*" Jimmy Terkel muttered, glancing automatically at the heap of orange life preservers on the shore. But no disaster occurred. The canoe made its awkward, lunging way into a cluster of lily pads, and we heard the delighted yells of the novice canoeists as they yanked up the tough-stemmed blossoms—an act that the camp staff, ardent conservationists all, had raised in our minds to the level of a felony. Then the boys in the boat all took off their shirts, and Marvin Jones stood precariously upright to paddle like a gondolier, a big lily coiled dripping around his neck. There was something barbaric and absurd about the sight of him paddling that overloaded canoe, which, as it wobbled heavily over the dark water, seemed a parody of a boat, something out of a nursery rhyme. As I watched, there came to me out of nowhere a surge of pure happiness. The other campers seemed to feel it as well; the faces of the kids around me were contorted with crazy laughter, and some of them were jumping up and down. Out of the corner of my eye, I saw one of the campers, from pure joie de vivre as it were, pick up a handful of sand and rub it into the hair of his bunkmate. Just for a minute, it seemed that the camp was a place where any mad thing could happen. While Jimmy Terkel stood on the shore with an angry smile on his face, campers and Thunderbirds alike were almost dying with glee.

That was the last, really the only, good time we had with the Thunderbirds. Later that afternoon, a scuffle broke out near the camp infirmary between two of the gang members and a stableboy. A burly counselor from Honolulu broke up the fight, which was just a matter of shoving and name-calling. The participants were made to stand face to face and explain themselves, and in the process they quite spontaneously shook hands and apologized. In ten minutes, the grapevine had telegraphed news of the scuffle to all parts of Grayfeather. It seemed that everyone involved in the fight had laughed it off except for Ned Woolworth, who had rushed to the scene and glared at the three boys as if he wanted to knock them all down.

The staff had scheduled a hayride for that night. Normally, the campers looked forward to hayrides: the dusky country roads, shrill with insects; the creaky wagon and plodding, pungent horses; the deep, scratchy hay that offered the opportunity for a little romantic improvisation (though Grayfeather, a camp of overeducated fourteen-year-olds, was notoriously backward in that department). Early in the evening, a subtle intelligence flashed through the ranks of the campers, a kind of mass intuition that suggested that things would be much better if we let the Thunderbirds go hayriding on their own. To the bewilderment of our counselors, who had no way of forcing us to accept a treat, all of the campers, gently but immovably, refused to go.

After dinner, Ellen, Chen-cheu, and I and the other girls from our tent took part in a desultory sunset game of Capture the Flag, as the Thunderbirds and their girls, escorted by Grayfeather staff members, boarded the wagon. An hour and a half later, the returning wagon creaked slowly up to the recreation hall. Norah Pfleisch, an excitable junior counselor, rushed inside and burst into tears on the shoulder of Ned Woolworth's wife, Hannah, who was directing a spur-of-the-moment Ping-Pong tournament.

"I've never, *never* had anything like this happen," sobbed Norah, resisting Hannah's efforts to lead her out of the rec hall and away from the fascinated gaze of forty campers. "They—fornicated! They lay in the hay like animals and just . . . did it! It started when we went under the old covered bridge. It was such a beautiful night. Usually we *sing* on hayrides, but this time I didn't know *where* to look, or *what* to listen to!"

We all rushed to the door of the rec hall. Outside, under a clear night sky streaked with meteor showers, the Thunderbirds and their girls, chattering loudly and innocently, were climbing out of the wagon, pulling hay out of each other's clothes.

Things fell apart completely the next day. That morning at swimming class, another fight broke out— this one between Femi, the camper from Nigeria, and an agile, pale-skinned, sullen-faced Thunderbird. On the shore in front of the swimming area of the lake, as the white rope and bright floats of the lane dividers bobbed gaily in the morning sun, two counselors held back the two struggling boys in bathing suits, Femi with a swollen nostril leaking blood. "I'll kill that filthy little nigger bastard," panted Femi in his Mayfair accent, wiping his nose with his coal-black arm. "I'll smear his dirty little arse all over the beach. He called me a monkey!"

"He spit on me," the Thunderbird was muttering, scuffling his feet in the sand.

Marvin Jones, his platinum streak glowing brilliantly in the blinding sunlight, was called over to make peace. "This ain't no way to act," he began, but his tone was insincere, the tone of a showman bent on pleasing everyone. He sent a quick, shifty grin over to the Thunderbirds standing near him, and one of them suddenly shoved a camper, who went sprawling into the lake. In the boys' swim group, a general melee broke out between campers and Thunderbirds, the tanned bodies of the campers mingling wildly with the small, dark, muscular Thunderbirds. The two counselors were themselves dragged in. Pairs of boys bolted, yelling threats, and ran off into the woods.

The girls at the lake, both Thunderbirds and campers, were quickly marched away to our tents, where we were told to sit quietly. Looking into her trunk, Chen-cheu found that someone had taken three of her prettiest T-shirts and a new bathing suit. When she complained loudly about it, she found herself surrounded by the three Thunderbird girls who shared the tent with us. They began to jostle Chen-cheu, and to pluck at her long, black hair. Chen-cheu promptly socked Belinda in the stomach. Our counselor, Molly, came running down the path from the rec hall at precisely the moment when Chen-cheu, propelled by a nasty push, came flying out of the tent and sprawled in the dust, shrieking out a string of curses that even Ellen and I had never before heard her use. Her beautiful face was contorted and almost purple with rage, but she wasn't crying. None of us were. After that, we were separated from the Thunderbird girls.

Meanwhile, the boys were being rounded up. I heard later that a number of them were found grappling in twos and threes in the woods; there were surprisingly few injuries beyond a few black eyes and bloody noses. "We had a plan," one of the boy campers said afterward. "We were going to barricade ourselves in the infirmary and fight 'em off from there. Firebomb 'em."

The Thunderbird boys, escorted by several strapping counselors called in from a tennis camp across the lake, were confined to the rec hall. By eleven o'clock on a fine, sharp, hot August morning, Camp Grayfeather had settled into a stillness in which the only sounds were those of a sublimely untroubled nature: birdsong, the harsh whirring of cicadas, the light slapping of waves on the lake shore.

None of us were surprised to discover that the Thunderbirds were to be sent home. I sat with nine other

182

girls on the sagging bunks of our tent as Hannah Woolworth, her kindly face pale and drawn with strain beneath its sunburn and freckles, talked to us. "We all feel that it would be better and safer for everyone," she said. "We don't want any of you kids getting hurt."

When she said "you kids," it was clear that she did not mean the Thunderbirds.

I looked at Ellen and Chen-cheu, and they looked back at me. Events were passing, as usual, into the unreachable sphere of adult justice, and though there was a certain relief in that, it also seemed sad. For a day and a half, the Thunderbirds, like a small natural disaster, had given an edge of crazy danger to life at Grayfeather; now the same powers that had brought them to us were taking them away.

"We didn't even get a chance to learn all their names," said Ellen slowly, after Hannah Woolworth had left.

A flicker of resentment ran through the group of girls crowded together in the tent, and Ellen and I began, with an obscure feeling of defiance, to teach the others the song that the Thunderbirds had sung for us under the oak trees the day before.

In about two hours, after we'd eaten a large pile of bologna sandwiches on horrid white bread, sandwiches that the camp cook had provided as a sort of emergency takeout lunch, we heard through the woods the unmistakable sound of a bus. "We've *got* to see this," I said.

Five of us—Ellen, Chen-cheu, and I, and two other girls—jumped up and, against the strict instructions left us by our absent counselor, took off toward the rec hall. We didn't take the path, but ran, dodging like Indian scouts, through the underbrush, stifling occasional nervous giggles and trying to avoid the poison ivy. When we got to the edge of the clearing, we stood discreetly back in the bushes and observed the scene. The midday sun gave the clearing a close, sleepy feeling. The Thun-

derbirds, their spirits apparently undaunted, stood in a rambunctious platoon behind a grim-faced Ned Woolworth, and the familiar graffiti-covered school bus was just coming to a halt in the parking lot.

We could see that the same tall, curly-haired man who had delivered the Thunderbirds was coming to pick them up; this time, he was wearing a green eyeshade, as if he'd been interrupted during a stretch of desk work. He came quickly down the bus steps and strode over to stand in front of the assembled Thunderbirds. "Well," he said, clapping his hands together. "What the hell have you guys been doing *now?*"

The Thunderbirds, all of them, broke into loud laughter, as if he had just told them the best joke in the world.

"We ain't been doing *nothing,* man," answered Marvin Jones, rocking on his heels. "Just being ourselves!"

The curly-haired man pulled off his visor and sighed so that even we could hear him, fixing his weary, skeptical gaze for a second on Marvin Jones's scarred face, and then on the golden hills and fields of the Delaware countryside rolling into the distance. He talked to Ned Woolworth in a low voice for a few minutes, and then turned back to his charges and sighed again. "Come on, get on the bus," he said. "We're going back to the city."

When we five girls heard the bus start up, we did something we hadn't planned to do. Without anyone suggesting it, we all took to our heels again and ran through the woods to a dusty crossroads far from the clearing, a spot where we knew the bus had to pass. Through some extraordinary, even magical, coincidence, the same plan had occurred to each one of us. When the bus came rattling up to the crossroads a few seconds after we got there, the five of us, like guerrilla fighters, dashed out of the bushes onto the road. "Stop the bus! Stop for a minute!" we shouted.

The bus slowed and halted, with a squeal of brakes, and the Thunderbirds stuck their heads out of the windows. We could see Marvin Jones's platinum streak shining beside Belinda's patch of dyed red hair.

"We wanted to sing your song," said Ellen, and without further ado we all began clapping our hands and chanting the profane verses that belonged to the Thunderbirds. "What the word/Thunderbird . . ."

We probably looked ridiculous—five girls in cut-offs, football T-shirts, and moccasins, clapping and trying to perform like a group of tough guys on a city street corner—but we felt natural, synchronized, as if we were doing a good job.

When we had finished, the Thunderbirds—still hanging out of the windows of the bus—gave us a burst of grave, polite applause. Marvin Jones leaned farther forward out of the window. "That sounded good," he said. "And we're sorry to leave."

The two groups looked at each other, and it seemed for a minute that some obscure misunderstanding was about to be cleared up, and then the bus started up and moved slowly away through the trees.

184

WELLFLEET AND THE BEACH OF THE INTELLECTUALS

NO LONGER GO THERE, SUMMER OR WINTER. The National Seashore, established in 1961, preempted so much land in the topmost reaches of Cape Cod (and a good thing, too) that I could not buy a house. Summer rentals, year after year, became just too tiresome, and contributed to the end of a marriage that flowered summer after summer in Wellfleet, but which even Wellfleet could not sustain.

But I often dream the place back, as one dreams intimate scenes with an old flame, so great a part have Wellfleet and the great ocean beach played in my life. I have never lived anywhere else in America where the sense of space, the freedom it brought, was so intoxicating. Wellfleet and its ocean beach still answer, at least in memory, to some long-buried need in me to live with the outermost land, the ultimate coast, land's end. As my friend Thoreau said in his book on Cape Cod, "A man may stand there and put all of America behind him." I have always had a thing about lighthouses; the very

ALFRED KAZIN

thought of my favorite, Highland Light off Truro, thrills me; it stands for so much that is human in a place I love for its very lonesomeness.

My wife R. did not care for lighthouses, or for Thoreau, "that neuro from Truro," as Edmund Wilson called him to her delight. She thought Melville's *Moby-Dick,* a book I had just edited, "a boy's book," and like a great many other bright, scathingly witty novelists fiercely ambitious for fame, she thought literary criticism—my calling and our bread and butter—existed just to give her a good review. But for a while at least, things were different in our beloved, dangerously exciting Wellfleet. Wellfleet and R. are so bound in my mind that just to think the name is to call her back. "I was always the smartest girl in class," pretty and cheeky, the life of the party at every party. How that girl loved parties! The summer crowd at Wellfleet made a point of cocktail parties on the dunes overlooking the ocean. R. regularly glowed there in her creamy white outfit, martini in hand, engulfed in banter and flirtations.

We started coming up to Wellfleet in 1953, the summer after our marriage, and continued year after year into the sixties. Before 1940, when I first saw Cape Cod, I had known only the mass beaches for a New Yorker off Long Island. What got to me was the unbelievable sense of space the minute you got away from Provincetown, the dunes right at the end of Commercial Street making a great desert—and ending in the longest uninterrupted stretch of beach on the Atlantic coast. Yet the whole length of the Cape, stretching into the ocean like a great arm enclosing Massachusetts Bay within its grasp, is only 65 miles long and at its narrowest point is only a mile wide. On my explorations of the Cape I was amazed to find how few of its external features had changed from the time, more than a century before, when Thoreau had recorded a journey along the "great beach."

What I still see when I dream of a summer afternoon in Wellfleet (Henry James thought "summer afternoon" were the most beautiful words in English) is a long stretch of tableland, high dunes overlooking the Atlantic, dunes half covered with poverty grass and beach grass where at the right hour people make love, even long-married couples. Behind this high bank is a path leading through patches of bayberry bushes straggling in the sand, tiny twisted shrub pine deep in the golden sand, not cute like minuscule Japanese "trees" grown in a pot but hardy and tough like the Cape itself, twisted by the sometimes violent winds that sweep the beach and the incessant shifting of the sand. I love the forceful play of wind and weather on the Cape, which is really one long sand bank anyway, a place composed entirely of sand, even to the depth of three hundred feet in some places.

Cape Cod used to be famous for the many vessels coming to grief on its beach. At one time its few inhabitants seemed to be mostly occupied in waiting and watching for wrecks, then pillaging. In the nineteenth century, when the Cape was utterly foreign to the rest of New England, Ralph Waldo Emerson, visiting it as one might now "visit" the Antarctic, was told that lighthouses were bad for the wrecking business and to be discouraged. Emerson relates in his *Journals* (my favorite of his books) that he was astonished by how much of the Cape he could see from Orleans in the middle. The whole place was that empty, apparently composed not of people but, in addition to the sand, of salt dust, gravel, and fish bones. "They say the wind makes the roads, and, as at Nantucket, the real estate was freely moving back and forth in the air."

Thoreau, arduously making his way from Eastham to Provincetown along the "great beach," marveled that there was not another beach so long and so straight, yet one from which you could see "two seas." The other "sea" is Massachusetts Bay. To summer in Wellfleet was to have your choice of the fierce, cold currents of the Atlantic, where it was possible to swim nude off an empty stretch of beach, or the more placid waters of the Bay, thick with weeds, where the beach was a favorite for picnics; the wind *there* would not blow too much on people making love in the dunes.

In addition, there were the "ponds," as they call even the largest lakes in New England. Gull Pond, the biggest, clear and deep, more than a mile in circumference; Newcomb's, Swett's, Slough, Horse-Leech, Round, Herring. In the old days all were connected—so I read—at high water. The way to R.'s and my favorite pond, Slough, lay through deep woods that were nonetheless filling up every year with more and more cottages, wartime Nissen huts, even some ostentatiously chic "country houses" before the National Seashore Law called a halt. The owners' names were gaily lettered on slabs nailed to the trees. It was like being a prospector who had struck gold to get yourself a habitation along those sinuous paths deep in the woods, so rapidly in the "radical" sixties, a time of unsurpassed government largesse to the many expanding and new universities, did Wellfleet become populated with tenured professors from universities as far as the Midwest, law professors, physics professors, newly rich psychoanalysts, imminent Nobel Prize winners from M.I.T.

Wellfleet presented certain difficulties to a young novelist. Although R. was a great favorite at the cocktail parties on the dunes and the afternoons on the beach itself—"la plage des intellectuels," as a famous historian's affected wife called it—she was compelled to make jokes, many jokes, because she would not read their books or show interest in their ideas. Limited salvation came from the only other novelist who was regularly at the "beach of the intellectuals," Edwin O'Connor, who inspired a conviviality that was a great antidote to the kind of psy-

choanalyst in Wellfleet who arranged chic candlelight processions on the beach in mourning for the dead of Hiroshima. We both loved O'Connor for his unpretentiousness—he openly laughed at the more ponderous academics as they left their books and departmental chatter to put a foot or two into the icy Atlantic—but he also had a weakness for flourishing in our faces the wealth he had gained from *The Last Hurrah,* about the last Irish Boston pol of the old style. Where once O'Connor had made it to the Wellfleet post office on a bicycle, he now arrived in a Porsche, and he gloried in his magnificently avant-garde house deep in the woods, built for him by a haughty Russian-born architect who never arrived on the beach without two enormous, restive, threatening German shepherds that frightened everyone around.

The "beach of the intellectuals" was not for the unknown, the still madly striving. It could also have been called "Who's Who in the Executive Assistants' Wing of the White House and at the Massachusetts Institute of Technology, the Harvard Government Department, and the Institute for Advanced Study." And I was part and parcel of the problems "intellectuals" posed for R. My books were getting me distinguished professorships at home and abroad. Postwar America had taken intellectuals and "the arts" to its bosom. High Culture was in. There on our section of the "great beach," almost any sunny afternoon in July and August, could be seen Arthur M. Schlesinger, Jr., and his wife Marian; the publisher Jason Epstein and his wife Barbara; the critic Irving Howe and his wife Arien; the psychoanalyst Robert Jay Lifton and his wife, Betty Jean; the radical polemicist Dwight Macdonald, so sharp in mind and manner that even when the intellectual set swam nude in the bay, you could see Dwight's pointed little beard wagging in political argument with another swimmer. How many others, how many famous names! The poet and man of letters Allen Tate, with his wife Isabella Gardner; the great

American architect Marcel Breuer and his wife, Constance. And amid so many *prominenti*, the great, the unique American critic and man of letters Edmund Wilson and his wife Elena.

What brought all these distinguished gifted and dramatic people to Wellfleet? Why Wellfleet? Intellectuals brought other intellectuals; the many groupings were not particularly related, just prosperous enough to be there. Before the war only writers, painters, and composers of an adventurous sort made it to the upper reaches of the Cape, at Provincetown, which had been vaguely bohemian and far-out ever since the Provincetown Players had inaugurated modern American theater on its famous wharf. In the days when Eugene O'Neill and Edmund Wilson were not yet famous and less than rich (Wilson never became the latter), the two had camped out for long stretches on the great dunes leading to the old coast guard station. They would come into town only to load up with groceries. At the end of Commercial Street John Dos Passos held out for years in Provincetown, as did the old radical Mary Heaton Vorse and the "tramp" writer Harry Kempt. Provincetown when I first saw it was full of Portuguese; Portugal was the very next stop across the ocean. The Portuguese bakery in town was famous; even Edmund Wilson would bicycle his way into town to carry away loaf after loaf.

Wellfleet was never bohemian. Wellfleet's intellectuals were so accustomed to seminars that Robert Jay Lifton even inaugurated a "Wellfleet Seminar." If the ocean, the bay, the ponds, the woods, and all the delicious paths between helped to perpetuate the usual American pretense that removing your clothes brought you "back to nature," the real passion of the place was the careerism made possible by the as yet unchecked prosperity of the academic intelligentsia—the top ones. Well into the sixties Arthur M. Schlesinger, Jr., was commuting between Wellfleet and the White House, the Kennedy top adviser Richard Goodwin was assuring us about Vietnam that "the little wars stop the big ones," and the radical young—radical so long as Vietnam lasted—modified their "threat" to the Establishment in order to live off their professor parents. Things could be astoundingly self-enclosed. Once, when children were making a rumpus outside one professor's house, his wife came to the window and pleaded: "My husband is writing a book review. I am sure that all your fathers and mothers have reviews to write!"

The conversations on the beach I recall best were brilliant hothouse affairs, intramural as you might say. When Nabokov's *Lolita* was still shocking the daily reviewer on the *Times*, the "beach of the intellectuals" knew it to be a masterpiece. Wilson had been reading some Jean-Paul Sartre and had to say "this new French fellow" was not bad, not at all. Only the "beach of the intellectuals" knew that President Jack Kennedy relished the *New Statesman* and a new biography of Lord Melbourne. And of course there was the endless gossip by the many "Kremlinologists" on the beach about Svetlana, daughter of Stalin, who actually appeared in Wellfleet to visit the Russian-Georgian writer Paul Chavchavadze, whose wife was a Romanov and who herself often modestly made her way to the South Wellfleet post office to receive letters from her kin in Buckingham Palace. It was said on the beach that Svetlana and Mrs. Chavchavadze had actually compared notes on what it was like to live in the Kremlin.

The contrast of all this talk with "Great Nature," with the always thrilling ocean raging away before our eyes, with the seaweedy bay and the many placid ponds! Edmund Wilson, living in Wellfleet all year, couldn't wait to see the summer crowd depart. As it grew larger and larger each year, resembling the overflow crowd attending some fashionable lecturer, Wilson went around growling that the place he loved had turned into "a fucking Riviera." Of course he was one of the place's attractions. His fame was prodigious, even international, and in a period when the nation's thinkers and even its writers were being steadily (and happily) absorbed into academia, Wilson's independence as an old-fashioned, doughty, even truculent free-lance writer and journalist kept the "beach of the intellectuals" all astir. There was never, never anyone like him, and there never will be—not for scholarship itself (he knew all the languages, and was even learning Yiddish and Hungarian before his death), not for the soundness of his learning, not for his political independence, quirkiness, perversity of opinion, and easy defiance of everyone in authority. And then there was the sight of him on the beach, especially in his middle to late sixties, with his long-stained Panama hat, his white dress shirt billowing, his well-filled Bermuda shorts, the handsome gold-topped cane that had long been in his family, and behind this getup, that high, painfully distinct voice and the manner, at once shy yet unmistakably authoritative, in which he listened without the slightest respect to institutional opinions being breathed to the ocean air.

And then there was the ever-present scandal and brouhaha of his relations with his third wife, Mary McCarthy. At one time or another, Mary McCarthy still held out in Wellfleet with *her* third husband, Bowden Broadwater. One school of thought in Wellfleet held it that Mary had gone back just to annoy Wilson in Wellfleet, a place she notoriously disliked and had made the usual wicked fun of in her novel *A Charmed Life* (1955). Wilson was undisguised, the only distinguished figure in this novel, which presented the rest of Wellfleet as a set of careless, usually drunken, destructive wastrels.

Although this side of Wellfleet was unfamiliar to me, I was all too familiar with the much publicized frictions in the Wilson-McCarthy marriage. The ill-fated marriage of male critic and female novelist bore some resemblance to the turmoil in our less famous home. R.

was very far from being as notorious as Mary McCarthy, though perhaps she would have liked to be. R., too, wrote fiction entirely on the basis of her intimate life, with no secrets barred. She had published without achieving significant reputation novels and stories in which the feminine protagonist always managed to describe my thick ankles and my clumsiness in opening cans. I so regularly served to represent the academic oaf in her fiction that she once cheerfully asked me to write in a bit of professorial dialogue—which I was indeed glad to do; it made her less mad at me than usual. Perhaps, if she had moved in a more reckless social set than my academic colleagues, women novelists as disgruntled as herself, she might have had really "scandalous" things to tell. Mary McCarthy, an old-time radical intellectual, had another advantage over R.: she knew what the highbrows in Wellfleet were talking about, even as she travestied their personalities. R. knew intellectuals only through me, and since she didn't *care* to know them, she observed only the usual careerist follies and petty adulteries common to the "academic" novel. When she published a novel about a "wicked" little girl who was the local "troublemaker," Arthur M. Schlesinger, Jr., laughed, "Darling! I can't wait for you to write about adults!"

Our marriage disintegrated poisonously, loudly, especially when my colleagues were there to hear. Each year, like us, the weathered old hut above the "beach of the intellectuals" sank more helplessly into the sand. Each year, as the regular cocktail party became friskier and more abandoned, R.'s sparkling personality and summer-gleaming flesh underneath her blonde hair became interesting to people who did not know she was a novelist until she told them. Our marriage became so meaningless that for a long time there was no need to end it. I came to think of R. not as a wife but as a brilliant, wayward daughter, so dogged that I would never be able to help.

End of summer. End of a marriage. How strange

it was at the "violet" hour of the day, when the light was fading and couples in odd corners were getting cozier by the minute—how strange it was to look out to the outermost Cape with nothing else in sight but a last fishing vessel. Somewhere out in that thrilling, frightening emptiness was Portugal, even Galicia in northwest Spain. How strange it was then to think that career can be the greatest passion, capable of destroying a marriage. How little, really, the intellectuals on the beach made of summer. They—all of us—used Wellfleet, that last great wilderness, in a way that cut us off from the primitive, everlasting heart of the world beating in our ears as we gabbed on the beach.

193

194

My mother could not swim. The rest of us were like otters; we couldn't get enough. Our skin turned to prunes in late May and did not smooth out until fall. We would go in the morning, my brother and I, stay until noon, come back at two, swim all afternoon. Swimming-pool chemicals turned my hair green and bleached out my bathing suits. Summer smelled like rotting mimosa blossoms, quick tuna fish, and chlorine. The one day a week when the pool was drained for cleaning, my brother and I rode our bikes, stayed in the house, fought like rats, and sulked. It was so hot! A detail man for a pharmaceuticals company, my father used to bring home blocks of ice to attach—I have no idea how—to the living room window fan. This cooled us off for a little while, until the ice melted. Summers, the swimming pool was our day camp, the lifeguard our baby-sitter. (When there was one. I remember occasionally swimming with only Drew, the black man who worked at the pro shop, to watch over us. Nobody told us whether or not Drew could

BEVERLY LOWRY

swim.) Our worst summer was the year of the polio epidemic, when all the pools were drained and closed. I remember thinking, when the announcement was made: But what will we do?

We had our specialties, my brother and I. He was the diver, I the swimmer. His affinity was, and continued to be, for tricks in the air—for danger and a challenge, wherever he could find it—mine for the comfort and saving grace, the natural replenishment and lapping rhythms of water—the element in which I felt most at home. I do not remember learning to swim; I only remember doing it. In water I knew I could take care of myself. Swimming, I felt strong and blessed. Doing a surface dive, I imagined myself a new Esther Williams. Plunging to the bottom of the pool, I thought I might discover there a glitzy Atlantis, peopled with sleek water-chorines and beautiful fishtailed boys. The only time I remember being afraid was once when—impatient with the draining and cleaning process—I broke the rules and went swimming while the pool was being refilled. The deep end—we called it simply the Deep—filled up first. A friend and I were paddling around down there. The water was swirling and roaring, too deep for me to touch bottom. ("Can you touch?" we'd scream to one another. "I can't touch, can you?") I reached for the bank. It was some six feet above my head. I knew I would not drown, but in a flash, I felt as powerless as a dead leaf to control my fate.

As usual, our father taunted my brother and me with his own skills—in water as well as in the air—which often put ours to shame. One of those agile, dance-your-eyes-out fat men, my father could float like an inner tube—from now on. His swimming stroke was powerful, if short. He could go under and hold his breath for a full minute, like a turtle. As a young man he'd been a clown diver; when in the mood he could still do tricks. (Once, when I was twenty-two and he in his early forties, he—

in his cups, on a Holiday Inn diving board, in the middle of the night—did his act for me and my new son. Fully dressed, in starched white shirt and tie, suit pants, and black lace-ups, he jumped on the diving board, once, twice. The third time he landed on his behind, bounced up to his feet, bounced again, came down on his behind. Back on his feet, he leaned forward on the diving board, farther and farther, until only the tiptoes of one foot were not in the air. Helicoptering his arms, he yelled for me to save him. I screamed. Surely the jig was up. But gravity and time gave my father a break. He didn't fall in. When it was over, he swaggered. "I haven't done that," he sighed, "in twenty years.")

Ours was a city kind of summer life. There was a lake nearby—on which the town in fact was built—but, as a child, I rarely went there. Our life was people, us and them: their rules and regulations and everyday habits, our wildly fluctuating regard and disregard for those rules and habits, our need to belong. We lived on the block.

But my mother. We—my brother and I—preferred to swim in the Deep. Down there, with no babies to get in our way, we could have fun. I remember my mother standing in the Shallow, hairdo dry and perfect, circling her arms on the surface of the water to keep her balance. We wanted her to come be a part of our games. She held her hands in front of her face and begged us not to splash her. When my father arrived, he would do a noisy belly-buster and come up shooting water and making hippo sounds. If we begged, he took us for a ride. When he went under we held tight to his shoulders and screamed, screamed, screamed. What an act he was, how people loved him! When we swam away from our mother, she went to sit in the shade, to sip her drink and smoke her cigarettes.

Once I saw my father dunk her. He gave her a warning. She begged him not to. (As if begging would help, instead of only make for a better show.) He placed his big hand flat on her head and said, "Hold your nose." In terror—in case he actually did it—she pinched her nostrils together. My father pushed. For a moment or two my mother disappeared. In seconds she came up sputtering, mortified and furious. Her hairdo was ruined. I was relieved but puzzled. What was she afraid of? Why was she gasping? She did not speak to my father for days.

In pictures she looks like an outsider. There are these three dark-haired, brown-eyed people, whose skin takes to summer as if the sun were their new best friend. We look revved up and hopeful: ready for the next thing. In the middle—or on the end—is a small, pale, blue-eyed, blonde woman. She looks if not worried then intensely *focused*, as if concentrating on something the rest of us cannot or do not see. In the sun my mother blistered, burned, and freckled. She and I used to get towels and lie in the backyard early in the season, to get a jump on our tans. While I lay there in bliss, face to the sun, happy as a lizard on a rock, my mother sweated. How she sweated! Pearls gathered on her forehead, small rivers ran down into her hair, her towel became a puddle. The next day I'd be golden honey; my mother, crab claws. After she peeled, she'd be white again.

For the rest of us, summer was the season our year looked forward to. My mother preferred the gentler months: early spring, late fall.

It wasn't just that she couldn't swim. She was afraid of water. Really afraid. I think I vaguely knew this, but we tried not to pay much attention to my mother's fears and eccentricities. She had too many. Besides which, her fears and eccentricities were inconvenient; they slowed us down. What was there to be afraid of? In her early twenties, she'd had polio. The virus left her with a shriveled right calf, an all-but-useless foot, and a crooked spine. If she'd been afraid of water before the polio, after it she was terrified.

I have done about every kind of swimming there is. When I was twelve and thirteen I was on the local swim team, my specialties the 100-meter individual and the lead-off position on the relays. In high school, I lifeguarded every summer. When my second brother was born, I taught him to swim. In New York I ballet-swam to the pas de deux from *Swan Lake,* on Fifty-ninth Street, in the Coliseum. Lately, I have been doing lap swimming to keep in shape. Toting goggles and swim bag, I travel from pool to pool—indoors and out—to go back and forth along a lap line, 72 lengths in a 25-meter pool, 36 in a 50. I have used equipment to vary my workout, from kickboard to pull buoys to paddles. Sometimes I divide the workout into three parts: arms, legs, the crawl. But really, it's all the same: back and forth along the line. Back and forth until it's over.

While my love for water has never abated, I have, in time, grown weary of swimming pools. For me a pool is like Sears to a sales clerk, a place where you go to work. Winters, when I have no choice, I make do in one; I swim my laps and go home. When the weather warms, I happily take to the river I now live on.

It's a good river, spring-fed and cool, milky green and accommodating. I go against the current first: at a certain stand of elephant ears, push off—eight or ten strokes before taking a breath to get a good start against the downriver pull—moving diagonally across the river to a certain weeping willow. There, I turn directly upriver. The branches of the willow hang low. I have to swim through them—always hoping no coiled water moccasins are up there waiting to drop on my back. Turtles on rocks flop into the water at my approach. Another twenty yards on, I pass a dead tree lying parallel to my path. The tree is my guidepost: I am about two-thirds there. As the river is shallow on its right bank, I

197

hug the left, where the deeper channels are. At a large cypress tree, the water is so shallow my fingertips scrape bottom. There, I turn around and come back downriver—fast, like a champion. At the elephant ears I go upriver again, then back down doing the breaststroke. Upriver and back again. From the time it takes, I figure it's something close to a mile. This is great swimming. When I'm finished I always feel nourished and strong.

Summers we spend a lot of time in our river. On hot days we drive our pickup truck to a low-water crossing and float in inner tubes back down to the house. In the shallows, the river is only maybe two inches deep, and so traffic is limited to tubers, canoers, and kayakists.

Living on a river teaches you about water. I have seen this quiet green river turn dark and muddy from a rainstorm. I have watched it rise some twenty feet out of banks. I have stood on my porch and watched whole trees float by. I have heard our new barn crack, yield, and go, as the water took it.

Watching the water reach up and grab things—we have had to rebuild our fence eleven times in seven years—I think of my mother. When the water comes up, there is nothing to do but take to high ground, stand there, and be amazed. No amount of skill or argument can help. You just have to wait for it to be over.

Recently I made a trip to the Pacific Northwest. With a friend I ate lunch at a restaurant whose windows overlooked a glacier lake—cold, inky blue, and, at its heart, 600 feet deep.

"There are stories," my friend told me. "They say there are trains at the bottom. Cars and logging trucks. Nobody can get to them."

A motorboat whizzed by. In its wake the water turned an even darker blue. The curl of water lapped over and then disappeared.

I shivered. "I have never," I said, "been this close to water I instantly feared."

"There is something ominous about it," my friend agreed.

Every time my brother and I threw ourselves fearlessly into the Deep, this must have been what my mother saw, a cold blue bottomless lake too deep to drag. We were blithe, agile, and certain; she was not. We thought water would—could—never hurt us. She knew better. It must have been terrible for her, holding back, all those years, to keep from screaming.

199

FIRST SAW NEW YORK IN THE MONTH OF AUgust when I went as a boy with my family to the 1964 World's Fair. Forever afterward the thought of summer in the big city stirred my heart with insane winds. The romantic idea of a New York summer as the setting of freedom, desire, longings for which I had no words, was fed by a hundred popular images, every one of which I absorbed like gospel. I grew up on moody black-and-white television programs, dramas I sneaked out of bed to watch, shows with a social conscience like "East Side, West Side," the opening of which had Cicely Tyson crossing a bridge against a fierce, menacing urban scene. I knew from television that in New York City people hung out in coffee shops, did strange things like ignore the Surgeon General's warning on a pack of cigarettes, got into trouble, reinvented themselves, and stayed up all night. My hometown, Indianapolis, was bereft of opportunities to be a genuine, heedless delinquent. There were no vigilante gangs of youths like the Dead End Kids

DARRYL PINCKNEY

who snatched fruit from carts, talked back to cops, and didn't have to tell their mothers where they were going every time they touched the door. There wasn't much of the Twilight Zone about Indianapolis. No jazz moaned out of the cellars, nobody sat around in his undershirt in an apartment kitchen, children didn't splash in the borrowed cool of hydrants, no aliens peeked around the corners of the alley.

By the time I was making college interviews, this dream had deprived me of my reason. I had *Breakfast at Tiffany's* swimming around in my head, mixed up with photographs of students with their feet up on the university president's desk, smoking his cigars, of Angela Davis being led in handcuffs from a midtown motel. Kerouac squinted at the rusty fire escapes and patched-up rooftops of the forlorn city, in the distance the skyscrapers had names like Gatsby, and over the brownstones I saw "Sister Carrie" instead of "Apartment to Rent," signs that are now a thing of the past. My vision of New York was a jumble, an ahistorical mess, probably because I first saw it in summer, that season when time stands still, when nothing bad can happen, when the mornings with the sun buttering the treetops represent a chance to start over, to begin again. Everything seemed possible in broad, uninterruptible New York after I'd made big Negro eyes at the college admissions nice guys all day. I walked back to my dreaded stepgrandmother's pigeon coop with a stolen, specimen night on the town in my pocket—Washington Square, I found it, but tell me again who had lived there?—walked under the train tracks over upper, upper Third Avenue, my huge bell-bottoms floating above the pavement, above the beautiful designs of broken glass.

Alas, the messages of the moon were not meant to be. Once I got myself to school in New York, my parents pulled the plug on my fantasies every May. I was not allowed to spend the summer in New York, and of course those months of perilous separation wielded the power of the forbidden over my imagination. Life would spring forth from the shining paths in Central Park, from the desert of the piers, from the insouciant discos of Sheridan Square—someday. Have patience, just wait. How long? Not long, and for many years I lived out summer in the ostentatious isolation of Manhattan.

Sixty millions, all fools, Wilde said of America, and coming from the Midwest I believed him, believed in travel books with titles like *New York Is Not America*. Not a blade of grass to remind one of home, no ants, no Ku Klux Klan, just roaches scattering from under the warmth of the electric kitchen clock. My first summer in New York, with the gates of school closed behind me, my introduction to the great world, a time more melancholy than autumn and more tender than spring, I passed in a state of ignorance and jubilee. I could go anywhere at any hour because most people assumed that I, the scruffy black kid, was the mugger. I'd known summers ruined by too many plans, and my first season of homesteading in the swelter of New York I celebrated my birthday alone. Summer, if you know how to work it right, can bring more privacy than you bargained for, and sometimes I thought the whole city was taking off its clothes just to torment me. In this grace of undress, letting it all hang out, New Yorkers seemed to be, at last, their true selves, unburdened of winter cares and layers. Strange that New York seemed to me more uniquely itself at a block party than during a snowstorm or a Christmas sale, but then, summer is the voyeur's paradise. That is what I stayed in New York to see: the great trek, the movement of life from indoors to outdoors, whole streets turned inside out, as if at every window people were shaking out the contents of shoeboxes, suitcases, closets.

To live alone is to be like an empty room. There is no furniture, no comfortable, familiar objects to absorb sound. Impressions, drifting thoughts, they enter your head, your spirit, and echo with that acoustical exaggeration. Everything stands out because no one is around to hint that you're nuts, to tell you to shut up. Nothing distracts from what is going on outside. I lived alone my first summer in New York, like a grown-up on television, I thought, lived alone with an overly alert ear for the voices in the street. Day and night the city came to keep me company, admitted me to intimacies through windows and thin walls, and the traffic, the delivery trucks hacking in the street, became a lullaby.

I was on a mission to rediscover the city. What lay hidden under the inhospitable stare of winter, what seemed too far away, was suddenly there, within reach. It was nothing to walk from 116th Street and Broadway all the way down, in a hot, blazing curve, to Stanton Street below Houston, where illegal cockfights were held in aimless yards, nothing to turn in any direction and find either the vibrating walkways of the Williamsburg Bridge or the silent canyons of Wall Street. Anything that you liked you promoted to the status of landmark, and even if you never went inside the Metropolitan Museum, it was enough to know it was there. Sometimes I went in the opposite direction to make friends with Harlem. I wanted to turn a corner and be astounded by the Negro Capital of the World, by the Seventh Avenue that boasted fifty-two Easters a year, as my elderly relatives said it did when they first came out of the subway in the 1920s and saw a black policeman directing traffic, a West Indian orator on a soapbox, felt the surge of surprise, wariness, and pride recorded in so many of the novels and poems of the Harlem Renaissance. That Harlem had moved away long before my time, had moved to the rare books desk of the Schomburg Collection, leaving side streets of stumbling shadows, indifferent, wide avenues of record shops, funeral parlors, fast soul-food joints, and faces whose stories were not for sale.

All cities smell in summer, I'd heard, but what could have prepared me for the onslaught of odors, one of the ways you know when you detach your matted hair from the wet pillow that you are well into June, trapped in July, ready to shoot yourself in yellow, merciless August. Fulton Fish Market, the vendor with his steaming hot dogs, the stinking back doors of fine restaurants, the subways with human beings jammed into something called five o'clock. Once upon a time not every car was air-conditioned, and you squeezed in and knew that you had gone to hell. Underground at high temperatures, you and the stranger glued to your stomach were on the verge of disgrace. Who ate garlic, who drank, why did she use that hair cream, and why could I not stop inhaling it. I stayed out of the subway after I witnessed two guys snap like rubber bands. The ingredients of a freak-out were simple: take too many people, stuff them into a subway car as hot as an oven, stall said car in a dark tunnel, and wait. This particular afternoon a fistfight broke out and the guys swung wildly at each other over the heads of shrieking secretaries who at least had a good reason to scream their makeup off.

What a miracle it was to come home and take the day out of my pocket, to lay it on a table like coins, keys, paper clips, and folded lunatic leaflets. The roaming around added up to something—but what? The answer would reveal itself in time. To do nothing has advantages that should not be abused, they say. The main thing was to live as variously as possible, to test every line I had ever fallen asleep over, to lean against the doorway, hero of my own film noir, to be unworthy of the blue-and-white china, to let a glance at the anchor man's mouth reassure me that the century of war and revolution would

203

flourish without me, and then to break off connection, to go on without radio contact, to climb the weeks that made a slope called job, rain, bills, guests, stupid hopes, to leave your clothes hanging on the branches, to do a free fall into the first heat wave: last seen swimming strongly.

I lived for over ten years in the same apartment. The young do not move as much as people think. It's too risky. These days many marriages and marriagelike alliances are held together by the sheer scarcity of rooms with a view, by the high price of giving up that unhappy, decent address. I was lucky, holed up in a house of only two apartments, one of a row lost on a side street of the Upper West Side. I washed my panes under pressure from my neighbors, and when I forced open a window the world flew in. I witnessed the scorchers and roasters from this constant perspective, leaned out into the thermal joke with the same expectations year after year, each time utterly convinced in some visceral way that every evening held magical promises of renewal, that this would be the night the doorbell would ring or the corner would turn and my life would change. Summer, in that sense, became like a neurotic pattern: you can't see the repetitions in your behavior; repeated actions come to you as a startling new episode. You do the same thing again and again and each time think the result different, significant, worth chewing over until the stars fold up.

The torrid, sticky, humid seasons in New York had their themes. My first summer in the city I could call the Fall of Indochina; the next is labeled in retrospect the Bicentennial Summer. Then, in 1977, came the terror of the Lovers' Lane murderer, Son of Sam, when women in the bookshops were afraid to walk home alone. To the unsavory hysteria of that summer was added the Blackout. The power failed all over town. Some people sat with admirable nonchalance in the candlelight of bars, others were to be seen on Broadway making a quick fortune in flashlights, candles. Some store owners, to defend their property, sat on stoops with handguns and shotguns on their knees. Buildings turned into indistinguishable hulks and Amsterdam Avenue looked as though it had sunk to the bottom of an ocean. Later that night, when the fun of exploration had worn off, when the challenge of resourcefulness had taken on an unwanted edge, I heard, in the shelterless dark, the sirens, shattering glass, and marauding voices. The next day the supermarkets were filled with the passion of those who had been trapped in elevators or underground. The summers came, accumulated like pennies, and not every theme was big or international. One year might be labeled Solidarity, some election summers felt like the end of the world, but then I think of some summers simply as the year the people's garden at Ninety-sixth Street and Broadway became an ugly co-op, or the moment when St. Mark's Place became the new Forty-second Street and New Wave took on an act for commercial purposes.

It's easier to remember people than it is to recall headlines, and if I could walk over to a shelf called "My Summers in New York," the boxes would have on them the names of family, friends, or names that don't mean what they used to mean. When I think of these people, summer scenes are often attached, like tin cans, scenes complete with music and plot. They come at random and I can go in an afternoon from the summer one friend moved to the happening intersection of First Avenue and St. Mark's Place, with the St. Mark's Bar and Grill here and the Holiday Cocktail Lounge just around the corner, to the end of the club era, to the last of the so-called outlaw parties, when huge amplifiers were in place in a kind of forum in the middle of a traffic oval leading to the West Side Highway for a bash that didn't come off

205

because the police had wised up and didn't make a move to bust it up, which was the point, the highlight, of these word-of-mouth gatherings.

Visitors from out of town arrive as an imposition, an intrusion on your routine of doing absolutely nothing worthwhile, but by the time they leave they have given you a gift, that of having seen something you would not have looked up on your own, a glimpse of the city from an angle you have been too savvy to bother with. New York was almost like the television fantasy I conjured up in my childhood when I gazed upon it from the hotels my mother was too frightened to leave. Would I have gone to the Caribbean Festival in deepest Brooklyn in 1977 had a friend from New Hampshire not insisted? One summer my sister wanted to see the Cloisters, where I'd never been, and another time a friend from Holland came with a guidebook decorated with checkmarks, among them a ride on the Circle Line, to be followed up by a voyage on the Staten Island Ferry. Visitors can get you out to exhibitions, concerts, and plays in the park that you don't have time for otherwise. They want to take a helicopter ride around Manhattan and you want to have lunch all day.

Once you surrender to living in New York, you cannot see it again through a nonresident's eyes, even if you never tire of pondering the banalities and calamities of the everyday. You can go away, get on a plane to another city, another country, take the Metro liner down south, or the jitney rattling with Perrier out to the Hamptons, but as soon as you return, disembark, your time away evaporates on the sizzling pavement, your time off is swallowed up by the mean, leaden sky, you fall back into your routine or lack of one as if you had never packed your bag. The same doors are waiting for you, and if not literally the same door, one very much like it. I still know people who wouldn't dream of leaving New York during the summer. Of course, they weren't born there—who was?—and they work, work all the time, late, on weekends. Not for them the shared house in an unspoiled town on the unfashionable fork of Long Island. They don't care how cheap the seats are going for in economy class, or how much the land is worth up in Maine. Give them a bicycle, Tower Records, the fresh vegetables at Fairway, the movie listings in the *Village Voice,* an unmolested phone booth, and they're set. I understand their pleasures, their joy in the consolations of a New York summer—at least I once did. What happened?

Many of my generation, primed on the ideology of marijuana, with many lazy, drowsy summer days long smoked up, were, by 1986, deranged and derailed by cocaine. The clubs became unbearable, closed down, live music disappeared, the nights got longer and emptier. Just when everyone began to shape up, eat right, say no, and go to bed, portable, inexpensive crack appeared, as if decreed by business strategy, by the saturation and revolt of the upscale, glamorous, supposedly nonaddicted market. Crack surfaced like a poison in the city's bloodstream, destroyed summer in many parts of the city as those who had been hidden in various warrens and dens emerged to gather in the shade of Bryant Park, to call from boarded-up entrances on East Twelfth Street. They fired up glass tubes on the sidewalk, up and down East Third Street. Crack dealers ran in and out of the welfare hotel on West Twenty-second Street, sold from secondhand cars at stoplights, carried beepers around East Fifty-third Street. Crack addicts tried to hustle a few quarters by acting as porters at Pennsylvania Station, and worse.

They, the crackheads of the Upper West Side, were out there when I got up at dawn to run in Riverside Park. They were loitering in front of the Japanese fish store, waiting to make a buy. They were dealing in front of refrigerators of beer in the Dominican bodega, behind the cookie counter in the Korean deli. They were standing

206

in herds outside the windows of new restaurants on Columbus Avenue. Police cars and undercover cops were no deterrent. Hundreds of people congregated on Ninety-sixth Street, on Broadway, West End, for their favorite dealer, as if they were lying in ambush for a rock star. Amsterdam Avenue, during the late afternoon, was a river of appliances as people rushed to the pawnshops before closing time. Broadway, at night, also had its commerce. I saw a man carry his box springs to a dealer to make a trade for a three-dollar vial. The men who cruised Broadway paid the prostitutes in crack, and women who were not whores resorted to walking the streets, an influx that led to ugly scenes of rivalry. In the playgrounds, dealers demanded oral sex from girls.

The eruption of the crack epidemic told us that we were not alone, and the drug was a class and cultural line that one crossed at one's hazard. Another New York had been waiting all winter, screaming to get out into the open air. Some streets one could not enter. They had been given over, even by the people who lived barricaded behind tenement doors, to crack bazaars where middlemen, runners, hawkers, crackheads themselves, sang over and over into any passing ear, "Jumbo, jumbo, jumbo," flashed plastic bags in their pockets, where hundreds of plastic vials with red, green, gold, and blue caps teemed like termites. The tobacco shops were doing a brisk under-the-counter trade in torches, pipes, Bic lighters, baking soda, butane gas. Cars were broken into, everything removed, and one night I heard a voice alarm on a violated BMW repeat in a deadpan, "Intruder, intruder." In front of McDonald's lady panhandlers with wigs slipping off their scratchy heads became aggressive, got out of hand, followed terrified mothers halfway down the block, extorted a dime here, a nickel there, and with a handful of change ran to the black door next to an innocent-looking flower shop. One policeman told us that a teenager had been shot through the head because

he tried to usurp the corner of another dealer, a corner where one could make $6,000 in three hours.

I was wrong: you do not grow up with a city; it grows away from you, a speeding landscape that veers off to present itself to someone else. Crack overran the Upper West Side, violence blew down the streets with the newspaper, and I discovered simultaneously another vulnerability: I was poor. I hadn't paid attention, and one morning I woke up to find that I could not flop into restaurants, go here, go there, buy this, buy that, do whatever came in my head in honor of summer on a budget that was fine for the 1970s, but pitiful for the 1980s. Poverty, among other things, makes you self-conscious: you don't look right, and after a while you begin to think that you don't sound right. Many doors are barred to you, or you bar them to yourself, even in the summer, that democratic season, when, once upon a time, what the city had to offer seemed available to all. It did me absolutely no good to rant and rave that the cultural center I'd come to town to be a part of had pulled up stakes and disappeared, not when so many were continuing to have a perfectly wonderful time. Then it happened: my apartment went co-op and eventually it was sold out from under me. I knew I would never find a landlord who loved me so unconditionally, no matter how far behind with the rent I was. Not being able to afford an apartment in New York is like not being part of the gene pool.

Maybe I could have stayed, could have found some other window from which to greet the torpid mornings and busy, hopeful dusks of summer. Maybe it was time to say "so long" to youth, to those fantasies going round and round like a stuck record. I still cannot explain to myself, in all the weather of self-exploitation, why it is I felt so forcefully that the jig was up. What had begun as a game, a curious journey full of arch nonsense, turned

207

out to be altogether serious, like life, after all. Maybe it has something to do with the fact that some I had gone through many summers with—parties, strolls, late nights, barbecues, club hoppings, phone calls, taxi rides—aren't here anymore. Summer was a different place then, when Christopher Street was a sea of white T-shirts. They die all year, someone's brother, someone's son, a friend's friend, someone famous, then your best friend, but in summer, like coming across a photograph that recovers, for a moment, the stray information of his face, his bookcase, what was on his wall, you think hard about the end that, even now, you refuse to believe was his. It was wrongly assigned or given out too soon. Maybe he's just away on a trip, and will one day soon be stopping by with an anecdote about August in another place.

THE STORMS OF SUMMER

T MIGHT HAPPEN IN THIS WAY: OUT OF THE stillness of a humid afternoon, in the midst of which you sit with a gnat whining at your ear in enhancement of your solitude, you hear a rending as of a tree splitting down its middle, and then an explosion like a crate of dynamite goes off. After you recover, and begin a tour of the house to close the windows, the rain starts, or the hail, or a combination of them, and you might wonder, fearing a tornado, why it is that you've never trained your family to take a quick route to the safest part of the basement when they feel a trembling through the house like the approach of an overloaded locomotive.

What causes summer storms to seem so pernicious is the resistance in our nature to admit them. We acknowledge the possibility of storms in the spring, yes, when rain on the roof can assume the sound of a waterfall; or in the winter, with a howling wind accompanying drifting snow; or even in the fall, when heavy-bodied rain tears off the last of the leaves and pastes them over spearing stubble. But

LARRY WOIWODE

summer is the season we're to be let off, to be free of this, in the same way that we expect, after the ingrained conditioning of years in school, to be freed from all our onerous chores. So summer storms set us outside our expectations, and often isolate us physically, since we don't take the precautions we do during other seasons; we expect to bask in stillness, inviting the summer elements as recklessly as—well, that storm on its way.

It was the summer of 1980, the same season in which I watched twin tornadoes set down from a black-green sky and finally spin themselves out without harm. I was working in an outer shed on our farm in North Dakota when I realized that I had been enveloped in utter silence. Then in the distance I heard the rumbling of that approaching locomotive. I thought of my family in the house, went for the door of the shed, and opened it against a sound like rifle fire. Hailstones the size of marbles, then golf balls, were ricocheting off everything in sight. A few hit my hand on the half-open door. I pulled it shut, and through one of the high windows, which I had newly installed that summer but hadn't yet equipped with locks, I saw the anvil-shaped cloud, and then, with a sudden drop in pressure I could feel inside my ears, all four windows sprang wide, wobbling on their hinges, and pages of a handwritten manuscript started climbing out the closest opening in a chattering stream.

I grabbed at the pages, batting some down, but only stirred things up worse, and now the shed was shaking, and everything loose or on a surface was springing for the windows in a rattling swirl around my face. The hail had forced the door inward, I saw, and went for it, but so much ice had built up I couldn't get it closed, and suddenly a fresh wash of rain, mixed with hail, sprang from the exact direction to enter the door, and a carpet I'd lugged all the way from New York rumpled up and lifted against my legs with the driving wind. In seconds I was soaked and dripping. "And it's summer!" I almost cried out loud, as if my statement could bring this incongruous situation to an end.

After the small tornado, I gathered from our fields as much of the manuscript as I could immediately get my hands on, and then my daughter and my niece, who was visiting, began to make wider rounds. Over a hundred pages were lost, but by the time the two of them had covered about a hundred acres, alert to the glints of pages, the task of reconstructing the manuscript began to seem less hopeless. Each sheet had to be spread out to dry, and some were battered so badly it took tape to reassemble them, but I had written in pencil, not ink: nearly everything was legible, and as I continued to recover more pages or shreds of them over the summer, I began to think that nearly nothing was irrevocable.

I have been in summer storms as bad, when a house trembled above the corner of the basement where my family huddled, praying; when a waterspout developed off a beach on Lake Michigan, so distant over the water a group of us blithely went on with our picnic, only to watch it suddenly swerve inland, tilting and swaying at its top. It started up the beach as all of us scattered, everything from the tables going up, and soon became so overweighted with sand it gave out with a sound like the contents of a swimming pool falling from five stories.

The glory of summer storms is their diversity: heat lightning traveling like networks of nerves through evening clouds; the hazy pinpricking rains of the Pacific Northwest; bronze-tinged banks of smog over L.A., and the dangerous wind-driven sea past Catalina Island as the smog moves off; storms of cottonwood pollen along inland rivers, called "summer snow" by French voyageurs, and the sudden actual startling August snows of the upper Rockies; firestorms in western forests darkening a dozen states with pine-sweet smoke; sleet ticking against steel derricks and oil drums in Manitoba; the magnetic storming of northern lights over the upper latitudes, igniting

213

the entire dome of heaven with pulsing currents of gold and pastels; a cloudburst descending from a lime-green sky along the Texas gulf—a gullywasher in which torn-off leaves skate down a clay-brown current laced with foam; the windstorms, termed "monsoons" by locals, that travel across the Arizona desert in late July, piling up such towering clouds of dusty silica that the dimmed sun shimmers like a coppery star; the tropical rains of southern Florida that come like clockwork, every day near noon, falling in quarter-sized dollops of drops and then rising in steamy humidity to fall at the same hour the next day; atmospheric inversions over Chicago and the stilled, muffled air that tastes of ozone; the rains that transform New York into an equatorial capital in August, when even potted ferns outside a hotel appear to wilt in the sticky texture and all of the best psychiatrists, even those who served residencies in Vietnam, take off for Europe or the Cape.

And then there is the peculiar summer storm that most of us have experienced at least once. You rent a house or cottage or cabin for a week at the ocean or on a lake or cape or bayou or bay, and arrive with the whole family, one of the few opportunities you'll have to enjoy summer together. The first night, as you lie in bed trying to sleep, you become aware of a sound like squirrels scrabbling on the roof. Rain. You fall asleep to the sound and wake to blue light and go to the window; it hasn't let up. It's a gentle summer rain, such a dallying drizzle you can scarcely make out the drops, the kind of rain you look forward to for your lawn's sake—but not here. The children are arguing. You get out the broken and taped boxes of picture puzzles, reproduced in the garish colors of the forties, pull an old murder mystery from a bookshelf, and crawl back into bed to wait this out.

It doesn't let up. At the grocery or general store the locals are exultant; this will be great for the crops, they crow. Such a *gentle* summer rain, they say. Back at the rented place, your spouse complains that you're mixing the drinks too stiff and having one right after the other. The children won't stop arguing. You suggest that they run out and play in the rain, splash in puddles, and at their looks you realize they've aged. And you remember that it's in the spring, anyway, when puddles attract them; by summer they want the real thing. They're *bored,* they say, and you wonder why it is that when you talked for weeks about this vacation, you found it necessary, like a bland travel poster, to emphasize the sun so much. You go to the window once more and experience the perverse joy of the natives; there is no sign of this letting up, and the grass and leaves everywhere look bejeweled with billions of drops. To break up the worst of the children's fights you take down a chess set and call a son to you at the card table you've set up. The rain sounds overhead until the last day of your rental.

Out on the beach, finally in the sun, you're grudgingly grateful at least for this, and you realize that the time has been instructive. You'll have to stop drinking. Your wife, you've learned, wants a new car, since it's largely fallen to her to transport the children everywhere, and your youngest son, about whom you've harbored a secret fear of his being slow, is more than your equal at chess, and has perhaps always only needed your concern and encouragement. And the daughter you thought was becoming a slugabed actually gets up as early as always but now spends an hour each morning at the reading you've recommended, and nearly another hour at the mirror. Of all of the children, she is the one who has most grown up—suddenly a young woman—and you might have missed this, along with the way she's beginning to take on half of your characteristics, if it hadn't been for this season of enforced closeness caused by the gentlest of summer rains.

* * *

But the definitive storms occur in isolation, as the one that struck when I was thirteen—perhaps the most susceptible age. I was working that summer on a ranch near the Montana border, twenty miles from the nearest town, riding a horse every day, helping with the livestock and haying, and I was interested in a girl— the daughter of the nearest neighbor, several miles up out of the river valley the ranch lay in, across coulee-intersected hills. Siobhan, I'll call her. Her father, a Skoal-dipping cowboy, was known for his skill with the fiddle and for his temper, and Siobhan was said to have inherited the temper. I rode with the family in their car every Sunday to church, a forty-mile drive. If Siobhan's brother got close enough on the back seat to touch her (I sat at the opposite window, in torment at her nearness), her freckled face flamed to the roots of her black hair, and she let him have it so hard with an elbow he doubled over. She was fifteen.

She was celebrating her birthday that summer, and invited me to the party, which I thought meant *me;* that is, I figured I was her date. But the wife of the rancher I worked for said, "Oh, if I know Siobhan, she's invited every man and boy who can stand upright, from here to Miles City."

On the day of her party a wind started up, the kind of summer wind that plagues the western plains like an endless sirocco. I began dressing two hours early; I'd bought a new pair of boots from a mail-order catalogue, a new cowboy shirt, buckskin riding gloves, and one of those basket-weave cowboy hats, spray-painted white, that were the style. I saddled up Lady, an aging mare who was mine to ride that summer, and saw from her skittishness that the weather was getting worse. Rapid black clouds were stretching so thickly across the sky it was turning dark. By the time I led Lady to the ranch house it seemed we were in the middle of an eclipse.

"Should I go?" I asked the rancher, who had turned on the pole light and stepped outside.

"Why wouldn't you?" he asked in the cheery, encouraging way he had of dealing with everything, even nature.

"It's so dark—" I wanted to mention the storm.

"Lady knows the way."

His wife came to the screen door, in yellow kitchen light that seemed to contain warmth, and said, "You wouldn't want Siobhan to think you aren't man enough to ride a few miles to see her on her birthday, would you?"

The rancher helped me mount; I couldn't reach the stirrups. "Go to the spring and take the trail east," he said. "It hits at their gate. Snug the gate up good."

He stepped back as he spoke, and I could barely see him below his hat brim. I swung Lady around on a road I couldn't see—it was so dark—and was about to turn back when I saw the rancher's wife still at the door. I gave up trying to make out the road, and kept Lady true to course by the sound of her hooves on packed ground. And when I was off the road? In my hesitation of thought, Lady pivoted and headed for home. We were beyond the stand of trees sheltering the house, and with the wind tearing at my hat and clothes, it wasn't easy to turn her back. She was headstrong if she sensed you didn't have the upper hand—"muley," the rancher called her— "ridden by too many children."

The spring was a half mile off, and by the time we got there I was tired of trying to hold my hat on and keep her headed right. While I looked up the darkened valley, she found the spring, from the way her head went down, nearly jerking the reins from my gloved hands, and I let her drink. The spring was in the crevice of a valley extending to the hilltops, and the trail, I knew from herding cows, ambled along the topside of the valley. I started her up and she resisted, so I prodded her flanks, and then my hat went as a wind whooped down the draw, hitting us broadside so hard Lady crowhopped. I slid off, shaking, and gripped the reins, my lifeline in the

216

dark. There was my hat, a dim glow in the darkness ahead. I reached for it and struck stone—a boulder, a mistake, the sort of place rattlesnakes hid.

I finally found the hat wedged in a stand of buck brush that scraped at me as I extracted it, and shoved it inside my shirt and snapped the shirt shut. I was able to remount by climbing the hillside and leaping across the saddle. Lady took off at a gallop, as if she'd received her reward in a drink at the spring, and was now bent on getting home. We were halfway back before I got her stopped and turned in the right direction again.

She started up the valley with her head down into the wind, as if each step would be her last, and I could hear the fluttery clatter of the leaves on the oaks to my right. There was a break in the clouds, and for a moment I saw the treetops bending like whips. As we came over the crest of the hill I had to gasp to get my breath; in my battle with Lady I hadn't noticed that the wind had grown so fierce. It felt as if gusts of it would lift me out of the saddle; with a popping sound my bulging shirt flew open, and I grabbed my hat but spooked Lady, who seemed to be going sideways about fifty. I could hear the trees again and was frightened, not so much by the shapes I imagined they were assuming as the actual whipsawing I had seen, and they were louder now. One could break off. Lady stopped. I slapped at both sides of her rump with the reins, but she wouldn't move. "Lady!" I yelled, the word tearing away, and she yawed to one side as if she would go over, then backed into the wind, her head down. There was the sensation of a hand smoothing the back of my shirt, and I swung around and slapped at it. Her blowing tail. No matter what I did I couldn't get her to move, and she started trembling underneath me.

"All right," I said, and slid out of the saddle. "You'll have to show me the way."

I stumbled through the dark, gripping the reins, and occasionally Lady nudged my side as if to say she appreciated it that I was down here with her. Wherever "here" was. I couldn't see the ground. But I could feel it, rough; my boots would be ruined, if I got through this. She stopped, balking again. I turned my back to the wind, pulling at the reins, and ran into a barbed-wire fence. I put my hand out and felt a gatepost; in our struggle she had directed me here and was telling me to stop. I got her through and cinched the gate up, and after we'd walked a ways I saw a line of light above us. It was a hilltop, and over its crest I saw gold shafts slanting from every window of the house and the barn at Siobhan's. Her father was scheduled to play the fiddle for her birthday celebration and dance.

I ran into a boulder big enough to serve as a mounting step, climbed up on Lady, pulled out my hat, and held it on with one hand as I let her have her head. At the barn I leaped off in the midst of Lady's halting, as Siobhan's father did, but no one was there to witness this. No welcome. I eased open a sliding door and saw Siobhan in the alley of the barn, in the calico shirt and tight jeans she wore to church, standing on straw bales in a blaze of light.

"Well!" she said.

"Am I late?"

"Sheet! And don't bring that damn clubfoot old mare in here!" she cried. "Tie her up outside!"

I did, and Siobhan slid the door shut as I stepped inside, into warmth. I pulled off my mangled hat.

"That damn storm's about done it," she said, and glared at me with half-crazed eyes, as if I were the storm.

"What?"

"Daddy's in the house so drunk he'll be lucky if he sees Tuesday!"

What day is it? I almost asked, remembering her party was to be on Friday; I felt I'd been riding a month.

She strode over to the bales, the boots under her jeans swooshing in hollow sounds with each step, and jumped up on some boards laid over them in a platform,

217

then turned as if in expectation, her fists on her hips. I walked over to her with my hat in my hands, hoping she might teach me to dance or, better, allow the stormy correspondences I saw in her so often to break over me.

"That's it!" she said. "We might as well go on into the blame old house and tie this birthday off."

"What?"

"With Ma and the kids. End it!"

"Your birthday?"

"Don't you get it? Look around! You're the only damn person here!"

So we wait out storms sometimes to be reminded of their power to isolate, a knowledge that's been borne in on me further as I've worked in isolation to gather these pages out of the storm of my life. After that summer night, no storm in or out of nature ever threatened me as much, because Siobhan's dismissal of me was also a blessing on my tenacity, or foolhardiness—the essential nature of one now willing to strike through any upheaval, knowing that there is another side and knowing, too, what is there: always another survivor.

218

220

HUMMINGBIRD

for Tess

Suppose I say *summer,*
write the word "hummingbird,"
put it in an envelope,
take it down the hill
to the box. When you open
my letter you will recall
those days and how much,
just how much, I love you.

RAYMOND CARVER

222

from the melon collection —

Unlike most citizens of these United States of America, I do not grill. There is no hibachi in my garden or anything else like it. When I moved into my garden apartment I was given a fancy barbecue, and as far as I know it is still in the cellar collecting dust and mold spores.

Grilling is like sunbathing. Everyone knows it is bad for you but no one ever stops doing it. Since I do not like the taste of lighter fluid, I do not have to worry that a grilled steak is the equivalent of seven hundred cigarettes.

Of course this implies that I do not like to eat al fresco. No sane person does, I feel. When it is nice enough for people to eat outside, it is also nice enough for mosquitoes, horse and deer flies, as well as wasps and yellow jackets. I don't much like sand in my food and thus while I will endure a beach picnic I never look forward to one.

My idea of bliss is a screened-in porch from which you can watch the sun go down, or come up. You can sit in temperate shade and not fry your

LAURIE COLWIN

brains while you eat. You are protected from flying critters, sandstorms, and rain, and you can still enjoy a nice cool breeze.

One year my husband and I rented a lake cottage—a rustic cabin set in a pine grove just a stroll from a weed-choked lake. With this cottage came a war canoe and a screened-in porch. The motto of the owners seemed to have been "It's broken! Let's take it to the lake!"

The dining room table was on a definite slant, and the plates were vintage 1950s Melmac. The stove was lit by one of those gizmos that ignite a spark next to one of the burners and was of great fascination to me. Near the corner cupboards lived an army of mice who left evidence of their existence all over the cups and saucers. Anything left around was carried away—quite a tidy little ecosystem. One evening we were visited by a dog who howled constantly as the sound of mouse rattling drove him into a frenzy.

Nevertheless, we ate on the screened-in porch all the time and with great success. Friends with beautiful houses came to our broken-down lake cottage to eat on that crummy porch and watch the sun set over the lake. All around us were grills; we could smell them, but we never so much as fingered a charcoal briquette.

Having said this, I admit to loving grilled food— that is, something that has been exposed to a flame. On a regular old stove, this is called broiling. English stoves have a special rack (a salamander) with a separate flame under which you can grill a chop or brown the top of a gratin. There is no better way to cook fish, steak, or chops.

I have avoided grilling by broiling, and I have never had to bother myself about getting in a supply of mesquite or apple wood, or old thyme twigs.

For a brief period of my life I thought to use the fireplace as a cooking surface. Years of ingesting gasoline at the barbecues of others led me to wonder if I could do it better. I decided to grill steaks on a rack in my fireplace, and by a stroke of fortune was given some apple and cherry to burn. The results were marred by nervousness, a syndrome that goes with the territory of the wood fire: constant cutting to see how far along your steak has come. I did not taste the merest breath of apple or cherry, although I have been told that you have not lived until you have tasted swordfish grilled over mesquite. This may be true, but, as Abraham Lincoln is said to have said, "For people who like this sort of thing, this is the sort of thing they will like."

But what to do on a clear summer evening? The sky is pink. The air is sweet. It is dinnertime and you are surrounded by hungry people who have just spent the day either swimming or gardening, or have just gotten out of a car or train or bus and found themselves in the country listening to the hermit thrushes.

Everywhere in America people are lighting their grills. They begin in spring, on the first balmy evening. I happen to live across the street from a theological seminary whose students come from all over. I know it is spring not by the first robin but by the first barbecue across the street on the seminary lawn. That first whiff of lighter fluid and smoke is my herald, and led one of my friends to ask: "What is it about Episcopalians, do you think? Is it in their genes to barbecue?"

It is not in the genes but it is in the American character to grill, a leftover from pioneer days, from Indian days, from the Old West. I have been able to buck this trend with Lebanon bologna sandwiches or mustard chicken.

Lebanon bologna is not from the Middle East but from Lebanon, Pennsylvania, in Lancaster County. It is a spicy, slightly tart salamilike cold cut with the limpness of bologna. I have never had the courage to ask what it is made of, but I am sure it cannot be good for anyone. The way to serve it is on whole-wheat bread spread with cream cheese into which you have mashed chives, thyme, tarragon—whatever you or your friends have in the garden. Spread the cream cheese liberally, but use only one (two if sliced very thin) slice of Lebanon bologna. Make an enormous pile of these sandwiches cut in half and serve with potato salad, cole slaw, or a big green salad. In the summer a large plate of sliced tomatoes is a salad in itself with nothing added.

If you feel you must make something more grill-like, spare ribs are always nice, especially if you have marinated them for a couple of days.

Some people like a tomato-based barbecue sauce, but I do not. Besides, these ribs are baked in the oven, not barbecued. I like them in what is probably a variation on teriyaki sauce.

For one side of ribs you need one cup of olive oil, one half cup tamari sauce, about four tablespoons of honey, the juice of one lemon, fresh ground black pepper, and lots and lots and lots of garlic peeled and cut in half. Let the ribs sit in this marinade as long as possible—overnight in the refrigerator is the least, two days is the best. Then put the ribs in a roasting pan (you can either cut them into riblets or leave them in one piece and cut before serving) and put them in a slow oven—about 300°—and leave them there, pouring off the fat from time to time, for three to four hours. What is left, as a friend of mine says, has no name. The ribs are both crisp and tender, salty, sweet, oily but not greasy and very garlicky. You gnaw on them and then throw the bones on the platter.

A finger bowl is actually appropriate here, if you want to be fancy, and so is the kind of heated washcloth you get in a Japanese restaurant. Plain old wet paper towels will do as well.

You can cook these ribs in the morning and eat them in the evening. They should not be cold (although a leftover rib for breakfast is considered heavenly by some people) but are fine lukewarm, and can be kept in a warm oven with no ill effects.

And as the sky becomes overcast and the clouds get darker, and the fumes of charcoal starter drift in your direction, you can sit down to your already cooked dinner in a safe place with the satisfaction of not having had to light a single match or get your hands all gritty with those nasty, smeary little charcoal briquettes. Furthermore, you will never in your life have to clean the grill, one of the most loathsome of kitchen chores.

Instead you are indoors while being out of doors. Your dinner is taken care of and you can concentrate on eating, which, after a long summer day, is all anybody really wants.

225

SAILING

AFTER

LUNCH

I t is the word *pejorative* that hurts.
My old boat goes round on a crutch
And doesn't get under way.
It's the time of the year
And the time of the day.

Perhaps it's the lunch that we had
Or the lunch that we should have had.
But I am, in any case,
A most inappropriate man
In a most unpropitious place.

Mon Dieu, hear the poet's prayer.
The romantic should be here.
The romantic should be there.
It ought to be everywhere.
But the romantic must never remain,

Mon Dieu, and must never again return.
This heavy historical sail
Through the mustiest blue of the lake
In a really vertiginous boat
Is wholly the vapidest fake. . . .

WALLACE STEVENS

It is least what one ever sees.
It is only the way one feels, to say
Where my spirit is I am,
To say the light wind worries the sail,
To say the water is swift today,

To expunge all people and be a pupil
Of the gorgeous wheel and so to give
That slight transcendence to the dirty sail,
By light, the way one feels, sharp white,
And then rush brightly through the summer air.

THINK YOUR MOTHER IS VERY BRAVE," T.'s mother said, cooking breakfast. "All the way to California, with two teenage boys, by *bus!*"

"My brother is only twelve," I replied, probably intending to score my mother's scheme with the mark of recklessness, even parental irresponsibility, although I'd certainly approved the plan at first. It was going to take me to Los Angeles, and from there perhaps as far south into film noir terra incognita as Encinada, in Baja, where Barbara Stanwyck got that perfume she didn't know the name of, the one that drove Fred MacMurray crazy in Billy Wilder's *Double Indemnity*. But that morning in August 1956, I wasn't approving anything that would take me from the splendor of Candlewood Lake, and away from T., the varsity "seeded" carrottop tennis star with whom I was in love, the way the wise tell you you are just once in your life, almost always in summer.

*   *   *

JAMES McCOURT

On our last afternoon together T. and I were lolling wordless in the boat, adrift in one of the lake's innumerable coves. T. had turned the Evinrude outboard motor off and tipped it back. Each of us was scanning a different stretch of landscaped shoreline. We'd been laughing about the difference between two high school sophomore classmates' lives (our lives), as illustrated by their parents' (our parents') disparate boy-rearing philosophies. Neither of us had or wanted sisters, nor did we care to know just then at the age we were—fifteen—how differently different girls were bred; it was the shared assumption and conceit of our fitful stabs at maturational communication that when we married and fathered we'd do as our father had done: we'd father boys. I envied T. his position as the teenage son of parents who still joked about turning forty, in a "sane" American family (even as I tended to think it was a family right out of television, whose interactions were nothing but auditions compared to the intramural histrionics I'd cut and gnashed my teeth on).

We'd compared the kinds of summers we'd experienced for the last several years. In childhood, after World War II, I'd lived much the way he had. I'd spent long vacations in Northport, on Long Island, in Windham in the Catskills, at the Jersey shore in settlements called Lavalette and Vision Beach. I'd picked berries, swum from Saint James Beach across Northport harbor to the Vanderbilt seaplane hangar in Centerport and walked on the beach, it was later revealed, where Eugene O'Neill had sat in declining health, glaring into a camera lens. I'd drifted too far out off Vision Beach on a rubber surf raft (on the sunny day after the rainy day spent looking at Marilyn Monroe play crazy at Richard Widmark in *Don't Bother to Knock,* while the rain pattered on the Quonset-hut movie theater's tin roof), been rescued, and been taken—as if being placated, as if the escapade on the raft had been some kind of threat—to the Roller Derby up in Asbury Park. These were our "normal" va-

cations, before my mother decided, in 1951, to improve on the situation by packing my brother and me and her sophisticated and talkative bachelor-girl pal Flo (an executive secretary at American Tobacco) into the Chevrolet and heading out to see the U.S.A., because America was asking us to call. America, the greatest land of all. (Another country: it was always understood that we, as New Yorkers, really did *not* inhabit America—either at home in Jackson Heights, or in our various vacation locales. Not even me, the Yankee Doodle Dandy, born on the Fourth of July.) America: the Eastern Seaboard, its battlefields, its monuments, its restored, renovated and maintained towns, its plantations. Salem, Plymouth, Lexington, Concord; Gettysburg, Williamsburg, Charleston, Atlanta. Charlottesville, Monticello, Mount Vernon. We "did" them all, and in the evenings we played quartet canasta.

T. always idealized my family: my faintly mysterious, dapper, "cool" father, who worked as a time-keeper on the New York waterfront, knew Toots Shor personally, and brought home things like cases of Hennessy V.S.O.P. that "fell off" the ships. My sophisticated, "bohemian" mother, also "cool," who played Broadway show tunes from memory on the piano at parties, of which my family had always thrown more than anybody else's. What T. didn't know about, I'd tell him, were the arguments between us, between parties. Arguments chiefly over what I read (*Bonjour Tristesse,* in French, for example, which she'd dug out from under the French 2 grammar in a pile on my private desk). Arguments about where my "life" was apparently headed, featuring remarks like "You can't shock me. I read Maxwell Bodenheim's *Naked on Roller Skates,* and all the rest of it!"

T. had never been caught reading compromising literature; he might safely stash the paperback of *Peyton Place* anywhere out of sight in his room, without fear of parental investigation, but neither did he "get to go any-

230

where," except in order to play championship tennis, because his kid brother was still too young.

"You've been to Texas."

"But not by *bus*."

We reviewed the week, a more manageable subject than parents, *Peyton Place, Bonjour Tristesse,* or sex per se.

The first day, when the boat had flipped over, and we'd come up under it at opposite ends, each fearing to find the other cut to bloody ribbons by the Evinrude's blade.

The swimming race across the widest part of the lake, which I'd astonished T. by winning by several lengths.

"Why aren't you on the *varsity?*"

"They said I'd have to give up smoking and drinking both."

"Bullshit!"

"Seriously!"

The double dates with the "fast" public school girls from New Milford. (We'd heard and compared the verdicts. On me: "He's *skinny,* but he's *cute* with that crewcut, those red Bermuda shorts and those white bucks. But he *reads* on the *beach!*" On T.: "He is an everlovin' livin' *doll—cute, smart, athletic . . . and* he can *kiss!*") We were both, T. and I, cheating on steadies back home, in Jackson Heights and Flushing, and the song that week was "Tonight You Belong to Me," sung by Prudence and Patience.

My imminent conquest of fabled California.

"You won't come back. You'll transfer to Hollywood High. They'll give you a swimming scholarship, and you'll train in Olympic pools in Beverly Hills. They'll let you smoke and drink all you want, and you'll get to drive to Las Vegas on weekends."

"I can't drive; you can't either. They had to drive us to the drive-in, remember? They thought it was 'a panic.' " (We saw James Dean, Natalie Wood and Sal Mineo in Nicholas Ray's *Rebel Without a Cause,* which we'd been seeing together on double dates all sophomore year, time after time, tracking it from theater to theater, in Jackson Heights, Flushing, Bayside, and Jamaica, until our steadies refused to sit through it one more time.)

"You'll be driving in a week. In convertibles. Just don't go drag racing on the cliffs in Malibu. You'd get your sleeve caught in the goddam door. You're like that, genius: two left sleeves."

"T.! Jimmy!"

"It's Mac." (T.'s older brother, whose given name was James.)

"T.! Jimmy! *C'mon!* You're gonna miss the *train!*"

"We better go."

Neither of us made a move to look at one another, or to tip the outboard motor down, until T.'s father's voice—

"Come on in, you guys; the party's *over!* It's *train* time!"

"We better go. I gotta get to practice, and you gotta get to California. . . ."

By the middle fifties, everything in our dog-tagged American lives was either brand new or "newly renovated": the bus stations, the buses, the roads, the idea of summer itself. We did not, for example, make the stop that summer morning we'd made in the madcap "Flo" years, at Edelstein Bros. in Long Island City, to stash the silverware and my mother's topaz dinner ring (Scorpio birthstone) in pawn. We were flush in 1956, heading out, with traveler's checks and sporty new Samsonite luggage, from the Greyhound bus terminal at Fiftieth and Eighth (the one immortalized, just before they demolished it, by Audrey Hepburn and Buddy Ebsen in Blake Edwards's *Breakfast at Tiffany's*). Walking into the elevated rear saloon of the Greyhound Scenicruiser, we

were dressed as if we were sailing on the *Île de France* or taking off on TWA from Idlewild. (I was "collegiate casual," in regulation pressed chinos, new white bucks, button-down powder-blue polished cotton shirt with sleeves rolled up three flaps, and "throwover" white high school sweater emblazoned with a purple-bordered gold *L.*—Forensic League—the arms encircled with purple stripes.) The ads said, "Leave the driving to us," but the subtext read, "And while you're at it, dress the way these passengers you're looking at in this commercial are dressed: as if you're going someplace, to *meet* somebody."

We'd scarcely cleared the Lincoln Tunnel before my mother, the New York Archdiocesan parochial sixth-grade teacher, was launched in conversation with two opposite numbers from the New York public school system, Staten Island division. My brother pulled out his EC and Donald Duck comics, and I, a seat apart, dove back into what I'd been reading on the beach at Candlewood Lake: Dostoevsky.

"I see you're reading *The Brothers K.*," remarked one of the teachers, who looked and sounded so much like Nancy Kulp on "Love That Bob" that, positive she was kidding me, I lost my composure.

"I'm *trying* to." What I *meant* (I thought in a matey way) was something like "If Marilyn can get through it . . . ," whereas what came out obviously gave her the green light to clock me as a snotty little contraption whose Vaseline brush cut and existentialist horn-rims might have them fogged in at home on Jackson Heights but (I realized as we crossed the Passaic Plain and headed into what I'd been trained in Gotham smart-talk to regard as the Midwest) wasn't fooling this cookie for a hot second.

We were sleeping on the bus the first night, staying in Saint Louis on the second, sleeping aboard on the third, stopping in Flagstaff, Arizona, on the fourth and day-tripping to the Grand Canyon; then heading into twilight and overnight through the Painted Desert up to the Hotel Sal Sagev in Las Vegas. ("The *Sal Sagev!*" I'd crowed. "That's like staying at the *Serutan!*") Finally, coming down through Marilyn Monroe's birthplace, Bakersfield, California, we'd be docking downtown in Los Angeles, a week to the day after leaving New York, and going to stay in Beverly Hills (on the right side of Wilshire Boulevard, as it turned out), our hostess my mother's old Yorkville acquaintance, a former operetta and vaudeville soprano, for whom she had on and off in the twenties played rehearsal accompaniment on the Strand Roof (at a time, we were let know, when Ruby Stevens, before she turned herself into Barbara Stanwyck, was frequenting the same hall).

The great Middle Atlantic States turnpikes of that bemused era comprised a ribbon-road prologue to the Civil Defense thoroughfare we now know as the Interstate: emblem and occasion, metaphor and setting of so much of everything there is to say about Nothing in the U.S.A. Every time I'd look out the window, I'd see road for the sake of road, and rather than torment myself with fantasies of the real road I'd never really ridden (the road of roadside attractions and roadhouses, the road of Jack Kerouac's desperate late-forties-latent-homosexual *On the Road*), I would float in my mind the Russian steppes, another plenitude of Nothing, but a negotiable one, for I'd decided, somewhere west of Paramus, to become Dostoevsky's Alyosha. (My father's middle name was Aloysius—T. even found that cool—but I was cross-casting the beatific A.K. with the Jesuit mascot Aloysius Gonzaga, whose role, it seemed, was edifying boys over eleven toward resisting reaching through the holes they'd poked in their pockets to . . . even more frequently, it was whispered, in summer.)

I'd gotten through the first-night, 4 A.M. some-where-in-central-Ohio rest stop and all, and had awakened into a morning that ought to have been washed in

233

the kind of serenity evoked by the following (recently found elsewhere than in the memory):

"The bus rolled westward across the farmlands as the wheat, corn and oats bent easily in the summer breeze. Barns and silos shrank before the vast sea of soil and grain that stretched as far as he could see."

(How I sometimes want—how I've always sometimes wanted—things to align themselves with the evangelical, American-summer-ripened simplicity of that paragraph.)

As far as I could see, that morning on that Greyhound bus, on the banks of the Ohio, over the rim of a page of *The Brothers Karamazov,* summer was a show I could pay a minimum of attention to, and still review. ("I had a very good time.") We'd come a long way from tending the Victory Garden in Northport to tossing a block of Birdseye into the double boiler at the end of a busy big-city day, and that was, metaphorically, what had become of summer too.

In the meantime, as far as I could tell from what I saw of, and in, any and all seasons (and their signal effects on the Something Called a Temperament I'd decided to become): reading was one of the only two ways there were or ever had been to keep from going completely crazy from the radical, and thoroughly unsatisfactory, difference between Life and Motion Pictures, and the other way—between movies and segments of reading—was rigorous concentration on One's Own Performance (as Martha Graham, that Fresh Voice From The Plains, had long since put it, "You're in competition with Nobody but yourself. Either do the work as it was meant to be done, or get out, and don't come back!"), particularly concentration on the fixity of one's self-installation, on the security of one's coign of vantage. (Otherwise the bastards would—so to speak—shake the full-leafed sycamore you'd foolishly imagined would hide and protect you in summer, until you fell out of it at their feet and broke your attractive neck.)

The speeding, air-conditioned Greyhound bus was a perfect armored perspective, safely away from the summer beaches where year after year I'd spent far too many overexposed afternoon hours in the sun that did my fair skin no good, longing for ten or twenty minutes in cool, commotional changing rooms that did my heart no better. There in the rear, reading, I could do more comfortably what I'd always done, wait for the summer night and sing to myself "One summer night I fell in *lu*-uv," or "The day is my enemy, the night my friend," depending on how sophisticated I felt like getting, how deep I felt like drawing on the Luckies, and whether the offer of a genuine cocktail (or a slug out of the bottle of Hennessy V.S.O.P. my mother kept tucked away as a specific against "travel cramps") could be descried in the offing.

It was farther west of Saint Louis, on what I ever after called "The Nightbus to Tulsa," that both the trip's vehicle provenance and its wardrobe contour swerved into alarming "Ozark" disarray. Up till then, in one long first act, the deluxe Scenicruiser conceit had held: all along the great turnpikes, with their gleaming Formica-table way stations installed with portfolio jukeboxes wailing Elvis Presley and the Everly Brothers, the great ship of the road had sailed. Through that vast sea of soil and grain: the waving wheat that sure smelled sweet, right out of *Oklahoma!* But I preferred the smell of paperbacks, of Luckies, of Hennessy, and finally, in a wild, yearning, Kansas-in-August seizure of American sentiment, my fellow man. (He'd come aboard at Saint Louis, in sailor whites, and was talking to, of all people, my little brother, still only twelve, asking to borrow a Donald Duck comic book.)

Then, suddenly, in a town I never knew, a breakdown, a deposition of baggage out onto the curbside of a dark and shuttered Main Street, whereupon we passengers were hustled from the wet heat of a southern

234

235

Missouri August night into the musky claustration of a late-forties-model Greyhound, its steamlines rust-pocked and dented (the kind of bus Barbara Stanwyck took out of town in *Clash by Night*, telling them she'd send for her things). I was beside myself. I'd been flung into the only America I'd ever believed in: the America of film noir, of Edgar G. Ulmer's *Ruthless*, of Russell Rouse's *Wicked Woman*, land of a decade of my troubled dreams. It was frightening, more frightening than summer, but I belonged there, more than I'd ever belonged, or would belong, in *The Brothers Karamazov*. . . .

Nobody wearing coordinated separates was boarding the bus at any stop along the road to Tulsa. The gospel of mix 'em and match 'em had evidently not been carried west of the Mississippi. A lot of women got on wearing dungarees, halter tops, ballerina "flats" and nothing else, and carrying only handbags. Men boarded wearing overalls. . . .

A woman got on with two small children; she was carrying very little luggage, nothing capacious enough to stash below. My mother started a conversation. They were laying over in Tulsa, then moving on somewhere, she wasn't sure where. All she was sure of ("All's I *do* know") was they weren't ever going back where they'd come from, and they sure as hell were through with *him*. He'd kept her "barefoot" in winter, but she'd been able to put by in the spring without his catching on, and now, in summer, they were cutting loose, getting so far away he wouldn't bother to look. They were of course headed west; everybody knew there was no percentage in going east. . . .

The sailor, having drifted to the last row, was beached opposite me, stretched out, legs spread apart, engrossed in Donald Duck. I kept smoking Luckies and reviewing the situation of the night in my mind, until the tide rushed in: a complex fantasy of vampirism, schizophrenia, and sex, accompanied by the voice-over of Vivien Leigh as Blanche DuBois taunting "at the 'Tarantula Arms,'" in counterpoint with another, more sepulchral voice from the same work, *"Flores para los muertos . . . Coronas para los muertos. . . ."*

The philosopher Ludwig Wittgenstein has said that of that which we cannot speak, we must perforce remain silent. The 1947 Vincent Sherman film noir *Nora Prentiss*, starring Ann Sheridan, issues the same directive, and so does the Tennessee Williams shocker *Suddenly, Last Summer* (which appeared some seasons following the events under consideration here). To invoke another auctorial precedent: William Maxwell, an American who writes definitively about, among many other things, adolescence, says somewhere, "When we talk about the past, we lie with every breath we take."

It may just be I've already lied to the absolute limit of suspiration. I can however designate, as in parables we're taught to do (always remembering—to paraphrase Maxwell again—that time has already, significantly, darkened it), the exact (metaphoric) nature of the lie of that night's ramble East of Eden, in the Land of Nod. I'll call it the very rapture of brain fever. Or, snatching another telling title, Henry Roth's, I'll *Call It Sleep*. ("We are such stuff . . .")

"She'll land on her feet; those women always do," my mother pronounced authoritatively, walking out of the Hotel Sal Sagev into the hallucinatory neon glow of downtown Las Vegas. "What I'd like to know is what happened to that poor soul the bus didn't wait for at the Grand Canyon. . . ."

When I'd remarked out loud of the Grand Canyon, looking down from a guardrailed protuberance into that very apotheosis of concavity, that all it reminded me of was a megatonic bomb crater somebody had gone crazy decorating with colored chalk, I was glad the so-

236

phisticated Staten Island schoolmarm was already a day ahead of us on her itinerary, because although only dimly aware why (or lacking the requisite actual grace or existential male fortitude to embrace an overwhelming *horror vacui*), I definitely wanted to be taken seriously, most especially by myself.

I was thinking about Thinking About Art, Art "threatened" by Nature. (Years later I'd write, and hold, "I prefer a picture of a tree to a tree. Does that give you a problem?") I was thinking about construction sites in Manhattan, places my maternal grandfather, one of those legendary ironworkers who built twentieth-century New York, had brought me to on warm sunny days as soon as I could walk, and I was imagining the Grand Canyon serving as the foundation excavation for the celestial-terrestrial city, a futuristic Ripley's Believe-It-or-Not Nineveh of my imagination. I was thinking of the toy I'd played with in summer on the beach at Northport, a yellow metal tractor, and of the tract-housing construction site behind the carriage house we'd lived in (the postwar image and situation that replaced the Victory Garden the same summer—the summer after the Summer of Hiroshima—we'd first heard the words "harbor pollution" spoken in the village). I was thinking of all that then, and then of Sorrow (in sunlight).

Las Vegas is either the Apotheosis of the Midway, or a detention camp for vaudevillians, or both. Its moon-crater desert situation and its grotesque night-for-day mise-en-scène made it for me the great grotesque parody of American Summer, a kind of hallucination, conflating Coney Island's Luna Park, Rockaway's Playland, Lou Walter's Latin Quarter, and Toffinetti's on Broadway and 43rd Street. No wonder the Mafia invented it; it is the great barococo revenge of the Excluded-from-the-Quite-White-American-Society Deer Park. Nobody brought up in New York, I decided, could take

it seriously for even an evening. It was worse than television; it was color television, a Mecca for enraged, depressive morons. And the gambling looked ridiculous: it had neither the sexual allure of Damon Runyon's back-alley Broadway (as designed by Jo Mielziner and staged by Abe Burrows in Frank Loesser's *Guys and Dolls*), nor the dextrously fabricated insouciant *frisson* of Nice and Monte Carlo (where, in those fabulous fifties, Grace Kelly, a Philadelphia girl out to *show* people, had made *To Catch a Thief* for Alfred Hitchcock and then gotten herself married to some kind of Camp-Royal croupier).

That said (about Las Vegas), we had a very good time. I had never before actually *seen,* in true car flesh, either an Edsel or a heliotrope Thunderbird, and that night we saw a lot of both. We went out to a "Night of the Stars" in a stadium there, and later collected matchbooks from the lobbies of those entertainment hotels better known nationally than the Sal Sagev.

I was feeling better and better about the West, because west of Oklahoma both elegant gleaming buses and carefully detailed costuming had come back. Native Americans had boarded wearing silver and turquoise bracelets, and the getups on weathered white people—cowboy hats and snakeskin boots: the watchword was "bedizened"—made them look what I called Western. Although nobody slung a gun, there were suddenly men coming down the aisles actually carrying lengths of looped rope. The Petrified Forest and the Painted Desert overlaid the Russian steppes in my fraught mind, and I forgot about being Dostoevsky's Alyosha. By the time we reached Bakersfield, I was very nearly convinced (as I have been time and time again the moment—always a reckless moment—I cross the California state line) that reading was not necessarily the way.

When we pulled out of Bakersfield in the white-on-white heat of a California summer midday, I was in

237

love with heat as I had never been in oppressive, humid, sweaty summer New York. ("It's why they called California California," declared Mac, the driver. "They named it after the heat.") I knew that Marilyn Monroe *was* California, *was* summer, and I knew too why she'd come east to stand, legs spread apart, over the subway grating. . . .

We didn't go to look at any battlefields in California that summer, but that night in Los Angeles my mother's friend and her husband took us out on the town to (or at any rate past) the Brown Derby, Ciro's, Mocambo and the Coconut Grove, and on subsequent occasions on location at the Planetarium in Griffith Park, high on Mulhulland Drive, on the cliffs at Malibu, and all along Sunset Boulevard—and the canonized James Dean finally, fairly, in ghostly single combat, once and for all vanquished his rival, the canonized Aloysius Gonzaga, in the war for my soul and spare parts. (I began to envision this melodrama in *moompix* sports newsreel terms as a hand-wrestling saga, shot on Venice Beach, between James Dean, as himself in a sailor suit, and Sal Mineo as Aloysius Gonzaga in cassock and surplice. Natalie Wood wasn't cast. . . .) I began to understand how it might come about that T.'s joking prediction about me in California would come true. (In the worried last scene of Joseph L. Mankiewicz's *All About Eve,* Barbara Bates, as the plaintive Phoebe, asks Anne Baxter, as Eve Harrington, if she plans to stay long in California. She's told, "I might.")

Even James Dean and Marilyn Monroe, working singly or as a team, couldn't have done it to me all by themselves; it was the sets more than anything else: the sets and the decoration of the sets. It was the streetlamps of Beverly Hills; it was the perfume of the night-blooming things florescent in every canyon. (There was no need to go to Encinada.) It was, of course, the view, from Mulhulland Drive, of the Grid lit up, stretching across Immensity to the shore of the Pacific, like the central-and-autonomic nervous systems of a supine, ultrasentient, intergalactic Somebody. . . .

I went back east to face T. and the others, and to commence dissembling, methodically, with increasing guile. I found it necessary to do so, and I credit California with showing me how.

I still don't drive.

SUMMER MORNING HAS ITS BIRDSONG, AND ITS clear pitchforks of energy. As the day lengthens in silence, we work at our desks while the sun struggles past Ragged to rise in the sky. Because we are protected by Ragged Mountain and by outspreading elderly maples, we don't take the sun's brunt until afternoon. The old house stays cool, almost cold, most mornings: a fire in the Glenwood. Even on the hottest days, when the New Hampshire midday reaches the nineties, our house stays cool except for upstairs.

Afternoons we go down to Eagle Pond; elsewhere we would be going to Eagle Lake, for it's not just a circle of water with a few ducks in it; it's twenty-five acres, shaped like a humpbacked whale, shallow and muddy at its edge and deep in the center. Half a mile northwest a small camel-hump hill is called Eagle's Nest, for the bird that lived there and fed from the pond twice a day in my great-grandfather's time. Great-Grandfather named our

241

DONALD HALL

house Eagle Pond Farm when he moved here in 1865. He was thirty-nine years old, a sheep farmer from Ragged with four children and more to come. My grandmother Kate, born at this place in 1878 when her father was fifty-two, never knew the eagle.

Pond afternoons begin at the end of June, maybe the first days of July, after the black flies have largely departed. At the little beach we cut into the east side of the pond, tall hemlocks and oaks screen the sun out until one or two in the afternoon. We walk down a steep slope over slippery needles and weathered oak leaves to our clearing on the mossy shore. A dozen birches lean out over dark water. The water is dark with minerals; exiting the pond as it goes south under the bridge, it turns into the Blackwater River. By the pond's edge under a birch a tiny ancient rosebush blooms pink and brief at June's turn into July. Ferns and oak saplings upthrust every summer. Moss sinks under our bare feet and sends up tiny red flowers. We sit in canvas sling chairs beside the picnic table or lie in the sun on Newberry's plastic chaises taking the breeze and the warm sun. These afternoons I stare a lot, moronic with easy pleasure, at birches and ferns, at Eagle's Nest in the distance, and at campers. There is a boys' camp on the west side of the pond, a girls' companion camp to the south, and both are remarkably unobnoxious.

I gaze at the landscape and at clouds; I look at a book; occasionally I write a line or a note toward a line, but I don't call it working. Jane reads and soaks sun in. We swim a little, but mush and mussel shells underfoot, not to mention green corpsefinger weeds straggling in our faces, make swimming less than perfect. With summer guests we laze talking and eat slow picnic suppers.

All summer the creation thrives, wasps and roses. Tiny ants plague the kitchen. A bundle of wasps models a new nest under an attic eave. By the road at the end of June single old roses, which budded late in spring, burst forth with petals of pink and white for the briefest season, ancient flowers my grandmother loved as a girl a century ago, doubtless sniffed by early settlers born in the eighteenth century. Shy, small, frail petals outcurl only to fall, to litter the green earth with their iridescence, making another beauty for an hour. While they bloom we hover above them, taking deep and startling breaths, for their odor is all the perfumes of Arabia, wave upon wave of velvety sensuous sweetness. We bend, sniff, shake our heads, walk away, and return for more. We cut a few—as abundant as they're brief—to take to church or to float in a bowl on the black Glenwood. Quick and fragile as the flowers are, the bushes are durable. All winter, snowplows heap dirty drifts on them thick with salt; sometimes the plow gouges their earth; we think they must have been damaged this year: come the end of June they raise to the summer air their proliferate odor.

Although the old farmers weren't known for their devotion to beauty, they loved their flowers. At least if they were Christian they could admire the Lord's creation, a pious aesthetic, while they gazed at Kearsarge, pond, birch grove, and old roses. While I hayed with my grandfather, working as hard as he did, he would pause stock-still from time to time—maybe as we worked the Crumbine place and looked across the valley toward Vermont's hills—and sigh and praise the glory. My grandmother interrupted the million tasks of her household— soap, pies, bread, doughnuts, canning, jam and jelly making, sewing, darning, knitting, crocheting, egg gathering, washing, ironing—to tend her flowers. She kept a small round garden in front of the kitchen window over the set-tubs where she spent so much of her life. I remember marigolds there, zinnias, pansies early, hollyhocks. Across the yard past the far driveway at the lip of the hayfield she tended a circle of poppies that dazzled their Chinese reds against the long wavy gray-green grass. Some summers now a lone poppy rises in the field. In a tiny round bed by the road I remember my grandmother placing, among the green things, silvery burned-out radio tubes

242

that she found beautiful. She loved a crockery birdbath that she ordered from Sears and set in front of the house and kept full of water where small birds routinely bathed. Also she stuck in the lawn painted wooden ducklings following a mother duck. In our back garden now we keep a wooden cutout of a girl in clogs watering a wooden cutout tulip. In front we favor whirligigs.

Where Jane grows her lilies, my aunts in the 1930s made a rock garden. I remember masses of pinks. Neither Caroline nor Nan married young. Both schoolteachers, occasionally they traveled in summer, and Caroline took an M.A. at Yale summer school, but mostly they returned to Eagle Pond Farm to their father and mother and nephew. The sisters cleared a beach near our swimming place, which they called Sabine, and when I was little, before I started haying with my grandfather in 1941, I spent my afternoons paddling and swimming with them, collecting mussel shells and turtles, scaring frogs.

The greatest crop in New Hampshire's July and August, now as for the last one hundred and forty years, is the summer people. Summer people were essential to the economy even before the collapse of farming. At the Pleasant Lake Inn—handsome with all its gables at the west end and a splendid view of Kearsarge rising beyond the water—my great-aunt Nanny cooked all summer. Families spent summers at the same address for a hundred years. Children from Massachusetts and New Jersey grew up identifying July and August with Lake Sunapee, with Springfield or Danbury or Enfield. These months made islands of guiltless hours away from school and the rules of winter; the summer place becomes a name for sweet freedom, innocent irresponsibility, imagination's respite, time for loafing and inviting the soul. Now in our backwoods of New Hampshire, many permanent citizens are emigrants or descendants of emigrants from city and suburb, and a small but valuable contingent are children of the summer vacationers who came to love the landscape

not only as interchangeable scenery—cards in a deck that flips through Switzerland, Mexico, Ireland, Peru, and Hilton Head—but as the heart's green and granite; and who, exposed to the rural culture, chose to join it.

On the other hand, many summer visitors care nothing for place or people, and people return the gesture. Every June we complain, at first of traffic and then of bad manners, discourteous behavior in the aisles of the supermarket, condescension, and arrogance. We have become the Natives, amusing rustics perhaps, more likely vendors suspected of exploitation. Year-rounders turn grumpy. Of course it is a perennial conflict wherever tourists congregate, as ineluctable as town-and-gown in the neighborhood of a college. When I feel scorn for July's hordes I try to remember that I started that way. Or almost. I grew up living the school year out in suburban Connecticut, Ardmore Street in Hamden, four miles from the center of New Haven, two miles from the Brock-Hall Dairy Company, which my grandfather cofounded and where my father worked. When I came north for summers I was not exactly a vacationer: I didn't go to a hotel or a rented cottage or a lakeside camp; I went to the house where my mother and grandmother were born and grew up; I worked in the hayfields; briefly I joined the back-country culture that was so alien to Spring Glen Grammar School and the values of the blocks. I inhabited for a while the universe of church suppers, Christian Endeavor, outhouses, cow manure, chickens, Civil War stories, fishing, poverty, straw-chewing, and Rawleigh's Salve.

All summer I worked but I did not work hard. The chicks were my domain, and I brought them water and grain at morning and at night. Afternoons were haying. I stood atop the old rack with its split-pole rails while my grandfather pitched hay up and I tucked it in place and trod to weave it together. On the way to the hayfield and on the way back my grandfather talked, told stories, and recited poems: this was the best part; but

243

even the work was good. I keep bright intact recollections of these afternoons: on a hot day I stand in the breeze on top of the hayrack looking down on valley and pond; I am thirteen and my grandfather will never die.

Because I did not belong to the country the whole year, the whole life, I was a summer person. A suburban child, I preferred the rural, archaic, old, and eccentric. I took my mother's New Hampshire over my father's Connecticut. I chose it and I choose it. When I was eleven or twelve I daydreamed living here year-round, a lonely trapper on the hill like all the bachelor solitaries who lived cramped into tumbledown shacks. By the time I was sixteen I daydreamed of living here as a writer; in my twenties I learned that this was impractical; in my forties I did it. Now if I grumble about summer people, doubtless I protest in order to separate myself from what I was or partly was. It is easy to make stereotypes, harder to make distinctions. Many long-term summer people feel connected to landscape and to people by way of rural culture; their summers are not only climate, pond, and hill but islands of country ethic and culture that they cherish against the life they lead at other times. They return to old cottages they renew each year, and they pay taxes and keep up their own land. Although in the stereotype summer people are rich, in truth many are not. I think of Clarence and Katherine Grimes, who came to Stinson Lake for fifty years. Clarence taught at Hamden High School in Connecticut, where I spent two years; Clarence taught German and French and music. Katherine was a painter and a cellist. On a high school teacher's salary they bought land in the thirties and built a camp and brought their children every year and later their grandchildren, and when Kay died in 1985 Clarence buried her in a tiny graveyard over their camp, where he stays summers still, lonely in his ninth decade.

On the other hand, a new breed buys condos and cuts off our view of a mountain. They purchase air and sun for their pleasure as if the creation were not common inheritance, glory, and obligation. Greed is not only theirs but also the farmer's who sells his land and the developer's who subdivides it, but it is also theirs who grant the farmer and the developer their money: their greed is for exclusiveness. On the west side of Newfound Lake there's a patch of road where I used to drive looking across choppy blue water at firs and hills on the other side; but now a sawtooth brown-shingle condo, between road and water, removes Newfound Lake from public vision. They bought the view; for the first time in millennia since the glacier set it there, the lake and the land are split apart.

John Morse hays our fields at June's end, cutting, turning hay that gets rained on, raking and baling it with a series of machines hooked up to his tractor: very like a horse. When he and his strong boys gather the bales onto a pickup truck, they work a long day shirtless in the bright sun and in the early evening stand resting in the long shadows. (In the fall after slaughter John returns our grass transformed into lamb roast and steak.) The stubble hayfield looks brown for a week or so; then it softens into green again, rises and waves when the wind blows. Where the long grass ripples my grandfather grew tall field corn; every summer when I was small I lost myself in it on purpose, in order to be frightened and enjoy the comfort of salvation.

For twenty-five years after my grandfather died hay remained abundant, growing from topsoil composed of a century and a half of Holstein manure. But underneath lies sand the glacier left. One year not long ago John stacked half as many bales as he had the year before, and we knew the goodness had leached out of the soil. Now John limes the fields in autumn; we talk of plowing, harrowing, replanting with new seed, and fertilizing. Whatever we do, we want to keep the fields. A hayfield grown up to bushes is melancholy. These summers I drive past dense groves of trees where I spent afternoons in the 1940s haying with my grandfather. Trees are beautiful and wood is useful but cleared land is a monument to the old settlers. Think of the labor that cleared it: cutting, stumping, burning the timber it didn't pay to haul; oxen sledding great stumps and granite boulders. How different the land looked a hundred years ago. On the slopes of Ragged, even of Kearsarge, stone walls border deep forest, stone walls that weren't built to keep pine trees in; somebody cleared it for pasture and kept it clear. Up on Highway 89 as you approach Hanover, great domed hills rise, clear with pasture and hayfield. The hills of our Ragged, and much of New Hampshire, domed clear and green under the yellow light of summer a century ago.

Mid-August is Old Home Day, Danbury one Sunday and Wilmot the next. Each town alternates the location among its tiny centers: Wilmot Flat, Wilmot Center, or North Wilmot; Danbury Village or South Danbury. Wherever it happens it repeats certain rituals; wherever it happens it is a diminished thing.

The governor proclaimed Old Home in 1899 because of New Hampshire's depopulation. For decades people had left the farms for the mills, where the hours were fewer and the pay steady; then the farms became increasingly poorer because on better and flatter land to the west farmers could use more machinery and fewer hands. My mother, born in 1903, remembers hordes arriving for Old Home when she was a girl. Wilmot's took place at the Methodist Camp Ground, where tiny cottages sprouted among tall pines like the mushrooms of a wet summer; the 1938 hurricane smashed pines onto tiny cottages and ended the campground. (We still travel Camp Ground Road.) Even I can remember two hundred gathering there in the mid-thirties: my grandfather bought me vanilla cones, my great-uncle Luther (who was a minister) addressed the multitude, and on the bandstand the old men of Moulton's Band from Sanbornton, blue caps and uniforms with red piping and epaulettes, played marching songs and hymns that marched. In my mother's day, maybe until the Second World War, local residents staged a play for the exiles' reunion, and a dance my mother couldn't go to. (Rumor had it some of the fellows drank hard cider.) Stagecoaches and primitive buses waited at the depot for the diaspora's return. There were prizes for those who came from the greatest distance—Pennsylvania, Tennessee, Ohio, even Idaho; for the largest family groups from great-grandparents to infants; for the eldest attending, usually in their late nineties or a hundred; and for the youngest, always a babe in arms.

We still give the prizes, but we are a remnant repeating a ritual after its purpose is mostly gone. Only forty of us gather: although the eldest is still usually a nonagenarian, the youngest is sometimes four or five; the farthest journeying comes from Boston; the largest family may be four or five. The original emigrants are dead and their children's children have lived in seven cities before they were ten years old, none of them in New Hampshire. Still, Old Home Day remains another pleasant and innocent excuse for gathering. Always a few old friends and former residents schedule an annual visit to coincide with Old Home. My mother, who lives in Connecticut, has not missed many. After the morning sermon we eat a picnic lunch and listen to the current Moulton's Band from Sanbornton playing Beatles' songs adapted for brass—and John Philip Sousa also.

Often on the weekend of Wilmot's Old Home the camps close down across the pond. Long lines of chartered Vermont Transit buses raise dust on Eagle Pond Road, and young campers crowd at the windows saying farewell for another year to Eagle Pond and Ragged Mountain. We get to stay. We linger at pondside for a few more weeks of warm water in perfect stillness. Then one night, warned by the *Concord Monitor*, we cover tomatoes with poly, and in the cold morning I scrape ice from the windshield. Two or three icy mornings turn the pond chilly; along the shore we spy the first gay fires of fall.

245

247

THE ILLUSTRATIONS

248

ALICE ADAMS was born in Virginia, grew up in South Carolina, and now resides in San Francisco. Her most recent book, *After You've Gone*, is a collection of short stories, and she is presently finishing a novel entitled *The Last Lovely City*.

ROY BLOUNT, JR., is the author of several books, including *Now Where Were We?, Not Exactly What I Had in Mind*, and most recently, *First Hubby*.

RAY BRADBURY specializes in short stories, but has also written numerous novels, plays, poems, and screenplays. He is perhaps best known for his science-fiction novels, including *The Martian Chronicles, The Illustrated Man, Fahrenheit 451*, and *Dandelion Wine*.

ANATOLE BROYARD was the daily book critic for *The New York Times* for thirteen years and the editor of *The New York Times Book Review* for five years. He now teaches fiction and writing in New York and Cambridge, Massachusetts.

MARY CANTWELL is on the editorial board of *The New York Times*.

RAYMOND CARVER published eleven books of short stories and poetry, including his last book, *A New Path to the Waterfall*, before his death in August of 1988.

LAURIE COLWIN is the author of two collections of short stories and three novels, the most recent of which is *Goodbye Without Waving*.

MICHAEL DORRIS, author of *A Yellow Raft in Blue Water, The Broken Cord*, and several scholarly books, lives in New Hampshire with his wife, Louise Erdrich. They are at work on a new novel, *The Crown of Columbus*, which will carry both of their names.

FRANCINE DU PLESSIX GRAY is a novelist and essayist, whose books include *Lovers & Tyrants, October Blood, Adam and Eve and the City*, and most recently, *Soviet Women: Walking the Tightrope*. She was born in Europe of a Russian mother and a French father, came to the United States in 1941, attended Bryn Mawr and Black Mountain colleges, and graduated from Barnard with a major in philosophy. She lives in Connecticut.

LOUISE ERDRICH is the author of three novels, *Love Medicine, The Beet Queen*, and *Tracks*, as well as two books of poetry, *Jacklight* and *Baptism of Desire*. She lives in New Hampshire with her husband, Michael Dorris, and their children.

VERONICA GENG is on the staff of *The New Yorker*. She is the author of two books, *Partners* and *Love Trouble Is My Business*.

MARIANNE GINGHER is the author of *Bobby Rex's Greatest Hit*, a novel, and *Teen Angel*, a collection of short stories. She lives in Greensboro, North Carolina, and has taught writing and literature at the University of North Carolina at Chapel Hill and at Hollins College.

DONALD HALL is a poet, whose most recent work, *The One Day: A Poem in Three Parts*, won the National Book Critics Circle Award in 1989.

DIANE JOHNSON is a novelist and critic. Her novels include *Persian Nights*, and the forthcoming *Health and Happiness*.

ELIZABETH HARDWICK is a critic and novelist. Among her works are *Seduction and Betrayal: Women and Literature* and the novel *Sleepless Nights*.

ALFRED KAZIN is a critic and essayist, whose books include *New York Jew, The Inmost Leaf: A Selection of Essays, A Writer's America: Landscape in Literature*, and a recently published work with David Finn, *Our New York*.

VERLYN KLINKENBORG is Briggs-Copeland Lecturer in English at Harvard University and is the author of *Making Hay* and the forthcoming book, *The Last Fine Time*.

ANDREA LEE was born in Philadelphia, educated at Harvard University, and lives in Milan. Her works include *Sarah Phillips*, a novel, and *Russian Journal*, which was nominated for a National Book Award and received the 1984 Jean Stein Award from the American Academy and Institute of Arts and Letters.

BEVERLY LOWRY is the author of five novels, the most recent of which is *Breaking Gentle*, published by Viking. She has written many book reviews, essays, and short stories, and is currently working on a Broadway musical.

JAMES MCCOURT is the author of *Mawrdew Czgowchwz* and *Kaye Wayfaring in "Avenged."* He lives in New York.

PHYLLIS MCGINLEY was a poet and essayist and the author of several children's books. Well known for light verse that celebrated life in the suburbs, she won the 1961 Pulitzer Prize for her collection *Times Three: Selected Verse from Three Decades.*

BILL MCKIBBEN is a former editor at *The New Yorker* and the author of *The End of Nature.*

STANLEY MEISES, a former rock-and-roll reporter for the *New York Post*, writes regularly about music and other subjects for *The New Yorker* and other periodicals.

W. S. MERWIN won the Pulitzer Prize for poetry in 1971 for his book *The Carrier of Ladders.* His many other books include *The Rain in the Trees* (1987) and *Selected Poems* (1988).

OGDEN NASH authored some twenty books of poetry, including *I'm a Stranger Here Myself, You Can't Get There from Here,* and *Bed Riddance.* His witty, unconventional rhymes frequently appeared in *The New Yorker* and other magazines.

DANIEL OKRENT is the author of four books, including three about baseball. He was also the founding editor of *The New England Monthly.*

DARRYL PINCKNEY has published essays in *The New York Review of Books* and is currently working on a novel.

JAMES SCHUYLER won the 1981 Pulitzer Prize for poetry. His books include *Freely Espousing, The Morning of the Poem,* and most recently, *Selected Poems.*

CHARLES SIMIC is a professor of English at the University of New Hampshire, Durham. He has published many collections of poetry, the most recent of which is *The Essential Campion.*

WALLACE STEVENS published eight collections of poetry during his lifetime while serving as general counsel to the Hartford Accident & Indemnity Company.

MARK STRAND is a poet and author and a professor of English at the University of Utah in Salt Lake City. His most recent works include *Rembrandt Takes a Walk* and *William Bailey.*

CALVIN TRILLIN is a staff writer at *The New Yorker.* His latest book is *Travels with Alice.*

GEORGE TROW publishes fiction and essays in *The New Yorker* and is the author of *Bullies* (a collection of funny short stories) and *Within the Context of No Context,* among other books. Long ago and far away, he was a founder of *National Lampoon.*

JOHN UPDIKE is the author of thirty-seven books, including thirteen novels and five collections of verse. Born in Pennsylvania, he has lived in Massachusetts since 1957.

MARJORIE WELISH is a poet whose work has appeared in *Conjunctions, The Paris Review,* and *Sulphur.* Her books include *Handwritten* (1979) and *The Windows Flew Open.* She lives in New York City.

LARRY WOIWODE'S fiction has appeared in *The Atlantic, Harper's,* and *The New Yorker. The Neumiller Stories* is his most recent collection.

MEG WOLITZER is a novelist whose most recent work is *This Is Your Life.* She lives in New York City with her husband and is the coauthor of a series of weekly puzzles for *Seven Days.*

250

GRATEFUL ACKNOWLEDGMENT IS MADE TO THE FOLLOWING
FOR PERMISSION TO REPRINT COPYRIGHTED MATERIAL:

George Braziller, Inc. for permission to reprint "Summer Morning" from *Dismantling the Silence* by Charles Simic. Copyright © 1971 by Charles Simic. Reprinted by permission of George Braziller, Inc.

Viking Penguin Inc. for permission to reprint "Season at the Shore" from *Times Three* by Phyllis McGinley. Copyright © 1954 by Phyllis McGinley. Copyright renewed © 1982 by Phyllis Hayden Blake. Originally published in *The New Yorker*. Reprinted by permission of Viking Penguin, a division of Penguin Books USA Inc.

The New Yorker for permission to reprint "Away" by Mark Strand. Copyright © 1972 The New Yorker Magazine, Inc.

Little, Brown and Company for permission to reprint "Summer Serenade" from *Verses from 1929 On* by Ogden Nash. Copyright © 1942 by Ogden Nash. Originally published in *Cosmopolitan*. Reprinted by permission of Little, Brown and Company.

The New York Times for permission to reprint "Without Air-Conditioning, The Gift of a City Breeze," by Mary Cantwell, August 4, 1983. Copyright © 1983 by The New York Times Company. Reprinted by permission.

The New Yorker for permission to reprint "Horse-Chestnut Trees and Roses" by James Schuyler. Copyright © 1987 James Schuyler. Originally published in *The New Yorker*.

Georges Borchardt, Inc. for permission to reprint "How We Are Spared" from *The Lice* by W. S. Merwin. Copyright © 1967 by W. S. Merwin. Reprinted by permission of Georges Borchardt, Inc. and the author.

Alfred A. Knopf, Inc. for permission to reprint "Sunglasses" from *The Carpentered Hen and Other Creatures* by John Updike. Copyright © 1982 by John Updike. Reprinted by permission of Alfred A. Knopf, Inc.

Atlantic Monthly Press for permission to reprint "Hummingbird" from *A New Path to the Waterfall* by Raymond Carver. Copyright © 1989 by the estate of Raymond Carver.

Alfred A. Knopf, Inc. for permission to reprint "How to Avoid Grilling" from *Home Cooking* by Laurie Colwin. Copyright © 1988 by Laurie Colwin. Reprinted by permission of Alfred A. Knopf, Inc.

Alfred A. Knopf, Inc. for permission to reprint "Sailing after Lunch" from *The Collected Poems of Wallace Stevens*. Copyright © 1936 by Wallace Stevens. Copyright renewed © 1964 by Holly Stevens. Reprinted by permission of Alfred A. Knopf, Inc.

Ticknor & Fields for permission to reprint "Summer" from *Seasons at Eagle Pond* by Donald Hall. Copyright © 1987 by Donald Hall. Reprinted by permission of Ticknor & Fields, a Houghton Mifflin Company.

251

SUMMER was edited by Martha Moutray.
Editorial assistance was provided by Johanna Van Hise.

Production was supervised by Lori Foley.
Production assistance was provided by Laura Noorda.
Manufacturing was supervised by Ann DeLacey, Hugh
Crawford, and Louise Richardson.

The design was created and executed by Brent Marmo of
The Brownstone Group.
Design assistance was provided by Christopher Bird.

The text of this book was set in Galliard
by NK Graphics of Keene, New Hampshire.

The separations were provided by Rainbow Graphic Arts
Company, Ltd., of Hong Kong.

The book was printed and bound in Hong Kong by C & C
Offset Printing Company, Ltd.